Federal Regulation and Chemical Innovation

Federal Regulation and Chemical Innovation

Christopher T. Hill, EDITOR

Massachusetts Institute of Technology

Based on a symposium

sponsored by the Division of

Industrial and Engineering Chemistry

at the 176th Meeting of the

American Chemical Society,

Miami Beach, Florida,

September 14, 1978.

ACS SYMPOSIUM SERIES **109**

AMERICAN CHEMICAL SOCIETY

WASHINGTON, D. C.   1979

178745

540,9
F293

Library of Congress CIP Data

Federal regulation and chemical innovation.
  (ACS symposium series; 109 ISSN 0097-6156)

  Includes bibliographies and index.

  1. Chemical research—United States—Congresses. 2.
Science and state—United States—Congresses.
  I. Hill, Christopher T. II. American Chemical Society.
Division of Industrial and Engineering Chemistry. III.
Series: American Chemical Society. ACS symposium
series; 109.

QD47.F4   540'.973   79-15407
ISBN 0-8412-0511-6   ASCMC 8   109 1–200 1979

ACS Symposium Series

M. Joan Comstock, *Series Editor*

FOREWORD

The ACS SYMPOSIUM SERIES was founded in 1974 to provide a medium for publishing symposia quickly in book form. The format of the Series parallels that of the continuing ADVANCES IN CHEMISTRY SERIES except that in order to save time the papers are not typeset but are reproduced as they are submitted by the authors in camera-ready form. Papers are reviewed under the supervision of the Editors with the assistance of the Series Advisory Board and are selected to maintain the integrity of the symposia; however, verbatim reproductions of previously published papers are not accepted. Both reviews and reports of research are acceptable since symposia may embrace both types of presentation.

CONTENTS

PREFACE

The past two decades have witnessed rapid growth in government regulation of the environmental, health, and safety aspects of industrial processes and products. The chemical process industries and the products they make are a major focus of the regulations administered by EPA, OSHA, FDA, and CPSC, and by their state-level counterparts. It is not surprising that these industries have received considerable attention from government regulators. The synthetic organic chemical, petroleum refining, and primary metals industries as well as such products as pesticides, pharmaceuticals, chlorinated hydrocarbons, and heavy metals can pose significant risks to human health, safety, and the environment.

The economic regulation passed in an earlier age is concerned with markets, prices, and preservation of competition. By contrast, a major objective of much of the "new regulation" is to stimulate firms to redesign or to change the processes they use and the products they sell. The chemical industries depend heavily on a continual flow of new processes and products to meet consumer needs; to control production costs in the face of higher prices for raw materials, labor, and equipment and to meet the challenge of foreign competition. Furthermore, technological innovation is often the means by which new firms enter the chemical industries and by which existing firms adapt and grow. It is also not surprising, then, that concern has arisen for the effects that environmental, health, and safety regulations have on the rate and nature of technological innovation in the chemical industries.

The importance of chemical innovation is not confined to chemical firms. It is equally important to the economy and to society as a whole. New technology provides the major improvements in productivity that help control inflation and that contribute to the nation's economic growth. At the same time, society needs new chemical technology to help solve many of the pressing problems of our time such as energy conservation and supply, production of food, preservation of environmental quality, and control of population growth.

Most of the papers in this volume were presented at an ACS symposium in September 1978. Perhaps a no more diverse and comprehensive set of papers on the effects of regulation on chemical innovation has ever before been assembled. They present a cross section of research results from most of the major schools of thought as well as the practical experiences and observations of people from industry and government. The disciplines represented by the authors include chemistry, chemical engineering, medicine, law, economics, business administration, and psychology.

The papers are arranged to provide (1) an introduction to the issues, (2) conceptual and analytical models and empirical results, and (3) policy implications and prescriptions for change. The first three papers provide a broad introduction to the issues. Eads covers the origins of the "new regulation," contrasts it with older economic regulation, and discusses how such regulation affects corporate decision making. Newburger discusses five real dilemmas society faces in regulating the conduct of firms and points out that regulation can be neither entirely just nor entirely positive in its effects. Leenhouts reviews and assesses the empirical evidence on the effects of regulation on innovation from the perspective of a chemical engineer in industry.

The next six papers present conceptual frameworks, theoretical models and empirical evidence, on the effects of regulation on chemical innovation. Ashford and Heaton and Iverstine and Kinard present evidence from surveys of firm-level responses to regulation. Both papers note regulation-induced changes in the level and nature of research and development, in the processes of decision making in technology areas in firms, and in the kinds of products and processes that are commercially successful. Cohen and Bennett provide first-person confirmation of the fact that government regulation creates new business opportunities to develop and sell new control technologies. Both Greenberg and Thompson present analytical models that are useful in examining responses of process technology to regulation. These studies are rooted in models developed by economists to study dynamic responses to price changes. DiRaddo and Wardell review past work and present new data on the effects of pharmaceutical regulation on the development of new drugs. Generally, more is known about the drug part of the regulation/innovation interface than about any other, since the regulations are older and the FDA new drug approval process automatically generates measures of innovation.

The final four papers move from theoretical concepts and research results to policy and prescription. Updegraff assesses the potential impact on innovation of the proposed Drug Regulation Reform Act. This Act originated, in part, from the recognition of the kinds of problems raised in the DiRaddo and Wardell paper. DeKany and Malkenson of EPA describe how EPA is implementing the Toxic Substances Control Act in light of the Congressional statement of policy that it not unduly impede technological innovation. Gerstenfeld and Nason find that regulation inhibits innovation, and to address this problem, present an 11-point program of government actions designed to improve the formal and informal processes by which regulations are developed. Schweitzer agrees that regulation is a problem for innovation, especially in the long term. Among other proposals, he recommends legislated changes in the Toxic Substances Control Act and formation of a national commission that would present recommendations for amending it. The commission would also evaluate the impact of regulation on society, including the chemical industry.

After digesting all the ideas in this book, however, the reader looking for a definitive understanding must continue to search. Despite the importance of both regulation and innovation to industry and society, and despite the hours that have been devoted to discussion of their interactions, there is still much to learn. Problems of description, definition, and measurement plague serious research in the field. Reasonable arguments can be made on theoretical grounds that regulation would inhibit or stimulate innovation, and empirical confirmation is available to support both sides. Furthermore, some participants in the debate confuse the impacts of regulation on innovation with the larger question of whether regulation's costs are worth the benefits.

Thus, there is still a great need for good empirical research on the effects of government regulation on chemical innovation. The papers in this volume provide an array of ideas that can be examined, expanded, and integrated to help improve our understanding of this interaction. With a better understanding, Congress and the agencies can better design regulations to meet important social goals, including the development of needed technologies for regulatory compliance, while maintaining the ability of the chemical industries to remain viable and grow.

I would like to thank David Gushee, former chairman of the ACS Industrial and Engineering Chemistry Division, for suggesting this symposium. I would also like to thank the authors and the reviewers for participating, and the Congressional Office of Technology Assessment and the MIT Center for Policy Alternatives for assistance in preparing the symposium and this volume. Betsi Wasserman helped immensely with the tasks involved in putting this work together. Finally, I would like to acknowledge the Division of Policy Research and Analysis of the National Science Foundation, which has funded or otherwise supported most of the research that appears in this volume.

Massachusetts Institute of Technology   CHRISTOPHER T. HILL
Cambridge, Massachusetts 02139
March 30, 1979

CONTRIBUTING AUTHORS

NICHOLAS A. ASHFORD (Chemistry, Law) is Assistant Director of the MIT Center for Policy Alternatives. He has worked at the ITT Research Institute, serves as the Chairman of the National Advisory Committee on Occupational Safety and Health, and is a consultant to several regulatory agencies.

ROBERT P. BENNETT (Chemistry) is Vice President and Technical Director at Apollo Chemical Corporation. He was formerly Director of R&D at Apollo, and has worked for American Cyanamid.

MURRAY S. COHEN (Chemistry) is Director of New Business Development at Apollo Chemical Corporation. He was formerly Technical Director for Borg Warner Chemicals and prior to that, Laboratory Director for Exxon Research and Development, Paramins Laboratory.

JOHN DeKANY (Chemical Engineering) is Deputy Assistant Administrator for Chemical Control in the EPA Office of Toxic Substances. He was formerly Director of Emission Control Technology at the EPA Mobile Source Air Pollution Control Program and has worked for Westinghouse Electric and Gulf Oil.

JEAN DiRADDO (Psychology, Neurochemistry) is Center Projects Manager at the Center for the Study of Drug Development at the University of Rochester's School of Medicine.

GEORGE C. EADS (Economics) is a Member of the President's Council of Economic Advisers and was the Director of the Regulatory Policies and Institutions Program at the RAND Corporation.

ARTHUR GERSTENFELD (Industrial Management) is Professor and Head of the Department of Management at Worcester Polytechnic Institute.

EDWARD GREENBERG (Economics) is Professor of Economics at Washington University in St. Louis.

GEORGE HEATON (Law) is a Research Associate at the MIT Center for Policy Alternatives.

CHRISTOPHER T. HILL (Chemical Engineering) is a Senior Research Associate at the MIT Center for Policy Alternatives. He has worked for the Congressional Office of Technology Assessment, Washington University in St. Louis, and Uniroyal, Inc.

JOE C. IVERSTINE (Chemical Engineering, Business Administration) is Professor of Business Administration at Southeastern Louisiana University at Hammond, Louisiana. He has worked for Allied Chemical Company.

JERRY L. KINARD (Business) is Professor and Head of the Department of Business Administration at Southeastern Louisiana University at Hammond, Louisiana.

JAMES. W. LEENHOUTS (Chemistry) is Manager of Business Development in R&D and is the Toxic Substances Coordinator for the Michigan Division at Dow Chemical U.S.A.

STEVEN MALKENSON (Economics) is currently at Blythe, Eastman, and Dillon. He was formerly in the Economic Analysis Division at EPA.

HOWARD K. NASON (Business, Chemistry) is President of the Industrial Research Institute, Research Corporation. He was formerly President of. Monsanto Research Corporation and Vice President of the Research and Engineering Division at Monsanto.

DAVID J. NEWBURGER (Law) is Assistant Professor of Law at Washington University in St. Louis and is an attorney in private practice. He has worked for the State of Ohio, the Department of Commerce, and the firm of Arnold and Porter.

GLENN E. SCHWEITZER (Engineering) is Senior Research Associate at Cornell University and Associate Executive Director of the Council on Science and Technology for Development in Washington, D.C. He was formerly Director of the EPA Office of Toxic Substances.

RUSSELL G. THOMPSON (Economics) is Professor of Quantitative Management Science and Director of Industry Studies in the College of Business Administration at the University of Houston. He is also President of Research for Growth and Transfer, Inc.

GAIL UPDEGRAFF (Economics) is Senior Economist at JRB Associates in McLean, Virginia. He was formerly Chief of the Economic Analysis Group at the Food and Drug Administration.

WILLIAM M. WARDELL (Clinical Pharmacology, Medicine) is Associate Professor of Pharmacology and Toxicology and Director of the Center for the Study of Drug Development at the University of Rochester.

Chemicals as a Regulated Industry: Implications for Research and Product Development

GEORGE C. EADS

Regulatory Policies and Institutions Program, The Rand Corporation,
Santa Monica, CA 90406

Governmentally imposed restrictions on private enterprise
are not a new phenomenon. For about 100 years, certain industries, such as the railroads and the electric utilities, have
operated under detailed regulation, and even the so-called "unregulated" industries have been subject to antitrust, securities,
tax, and labor laws. It is now widely recognized, however, that
government regulation has entered a new era. This era began in
the mid-1960s with the passage of a series of laws aimed at,
among other things, protecting the environment, insuring worker
health and safety, and assuring the safety and performance of
consumer products. This "new regulation" applies to all private
enterprise, and is administered by a multiplicity of agencies,
each interested only in specialized segments of a firm's operations. In further contrast with traditional regulation agencies,
the regulators in these new agencies have no specific mandate to
promote the industries they regulate or even to assure the continued existence of these industries.

A number of observers, both within and outside government,
have expressed concern that this new use of regulation is fundamentally altering the behavior and performance of U.S. private
enterprise, with potential repercussions far beyond the intended
scope of regulatory activity. One reason for concern is the fact
that the increase in regulatory activity requires that a larger
share of U.S. economic and social resources be devoted to supporting the regulatory bureaucracy, to assuring effective and
appropriate representation of firms' interests before regulatory
bodies, to gathering and processing numerous data requests made
by government agencies and their contractors and, finally but
certainly not least important, to complying with regulations once
they are promulgated. Estimates of these costs vary widely, but
some notion of their potential consequence is given by a recently
published study by Denison (1) in which he estimates that compliance with environmental constraints introduced since 1967
diverted nearly one percent of 1975 nonresidential business
resources away from final output, with another 0.42 percent
diverted as a result of compliance with regulations to improve

worker health and safety. This may seem like a small figure, but it is not. Denison estimates that by 1975, this reduction was equivalent to knocking 1/2 of one percentage point off the economy's annual growth rate. This, in turn, represents fully a 25 percent reduction in the economy's long-term rate of improvement in output per unit of input. Moreover, Denison reports that the share of resources being diverted has been steadily rising.

But the diversion of economic and social resources away from final production may not be the only, or even the most important, cost of the "new regulation." Virtually every aspect of the firm's strategic environment is likely to be affected. Of special concern is that the pace and direction of technological advance is likely to be altered in ways that are not presently predictable.

Historically, technological innovation has been a prime force in economic development. New processes and products have been credited with such diverse benefits as increased employment, increased labor productivity, new opportunities for preventing and curing disease, greater consumer comfort, and improvements in the balance of trade.

Of course, it is also argued that technological development is at least partly responsible for precisely the environmental, health, and safety hazards to which the bulk of the "new regulation" is addressed. Therefore, some of the changes that regulation may induce may be all to the good. But we need not deny the existence of technology created hazards in order to be concerned about the possible negative effects of this regulation on the rate of technological advance. The issue is not whether some regulation is justified, but what trade-offs our society is willing to make between the social and economic benefits from further high rates of technological advance and the losses associated with actual and potential new product and process hazards.

We are in the very early stages of research aimed at exploring just such questions as these. This paper is intended to describe some of our preliminary hypotheses and to expose our general approach to comment and criticism.

The target industry for our research is chemicals. This choice has merit for several reasons. Chemicals has long been considered a prime example of an industry whose success has been based on a continued high rate of technological innovation. Traditionally grouped among the "research intensive" industries, chemicals has been particularly noteworthy for the extremely low proportion of its R&D funds that have been federally supplied. Thus it is little wonder that researchers seeking to understand the process of industrial innovation have been attracted to the chemicals industry and, in particular, to its technologically most advanced firms.

But chemicals is distinctive in another way. The industry has been a prime target of the "new regulation." Indeed, with the possible exceptions of autos and steel, no previously "unregulated" industry has been subjected to a wider variety of regulations. Certainly among the high technology industries, it ranks first.

The chemicals industry also contains a sufficiently large number of firms so that a diversity of behavior likely can be observed. But more importantly, the chemicals industry, being highly dynamic, has always been in the forefront of managerial innovations. As Chandler has noted, a chemicals firm, Du Pont, pioneered the multidivisional form of corporate organization.(2) Chemicals firms were among the first to establish organized corporate research activities. And, as we have observed during our research, certain of the firms in the chemicals industry are taking steps to become active participants in the regulatory process. Therefore, if U. S. industry is indeed undergoing significant changes as it attempts to deal with the "new regulation," these changes should readily be observable in chemicals.

Maintaining this particular industry's past excellent performance is of obvious importance to the economy. We have already referred to the industry's high rate of technological advance. The new and improved products it has developed have, in turn, fueled productivity improvements throughout the economy. And, although more high-level policy attention is usually given to the problem and performance of such industries as steel, chemicals long ago surpassed most of these sectors in contributions to the gross national product. Furthermore, chemicals, stimulated no doubt by its enviable performance in developing new products, has continued to make a strong positive contribution to our balance of payments.

One element of the chemicals industry--pharmaceuticals--has already been the subject of intense study. Considerable attention has been given to the role that FDA regulation may or may not have played in an observed slowdown in the rate of development and commericalization of new ethical drugs.

This interest in pharmaceuticals has tended to draw research attention away from the effects that have been felt by the other segments of the chemicals industry. This is unfortunate for, whatever its importance, the effects of FDA regulation on innovation and product development in pharmaceuticals is likely to be quite different from the impact generated by the type regulation to which the nonpharmaceuticals portion of the chemicals industry has become subject. As we shall argue in more detail below, dealing with such regulations and with the entities that promulgate and promote them creates a fundamentally different planning problem for a firm than does coping with regulations administered by an agency which has a scope of interest and responsibility roughly corresponding to the boundaries of the industry being regulated.

In the next section of this paper, we discuss some of the characteristics of the "new regulation" that help to differen-

tiate it from the more traditional forms of regulation. Following this, we speculate briefly concerning how these characteristics are likely to influence the strategic environment within
which the typical firm in the chemicals industry likely finds
itself presently operating. Only then do we begin to hypothesize
as to the effects that regulation may have upon innovation in
chemicals. This may seem a rather round-about approach for a
paper whose stated purpose is only to examine the last of these
topics. But there is method to our madness. The approach just
outlined reflects our strongly held belief that in an industry
like chemicals, the research decision cannot be separated mean-
ingfully from other strategic business decisions. Thus, if we
are to understand in more than just a superficial way how the "new
regulation" is likely to affect the long-run path of innovation in
the chemicals industry, we must first understand how it influences the larger environment within which the chemicals firm must
operate. The road we have described is indeed somewhat round-
about. But, in our opinion, there are no easy short-cuts.

The New Regulatory Environment

One phenomenon that has been documented and attributed to
the "new regulation" is the recent rapid rise in the amount of
regulation. While growth in the overall level of regulatory
activity surely impinges upon the American economy as a whole, it
does not in and of itself imply a change in the regulatory
environment of any particular firm or even industry. When a new
regulatory agency is formed along traditional lines, with
interest limited to a single industry, regulatory activity necessarily increases but with a direct impact on only a narrow segment of the economy. Other firms and industries adapt in their
dealings with the newly regulated industry much as they do to
nonregulatory changes in their economic and social environment.
But, by and large, that is the limit of the impact on them.
The chemicals industry has not come under the exclusive pur-
view of any single new regulatory agency, but it has over the
last decade or so become a "regulated industry." This is not the
result of simple growth in the level of regulatory activity, but
reflects a new regulatory approach. We believe this approach can
be usefully characterized along four dimensions:

o   The jurisdictional boundaries of the new regulatory
    bodies;

o   The goals these bodies are directed to achieve;

o   The evidence they utilize in deciding whether and
    how stringently to regulate; and finally,

o   The instruments they use when they do regulate.

Each of these areas could--and perhaps will ultimately be--the
subject of its own separate study. But in the interest of brev-
ity, and in recognition of the work done by others (for example,
see (3)), we will confine ourselves to a brief description.

Regulatory Jurisdictions. The traditional motivation for
regulation was fear of "natural monopoly" or "destructive
competition"--market behaviors perceived to threaten consumers or
producers. This motivation was such that the "natural" jurisdiction of regulatory activity was a particular industry or, occa-
sionally, a group of related industries (e.g., transportation).
Consequently, the regulated industry was usually subject to over-
sight and control by a single regulatory agency authorized by a
single, comprehensive legislative or administrative action.

In contrast, the majority of the newer regulatory agencies
have been mandated to resolve social or economic problems wher-
ever they are perceived to arise. In some cases, the mandate has
resulted in regulations to which all (or a very wide range of)
industries are immediately subject. In other cases, agencies
have focused on a few industries at a time, but with the clear
prospect that all industries are potentially subject to future
action.

This change in jurisdictional definition has three important
implications for the firm: First, the firm cannot rely on a
regulatory agency to have a well-versed understanding of the
economic and social role played by it or its competitors or to
retain interest in the industry or firms long enough to
observe--much less accept responsibility for--the eventual implications of regulatory actions. Consequently, a major responsibility for assessing the broader implications of policy actions
and communicating these results of this assessment must fall upon
the firm or industry itself.

Second, while the very existence of an agency with a particular mandate (such as the protection of the environment) provides
a forewarning of the general issues that one day may confront the
firm, there is much uncertainty about the specific form these
issues might take or precisely when or by whom they will be
raised.

Third, the firm must accustom itself to dealing with
interagency (and sometimes even intraagency) conflicts. It often
is the case that one regulatory body will be totally unaware that
another body is contemplating (or, indeed, has already taken) an
action that impacts crucially upon an action that the first
agency is considering. In such cases, the firm finds itself in
the somewhat awkward position of explaining to the government
what the government itself is doing. Should it take the lead in
trying to point out such conflicts? Or should it wait until an
obvious conflict develops and attempt to exploit it to obtain a
more favorable decision from the viewpoint of the firm? The
proper answer is by no means obvious.

Regulatory Goals. The goals of the traditional regulatory
agencies required them to assure the long-run existence of the
industries (and, in some cases, the firms) they regulated. In
some instances, a promotional responsibility was directly written
into the statute establishing the agency.

But even where this did not occur, the goal of assuring
industry health was implicit. How could the FCC and the state
PUCs assure that adequate telephone service was universally
available at "fair" rates and charges if no company existed to
provide it?

The same cannot generally be said for the new regulatory
agencies. EPA's goal is to prevent damage to the environment.
It does so by limiting emissions deemed harmful. Its success in
this does not require the survival of the firm doing the emit-
ting. The Consumer Product Safety Commission's goal is to eliminate hazardous products from the marketplace. Achievement of
this goal may sometimes require the elimination of the firm that
produces the products deemed hazardous. OSHA must protect the
health and safety of workers. If this goal cannot be achieved
consistent with the preservation of firms determined to be
employing the unsafe practices, the agency is prepared to sacri-
fice such firms.

To a degree, Congress has recognized the difficulties
inherent in such mandates, and has placed limits on them. But
these limits are necessarily vague. Thus, the Williams-Steiger
Occupational Health and Safety Act of 1976 requires the Secretary
of Labor in promulgating standards dealing with toxic materials
or harmful physical agents to "...set the standards which most
adequately assure, to the extent feasible... that no employee
will suffer material impairment of health or functional capacity
even if such employee has regular exposure to the hazard dealt
with by such standard for the period of his working life."(4)
The courts, in interpreting this mandate, have held that under
this provision, a standard which is "prohibitively expensive" is
not "feasible." However, standards may be deemed "feasible" even
though, from the standpoint of employers, they are financially
burdensome and affect profit margins adversely. More importantly, to meet the test of "feasibility," a standard does not
necessarily need to guarantee the continued existence of individual employers.(5)

The Evidence on Which Regulatory Decisions Are Based. While
the issues dealt with by the traditional regulatory bodies have
been largely financial or commercial in character, those faced by
the "new regulators" generally have been more of a scientific or
technical nature. In keeping with the sort of questions
addressed by scientists or engineers, these issues have been subject to a high degree of speculation and uncertainty. The need
to make decisions involving such slippery matters, and the standards and evidence upon which such decisions have been based,

have distressed both businessmen being regulated and certain
scientists who fear the intrusion of politics into their "commun-
ity of science." (See (6).)

While exceptions can be cited, by and large it appears that
the regulatory agencies are dealing with such issues exactly as
Congress intended when it established them. The uncertain nature
of many of the hazards that were to be controlled was recognized
by Congress. The ambiguity of much of the evidence on which
decisions inevitably would have to be based was admitted. But
the risks of waiting until all the evidence was in was felt to
outweigh the harm caused by an occasional unnecessary regulation.
Thus, although the EPA Administrator is directed to conduct studies concerning the nature of the threat to the ozone layer from
fluorocarbons, to consult with recognized scientific authorities,
and to "consider" feasibility and economic impact, the final
decision about whether and how stringently to control these substances rests squarely on his shoulders. The standard he is to
use? Whether "in his judgment" such substances may "reasonably"
be anticipated to affect the stratosphere and whether that
effect, in turn, "...may reasonably be anticipated to endanger
public health and welfare."(7)

This is not to suggest that the institutions which we utilize to collect, assess, and update scientific and technical
information could not be vastly improved. Our point is that the
nature of the decisions the "new regulators" are required by law
to make are such as to preclude absolute certainty prior to
action. This is likely always to be the case.

Regulatory Instruments. The fourth area in which the new
regulation represents a break with tradition is in the instruments it uses to achieve its aims. Old-line regulatory agencies
such as the ICC, FCC, or CAB relied primarily on their power to
approve or disapprove specific requests relating to such matters
as pricing, entry and exit, and mergers. But their power to
influence specific firm conduct was severely constrained by statute. For example, the Federal Aviation Act states: "No term,
condition, or limitation of a [an air carrier's] certificate [of
public convenience and necessity--the operating license issued by
the CAB] shall restrict the right of an air carrier to add to or
change schedules, equipment, accommodations, or facilities for
performing the authorized transportation and service as the
development of the business and the demands of the public shall
require..."(8)

The "quasi-regulators" such as the Antitrust Division have
always employed a combination of specific enforcement actions in
the courts with statements of general policy in their attempt to
alter the general pattern of business conduct. They, too, left
the detailed day-to-day decisions concerning what a firm might
produce and how to produce it to the discretion of the firm and
its management. In contrast to the prohibitions cited above on

permissible CAB control instruments, EPA, OSHA, and CPSC can (and
do) dictate the most minute details of how a production process
shall be carried out, what inputs, outputs, and intermediate products will result, and what the precise characteristics and uses
of the final product will be. Of course, such activities require
the new regulators to know things they do not--and likely even
cannot--know about the details of individual firms' operations.
They are not unaware of that. But they struggle on anyway.

The four characteristics of the "new regulation" we have
just described combine to produce a major change in the strategic
environment facing the typical large business firm today. How
this happens, and what it means for the firm is the topic to
which we now turn.

Impact on the Strategic Decisionmaking Environment of the Firm

In recent years, the question of whether the United States
should engage in something called "economic planning" has generated considerable controversy with conservatives generally con-
demning and liberals generally applauding the idea. However, the
picture that emerges from the above description of the "new regulation" indicates that, in a real sense, the debate has been settled. As federal regulation has gradually come to affect more
and more areas of the typical firm's activities, the government
has acquired more authority to influence firm decisionmaking than
likely would have been tolerated had this country adopted an
explicit system of national planning.

But while the ability to influence is now present, the ability to comprehend the effects of actual and proposed actions and
to coordinate the various different activities being undertaken
is largely absent. In its current state, the government regulatory apparatus is like a benevolent, well-intentioned giant,
struggling to do good, but often wreaking havoc due to its sheer
size and power, its lack of the necessary sensory and feedback
mechanisms, and its only partially developed brain.

We will leave it to others to debate whether such an organ-
ism can ever either learn to control itself or be brought under
effective external control. Instead, we will confine our attention here to discussing how having to live with such a state of
affairs is likely to influence the strategic environment within
which the firm must operate certainly at present and perhaps
indefinitely into the future.

In the past, the principal factors that a businessman had to
take into account when plotting a future course of activity for
his firm were the attitude of the public toward his products and
the likely actions and reactions of actual and potential competitors. If he chose to engage in research and development, he
added a third category of worries--the possibility that nature
might prove fickle and prevent his scientists and engineers from
developing the new products and processes upon which his plans

depended.

The introduction of regulation--in particular, multi-agency, issue-oriented regulation--changes the businessman's decision-making calculus. This change is not brought about so much from the burden of having to spend time dealing with numerous government agencies. This aspect of regulation is accurately describable as a "hidden tax" and, as such, can be adjusted to relatively simply.

No, the "new regulation" is much more than merely a "hidden tax." Due to the characteristics identified above, it is the generator of a class of uncertainties quite different in nature from those with which the businessman has historically been accustomed to dealing.

Because government regulatory activities are so uncoordinated, it is difficult, if not impossible, for a businessman to know what the government's priorities are in regulating. Most legislation speaks in absolutes. Workers will be protected. The environment will be preserved. Energy will be conserved. Consumer products will be safe. But when conflicts develop, as they inevitably must, which goal is to have priority? As new goals are defined, how are conflicts with older goals to be reconciled? And as it becomes clear that the absolutes sought by the law are unreachable, how are the necessary compromises to be developed? Businessmen ask, "Doesn't the government know what it wants?" The answer is "no," primarily because, as far as regulation is concerned, there is no single actor that can be called "the government."

Even more confusing to businessmen is the matter of how specific targets for regulatory attention are selected. The wide latitude of discretion given agency administrators, the vague nature of their mandates, and the uncertain nature of the evidence with which they have to deal inevitably leads to actions that seem (and sometimes are) highly arbitrary. Indeed, the agencies' poor understanding of the industries they regulate means that they are often as surprised as the businessman being regulated to find that a particular class of firms will be impacted by what they are proposing to do.

Finally, the almost universal use of "command and control" techniques for enforcement once standards have been decided upon helps insure that ultimate regulatory outcomes will be uncertain. The stringency, timing, and even applicability of regulations to a particular firm or even to entire classes of firms is often in doubt until lengthy court battles have taken place. To be sure, business itself is the instigator of much of this protracted litigation. But the uncertainty this process generates in the minds of top executives, stockholders, customers, the firm's bankers, and employees cannot help but play havoc with a firm's ability to plan rationally.

But the picture may not be all that bleak, at least from the
viewpoint of the individual firm. The very fact that government
agencies are usually uninformed about the industries they regulate, that their priorities and procedures for targeting are so
ill defined, and that their enforcement processes so arbitrary
creates major opportunities for the regulatory process to be
influenced to the advantage of the firm.

The use of the regulatory process by "public interest"
groups to achieve their goals has been well documented. (See,
for example, (9).) Less well known or understood is its use by
individual business firms to create or enhance the market for
their products or to disadvantage a competitor.

The benefits can be substantial. In a recent article,
Fortune magazine estimated the subsidies created by Congress for
small refiners through the oil entitlements program at $2.5 bil-
lion per year.(10) This, plus the fact that the magnitude of the
per-barrel subsidy is inversely proportional to the size of the
refinery, has caused a boom in the construction of otherwise
highly inefficient units. Jackson and Leone, in a soon-to-be-
published paper, estimate the impact on individual establishments
in segments of the pulp and paper industry of the 1972 Amendments
to the Water Pollution Control Act.(11) Observing that the magnitude of the cost pass-through will be determined by the impact
on the average firm, they observe that some firms stand to have
their profits substantially enhanced.

We have encountered similar examples in our present study
for EPA of the economic impact of potential controls over
nonaerosol fluorocarbon emissions. As disadvantaged as certain
firms might be by such controls, others stand to profit hand-
somely by them. Indeed, this ability to profit from the current
chaotic state of the regulatory process has been suggested by
some as a reason why businessmen, who might otherwise seem the
natural allies of the increased use of more predictable economic
incentives, adamantly defend current regulatory techniques.(12)

The range of permissible conduct open to a firm in attempting to influence governmental regulatory activities is much
broader than when engaging in more traditional forms of competition. A businessman cannot conspire with his competitor to raise
or lower prices. He cannot engage in overtly predatory behavior.
He cannot merge if that merger will tend to create a monopoly "in
any line of commerce in any sector of the country."(13) But he
can attempt to influence the government to undertake actions
which have the identical effect. (See (14).)

Thus regulation, through its very arbitrariness and its sus-
ceptability to manipulation, emerges as both a major problem and
a prime opportunity for today's business firm. Through its regulatory activities, government has become both a creator and des-
troyer of business opportunities, a factor equal if not superior
in importance to the actions of competitors and the tastes of the
public in shaping corporate strategy. Tracing out the

implications of this fact is a task deserving of attention. But
this must be the subject of another paper. Instead let us at
long last address the question we originally posed: How does
this "new regulation" and the fact that it constitutes such a
change in the firm's competitive environment affect the firm's
incentive and ability to innovate?

The Impact of the "New Regulation" on Innovation: Some Tentative
Hypotheses

    While others undoubtedly could be suggested, we have identi-
fied five impacts that regulation as we have described it can
have on innovation for a typical large chemicals firm:

   o Regulation may divert resources that otherwise might
      be used to fund research.

   o Regulation may change the firm's ability to calcu-
      late the payoffs to investments in research and
      development.

   o Regulation may alter the proportion of benefits that
      are properly classifiable (from the viewpoint of the
      firm) as "externalities," and this may change the
      nature of research the firm is likely to undertake.

   o Regulation may change the optimal institutional pat-
      terns for performing certain types of research.

   o Regulation may politicize the research process.

    Although some might consider us excessively timid, we hesi-
tate at this point to declare whether, on balance and in the
longer-term, these various impacts are likely to increase or
decrease the incentive of the chemicals firm to innovate and thus
the level of funding that will be devoted to research and
development activities. We do believe that regulation certainly
will alter both the role research plays in the firm and the
manner in which the firm's research activity functions. Therefore, rather than devote much time to speculating about future
levels of research spending in chemicals, we will content ourselves with outlining in a semi-analytical fashion the various
impacts we have mentioned, reserving the more quantitative conclusions until our research is more complete.

    Diversion of Resources. We have already noted that this is
the aspect of regulation's impact on research activity in the
chemicals industry that has been most widely discussed. Companies that report large shares of their current resources being
devoted to responding to government requests for information and

to complying with regulations that have already been promulgated infer (if they don't directly state) that some portion of these funds would otherwise have been directed to increased expenditures on "productive" research and development.

The impact of this "resource diversion" argument on the firm's research and development activities would be greatest if, as some claim, the level of resources devoted to R&D were generally a simple function of net earnings. Certainly some firms take this "consumption" view of R&D. But, if we are to believe the results of those who have studied the innovation process, the vast majority of firms view R&D as an investment. In such a case, the resource diversion aspect of regulation affects R&D spending not because of its effect on current net earnings, but because it also promises to affect _future_ earnings from any new product or process developed as a result of a current expenditure of R&D funds. But note. This is equally true for _any_ investment the firm might make--in an advertising campaign, in acquiring a new subsidiary, or in expanding producton capacity. To the extent that the payoff to R&D occurs further in the future than the payoff to other activities, or to the extent that a differential risk premium is assigned to R&D projects, R&D spending might be particularly hard hit. But the net result on the firm's allocation of future resources across its full spectrum of future opportunities is not all that clear.

For example, in a world of rampant regulation where research can serve both to generate regulatory targets and to provide perhaps the most effective regulatory defense, the short-term payoff to investment in certain types of research may be immense. Consider fluorocarbons and products related to them. If all affected industries are included, tens or even hundreds of billions of dollars in sales are likely to be affected by whatever the ultimate regulatory decision is. The magnitude of these costs will surely play some role in determining the action that is taken. But the driving factor will be the state of information at the time a decision is made concerning the ozone-fluorocarbon relationship. Research to develop new uses for fluorocarbons may be in limbo pending resolution of the fluorocarbon issue. But research to investigate the underlying atmospheric relationships, techniques for fluorocarbon conservation, and substitute refrigerants, blowing agents, aerosol propellants, etc., has been greatly stimulated. Much of this research may appear (and even may be) "unproductive" from the viewpoint of those firms who had other plans for the resources and personnel now involved in it. And it certainly is not the result of any well-planned or logically conceived strategy that identified this as an area where concentrated scientific inquiry might yield especially promising results at this time. But it nevertheless is going on. And, inevitably, it will yield new product ideas that can be exploited by someone (but perhaps not the firms conducting the research) at some future date.

The one area where R&D spending might most be expected to be impacted would be basic research, since the benefits of such research are, by definition, undefinable at the time the research is carried out. Individuals who have studied firm behavior report that, in this instance, allocation of funds are often decided on a "rule of thumb" basis. This is not too relevant a consideration in the case of chemicals research, for most chemicals firms conduct little of what is properly termed "basic research." Mansfield's survey of seven major chemicals research laboratories showed that in 1966, only 7 percent of expenditures were for this research category.(15) And indeed, it could be argued that a private firm has little or no business engaging in such activities. (See (16). This suggests that the 7 percent figure cited above for chemicals industry "basic research" may be overstated.) However, as we will observe below, there are reasons to believe that regulation may be acting to increase the incentive for chemicals firms to engage in what otherwise would be considered "basic research," by changing its character so that it does promise to produce an identifiable payoff to the firm.

Changes in the Ability of Firms to Calculate Payoffs from Research. As we have already mentioned, most firms appear to consider their R&D expenditures to constitute investments designed to generate future streams of income. As such, their research decisions must meet the test of any investment--the discounted present value of their anticipated future revenues must exceed the discounted present value of their future costs.

However, investments in research and development are characterized by special risks. First there is the risk that the technical objective sought will not be achieved. Then there is the risk that the product or process cannot be profitably marketed. Mansfield's work makes clear that the latter are generally more important than the former (due in part perhaps to the small technical advances typically sought in industrial research projects) but that taken together, these risks are high.

(Mansfield studied three industrial laboratories, one chemicals and two proprietary drug. He found that 40 percent of the R&D projects that were begun were not technically completed; of those that were technically completed, 45 percent were not commercialized, presumably because of poor commercial prospects; and of those that were commercialized, 60 percent did not earn an economic profit value that is defined as a return exceeding that available from alternate uses of funds.(17) Thus the probability that a given project, once started, would be technically successful, commercialized, and profitable was 0.6 x 0.55 x 0.4 = 0.13.)

Regulation may alter these risks. In determining whether
research aimed at producing a new product can be deemed to have
achieved "technical success" and the resulting product considered
potentially "commercializable," attention must now be given to
whether the product can meet both current and anticipated tests
for toxicity, carcinogenicity, mutagenicity, teratogenicity, etc.
Like the costs of regulatory paperwork, this burden is not too
difficult for the firm to deal with. The cost of the tests are
well known. And, if they are at all "appropriate," the products
that are screened out are those that had no business being
advanced to the next stage of development. If the tests are
"inappropriate," but still serve a screening function that regulatory authorities and the courts consider adequate, only the
public is the loser. The firm's profits are likely to be relatively unaffected.

However, a product can meet the conventional standards for
"commercialization" and "pass" the battery of tests just referred
to and still run into trouble. A corporate decisionmaker, aware
of recent history and knowledgeable of the present somewhat con-
fused state of chemicals regulation, must consider the real possibility that, if he proceeds to authorize steps leading to commercialization, somewhere down the road a new and currently
undreamed-of hazard will be identified that will lead to severe
restrictions being placed on the marketability of his product.
This may represent the greatest hurdle of all to new product
development, for as expensive as the early stages of the product
development process (and even toxicity testing) undoubtedly are,
the real costs of bringing a new product to the marketplace only
begin once the decision is made to move it out of the lab. Mansfield has estimated that, for chemicals, 83 percent of the costs
of new product development occur after the applied research stage
and 57 percent occur even after the pilot plant stage.(18)

It is difficult to know how this latter category of risks
can be dealt with by a decisionmaker. Certainly increased testing of all new chemicals is one reasonable response. We are not
surprised to learn that at least one company is considering all
new chemicals to be potentially toxic and is subjecting them to
intensive screening. (See (19). Indeed, this seems to be the
path dictated by the Toxic Substances Control Act.) However, as
we have already suggested, this response, while perhaps laudable,
is insufficient. Accepted standards of toxicity change.(See, for
example, (20). This test may seem hopelessly primitive today,
but considering the advances in science, who is to say that 30
years from now our current testing methods won't be considered
equally primitive.) Furthermore, certain hazards are so remotely
associated with a given chemical that no conceivable test made at
the time of the commercialization decision was being made could
hope to discover them. The example of fluorocarbons'
hypothesized impact on the ozone layer is as good as any to cite
here.

What, then, is the conscientious executive to do? The most
reasonable course for him would be to employ a heavy additional
risk premium when evaluating any chemical that meets all
presently known tests and that shows strong commercial potential.
If the product passes even this hurdle, it may still eventually
encounter regulatory difficulties, but the chances are high that
it will have repaid its development cost and produced a profit
for the company by the time these difficulties emerge. The
impact of such a "regulatory risk premium" would be to slow--but
not necessarily stop--new product development.

Alternatively, the decisionmaker might impose a moratorium
on commercializing new products. This might prove superior when
the regulatory situation is in a state of extreme flux and is
expected to stabilize. In such a case, the appropriate risk
premium might be so high that the knowledgeable executive, hoping
that the situation is temporary, would be hesitant to impose it
and thereby weed out new product ideas that might prove acceptable once matters stabilized.

Casual conversations with chemical executives suggest that
behavior of the latter sort may be occurring at present. But
absent systematic investigation, we hesitate to give much weight
to such statements. Certainly this is a time of extreme regulatory uncertainty. Passage of legislation such as the Toxic Substances Control Act reflects Congress' feelings that some form of
regulatory screening procedures is absolutely necessary if sensible product introduction decisions are ever to be made. But it
remains to be seen whether the legislation will produce any
increase in predictability or, more importantly, whether generalizable procedures will emerge that permit existing chemicals to
be classified as to potential threat.

The preceding two categories of impacts have previously been
identified and their significance widely debated. The next three
we will mention have been much less discussed but are, in our
view, of even greater long-term importance.

Changes in the Nature of Research that Firms Undertake. The
mention above of the importance of developing generalizable testing procedures for chemicals gets us to the third of the effects
that regulation likely is having on chemicals research--its
impact on the nature of research that chemicals firms undertake.
We noted earlier that most chemicals firms do not actually engage
in much "basic research"--that is, research whose results are
intended to show no apparent applicability to the firm's
businesses. This is because such research generates no promise
of profit for the firm, and it is promise of profit, not concern
over the state of human knowledge, that motivates research spending by private firms.

Regulation alters this calculation by altering the payoffs to different classes of research. Although other examples surely can be cited, the one that comes immediately to mind is the explosive growth of industrial interest in the once obscure field of toxicology.

It is a mistake to assume, as some appear to, that chemicals firms gave no thought whatever to the possible consequences to the environment, to consumers, or to workers resulting from the production or use of their products prior to the rise of the "new regulation." Legal doctrines of liability, although perhaps not as strict then as today, provided such an incentive as did concern for the company's public image. (Remember the slogan "Better things for better living through chemistry"?) But there can be no doubt that the rise of the "new regulation" and, in particular, certain of its characteristics mentioned earlier, have greatly stimulated toxicological research.

The reasons are complex reflecting the complexity of the incentives presently generated by chemicals regulation. In part they are defensive. Chemicals firms, perhaps once content to draw much of their basic research from the universities, now want to stay abreast of research that can overnight direct the regulatory spotlight at important segments of their business. Given the nature of the adversarial process, they cannot wait until a research result is published in a reputable scientific journal and subjected to critical scrutinizing by disinterested colleagues.

In part, however, the reasons for interest in toxicology may reflect the power that such knowledge can give a firm vis-a-vis its competitors. Although individual firms will deny that they engage in such behavior, it is not unknown for firms to boost their own prospects by suggesting that a competitor's product may embody certain dangers.

Finally, research on toxicology may ultimately generate a level of understanding about the effects of chemicals on biological processes sufficient to permit the development of the generalizable testing procedures mentioned earlier. From the viewpoint of the chemicals industry, this would be a great boon, justifying the expenditure of considerable sums of money on research whose immediate applicability appears uncertain.

Changes in the Optimal Institutions for Performing Research. The same factors which alter the type of research that the firm has an incentive to undertake also alter the institutional form within which that research may optimally be carried out. Last year, major chemicals firms announced the establishment of an industry-funded institute to undertake research on toxicology.(21) This represents a sharp break for the chemicals industry which traditionally has relied most heavily on in-house research capability. It seems explanable in part because of the shift in what is properly classifiable from the viewpoint of the firm as "basic research." But more may be involved. There are strong competitive reasons why it is useful that all chemicals firms have equal access to any breakthroughs that might be made in identifying new classes of toxic substances or new mechanisms by which toxicity might be inferred. Such breakthroughs may "clear" entire groups of chemicals or place others in jeopardy. It makes good sense from the viewpoint of the chemicals industry to fund such work cooperatively. We are less certain that it is in the public interest, but leave that question to future research.

The Transformation of Research into an Adversarial Process. Regulation, and the increased attention it has focused on hazards to the environment, to consumers, and to workers, has altered the once prevalent view of the researcher as a dispassionate scholar, gradually developing a line of inquiry, publishing only for the benefit of his colleagues and in the name of advancing the state of human knowledge. This picture probably was never completely accurate, even in the academic world. It certainly never characterized industrial research. Nevertheless, the rise of scientific activism has greatly altered the nature of scientific inquiry. (See (22).) The ability (and willingness) of regulatory bodies to reach into firms to gain access to preliminary research findings, and the necessity that corporate researchers be willing to defend their work to the general public, not just to their superiors, is likely to change the nature of the research process as well as the type of individual who seeks out a career in industry. Changes such as these are likely to be the most difficult of all to verify, but, in the long run, may prove to be the most significant, both for the firm and the economy.

Conclusion

Much has been heard of late concerning the impact of regulation on industrial innovation. A consensus seems to be emerging that this impact has been negative and that, as a consequence, the "burden" of regulation should be eased. While we would agree that there is substantial room for improvement in the way our government regulates business conduct, we hope that this paper makes clear that we are skeptical of many of the claims that have been put forward to date--as well as of many of the proposed "solutions." Regulation is indeed likely to generate major changes--not all of them desirable from a social point of view--in business behavior in this country. But overly simplistic solutions to overly simplified characterizations of "the problem" will not help matters. We need to examine in a much more systematic way than we have done in the past just what these changes will be. For not until that has been done can we hope to advance solutions that have a high probability generating a genuine improvement.

Acknowledgments

The research upon which this paper is based was supported
partially by The Rand Corporation as part of its program of public service. The author would like to thank Adele Palmer, The
Rand Corporation, for her suggestions and helpful criticisms.

Literature Cited

1. Denison, Edward F., "Effects of Selected Changes in the
Institutional and Human Environment Upon Output Per Unit of
Input," Survey of Current Business (January 1978), 58, (1),
21-44.
2. Chandler, Alfred D., Strategy and Structure, M.I.T.
Press, Cambridge, 1962.
3. Weidenbaum, Murray L., Business, Government, and the
Public, Prentice-Hall, Englewood Cliffs, N. J., 1977.
4. 29 USCA 655(b)(5) [italics added].
5. Industrial Union Department, AFL-CIO v. Hodgson, Court
of Appeals, D.C. Circuit, 1974, 449 F. 2d 467.
6. Weinberg, Alvin M., "Science and Trans-Science,"
Minerva, (April 1972), 209-222.
7. 1977 Clean Air Act Amendments, Sec. 126, inserting new
Part B, Sec. 157(b) to Title I of the Clean Air Act.
8. 47 USCA 1371(e)(4).
9. Berry, Jeffrey M., Lobbying for the People: The
Political Behavior of Public Interest Groups, Princeton University Press, Princeton, 1977.
10. Alexander, Tom, "How Little Oil Hit a Gusher on Capitol
Hill," Fortune, (August 14, 1978), 148-154.
11. Jackson, John E., and Leone, Robert A., "The Political
Economy of Federal Regulatory Activity: A Case Study of Water
Pollution Controls in the Pulp and Paper Industry," preliminary
version.
12. Buchanan, J. M., and Tullock, G., "Polluters' Profits
and Political Response: Direct Controls versus Taxes," American
Economic Review, (March 1975), 129-147.
13. Clayton Antitrust Act, Section 7.
14. Eastern Railroad Presidents Conference v. Noerr Motor
Freight, 365 U.S. 127, 1961.
15. Mansfield, Edwin, et al., Research and Innovation in
the Modern Corporation, 34, Table 2.6, Norton, New York, 1971.
16. Brown, Alfred E., "New Definitions for Industrial R&D,"
Research Management, (September 1972), 56-57.
17. Mansfield, op. cit., p. 209.

18. Mansfield, op. cit., p. 118.

19. Newsweek, (August 21, 1978), 27.

20. Lowrance, William W., Of Acceptable Risk, 159-160, Kaufman, Inc., Los Altos, Ca., 1976.

21. Reddig, William, "Industry's Preemptive Strike Against Cancer," Fortune, (February 13, 1978), 116-119.

22. Goodell, Rae, The Visible Scientists, Little, Brown, and Company, Boston, 1975.

RECEIVED March 8, 1979.

A Reasoned Approach to Government Regulation: How Can We Separate the Good from the Bad?

DAVID J. NEWBURGER

Washington University, St. Louis, MO 63130

If statistics had been kept, I suspect that we would discover that the national sport gaining most popularity in this decade is documenting horror stories to show how awful government regulation has been for business. The sport has even gone professional with the development of research institutes at my university, at another here in Miami, and others elsewhere that are devoted largely to displaying regulation's folly. Like all other sports, this one would not gain in popularity without particular attraction to a vast portion of the citizenry. I believe that that attraction stems from a widely held view that government gets away with too much absurdity and well desires to be the subject of belittling, nitpicking, and guffawing.

Entertaining as the sport may be, however, I suggest that a more interesting subject for academic pursuit is how to eliminate untoward instrusions by government into business in general and into innovative activities in particular. I choose my words carefully, for at the outset I suggest we must distinguish those government intrusions that are wholly justifiable crosses that some among us must bear, from the untoward intrusions that impose limitations and requirements without justification. Thus, we need to develop some working criteria for separating justified regulations from those that are not. Then, we will be prepared to attempt a brief systematic review of the mechanisms of regulation to see how untoward intrusions might be minimized.

The whole point of any regulatory regime is to get some or all of the populace to conform to standards of conduct that they might not otherwise. Therefore, any regulation intrudes upon the right of individuals to exercise their own free choice. The interesting question is not whether some intrusions on personal freedoms should be allowed, but which should be. In our own system of government, I define a regulation as justified if it induces conformity with some standard of conduct that, through deliberations of the democratic process, we have come to prefer. If we can agree that that is a reasonably noncontroversial definition, we can turn our attention to the questions implicit in it:

0-8412-0511-6/79/47-109-021$05.00/0

how can we tell what conduct a regulation induces, what conduct
we prefer, and whether we arrived at that preference through suitable democratic processes?

Determining what conduct an existing regulation induces is a
relatively straightforward empirical matter, although separating
regulation from other forces that drive conduct may be difficult.
Certainly, ascertaining what changes in conduct a new regulation
will induce, deciding what conduct is preferred, and figuring out
whether decisions were democratically arrived at are all vexing
problems.

Inherent Dilemmas of Regulation

These problems are so difficult because they reflect dilemmas
of regulation with which we must live. Consider several such
dilemmas. First, regulations do not necessarily induce desired
conduct. After all, all that a regulation does is to set new
constraints and, sometimes, opportunities on the decisions of
people who operate, in any event, within a wide range of opportunities and constraints. Depending upon the particular mix of all
these, a person may resist complying with a regulation, he or she
may comply, or he or she may avoid the imperative to comply by
leaving the area of conduct all together. Thus, we are aware of
truckers who characteristically exceed highway speed limits because they believe their business requires it; we are aware of
firms that install waste water management facilities to meet
specified standards; and we are aware of firms that terminated
R & D efforts in chemicals that are more likely to be carcinogenic.

Consider the second dilemma. The standards set in regulations
and the devices available for enforcing those standards often only
remotely reflect the purpose of the regulation -- especially where
the risks that the regulation is to protect against are, in proba-
bilistic terms, remote. The regulation of recominant DNA research
for investigators under federal contract is a case in point. The
NIH Guidelines require that certain experiments be carried on in
limited quantities of material under high degrees of isolation
from the environment. Yet, because of our primitive knowledge of
the threat of new recombinant creations, we do not understand the
degree of risk associated with research in large quantities of
materials or in low level containment facilities. We do not know
whether complying with the Guidelines is useful in protecting
public health, unnecessary because the perceived risk of such
research greatly exceeds the real risk, or inadequate because
possible products of the research will breach the containment
facilities required even if they are produced in small quantities.
And, on the enforcement side, we have no assurance that the threat
of reprisals in government contracting will deter those who are
set on violating the Guidelines. Thus, neither the standards nor
the mechanism available for their enforcement assure us that the
standards will promote the Guideline's ultimate purpose -- protec-

tion of the public health and safety.

Third, perceptions about the content of regulations -- and
about how they might change -- may induce unintended reactions.
For example, most firms depend on a continued growth in performance to support their continued profitability. Interruptions
in the constancy of the flow of business endangers that continued
growth; and new regulations and new interpretations of them
threaten such interruptions. Therefore, firms must assess the
risk that regulations may change and consider withdrawing from
areas of business activities where developing regulations threaten
uncertainty and interruption: the less stable a regulatory regime
is, the more incentive firms have to avoid the activities that
regime might affect. This suggests that where we introduce new
policies -- for example, cleaning up air, reducing public or
worker exposure to a wide range of toxic chemicals, or limiting
payments abroad that would be viewed as unethical at home -- we
necessarily create incentives for avoiding activities that most
likely will be affected. This is good to the extent that it controls conduct we want to circumscribe, but it is bad to the extent
that it affects conduct that will not be intentionally limited
once the regulation has crystallized into an understandable and
stable regime.

Fourth, recalling that we live in a world of scarce resources,
we know that not all social goals can be obtained. In time of
war, we speak of this as the dilemma of choosing between producing
guns or butter. The problem, we know, pervades all times. It is
the basic premise of our economic system. And, it pervades the
study of effects of regulation. Thus, any decision to regulate
a firm creates a new cost of production. That, in turn, lowers
the firm's potential sales. The new cost, on the other hand,
usually constitutes a payment for some other resource. Thus,
environmental regulation may reduce industrial output -- and jobs
-- but may produce more clean air and water. The fact that we
live with scarce resources implies that, in creating a regulation,
authorities must balance choices among values that are all desirable. And, since this decision requires accepting less of
each of the desired results, no choice is satisfying.

Another feature of this dilemma exacerbates the problem.
While we can discuss net benefit/cost trade-offs of a regulation
for society as a whole, we must recognize that the victim of any
cost may not be the beneficiary of the benefit traded for. Thus,
in the jobs and clean air or water exchange, the question becomes
whether a relatively few people are required to find new means of
livelihood so that many people may have a slightly healthier or
aesthetically more pleasing environment.

The problem of scarce resources plays out in other areas.
For example, it is a matter of political fact that regulatory
authorities have scarce resources to enforce standards. If they
devote their all to one problem, others will suffer. Therefore,
they may have to be satisfied with less effective enforcement of

all regulations.

Consider the outstanding case of OSHA. At one time its administrators calculated that on a random basis a firm subject to that regulation was likely to be inspected once every 28 years. No doubt the number continues to be about the same. Without inspections OSHA cannot use personal interaction between firms' managements and OSHA officials to guide firms to understand the scope of response the agency expects. This may explain why OSHA decided early to adopt meticulous regulations. It may also explain why Congress required OSHA inspectors to issue citations for every violation found, even those that are inconsequential. By making expectations crystal clear and creating a strong likelihood that those in violation will be punished, Congress and OSHA may have offset the fact that enforcement is so episodic and, therefore, may have secured compliance similar to that that would have been achieved if annual inspections were feasible. However, doing this implies that the particular firms that happen to be inspected may find themselves subject to far more rigorous enforcement of the rules than reasonable protection of worker health and safety requires.

The fifth and last dilemma of regulation that I am reviewing here is one of moral proportion. We cannot ensure that regulations will be just. To even approach the question of whether a regulation is just, we must recognize that justice has many faces. To be just, a decision must surely have at least been (1) fair for the person affected, (2) fair from the point of view of the myriad different interests in society, (3) predictable, (4) made after adequate deliberation, (5) made by a wise, morally upright decisionmaker, and (6) substantively correct. Yet, not all of these elements can be achieved in a given case, and, indeed, sometimes they are mutually inconsistent. Consider, for example, the Tris-treated sleep wear problem where banning the garments was probably substantively correct from a public health standpoint but was certainly unpredictable and probably unfair from the manufacturers' viewpoint. Where there are competing interests, it is often impossible to treat all justly -- King Solomon was lucky.

Coping With The Dilemmas

Recognizing that these dilemmas exist, we can approach regulations with a more tolerant, if skeptical, perspective. By now, I hope we have learned that regulations cannot be "right." Assuming we continue to need some regulation -- and there is no doubt about that -- the question becomes how we will decide what regulation is adequate. I suggest that this can only be answered on a case-by-case basis for each particular social problem regulation is to address. And, I suggest this must be done by examining the consequences of imposing each of the possible forms that regulation might take with an eye on the particular problems of the case and on the irresolvable dilemmas of attempting to regulate.

Time does not permit a detailed analysis of the different possible features that regulations may take, although I would suggest that a better understanding of the subject by those in both the private and public sector who are involved in developing regulations would be refreshing. In briefest outline, we should observe that two elements comprise regulations -- standards for conduct and devices to enforce compliance with those standards.

Alternative Methods For Standard Setting

The source of the standards for conduct may be laws, judicial decisions, rules of administrative agencies, or formal or informal directives of such agencies. Usually, the greater the generality of the standard, the less likely it is that we will be able to understand its applicability in a given case without further enunciation, but the more likely it is that it will cover more cases. Thus, a standard that prohibits chemical manufacturers from negligently producing drugs applies to a wide number of cases, but is less than clear about just exactly what is expected of the manufacturer in each case.

On the other hand, as standards are made more particular, it is easier to ascertain what is required, but what is required may stifle innovative alternatives or serve no useful purpose. We are all familiar with the old design standard building codes that required, for example, ceiling joists made to some specified dimensions and of some specified type of wood. These stood in the way of architectural innovations in alternative dimensions and with alternative materials, such as steel, glass, concrete, and plastics. Such regulations did sometimes achieve the standard of conduct sought. Ceiling joist requirements in building codes probably did ensure the sturdiness of floors and ceilings. But, they also prohibited alternative choices that would have been equally adequate. These specific standards also run the risk of requiring conduct that it not even consistent with the ultimate goal. For example, the purpose of the famous Delaney Amendment to the Food, Drug and Cosmetic Act is to protect the public from cancer and, presumably, to protect the public health. The current debate over a saccharin ban suggests that the Amendment may ban a substance even though that substance may not, in fact, cause cancer in humans and even though it does have other public health benefits.

Thus, we have the alternative of setting standards with varying degrees of generality, and none of the choices are entirely satisfactory. Review of the circumstances in each particular case may suggest which is best among inadequate alternatives.

Alternative Methods For Enforcement

Selecting means of enforcement is also difficult. In the

United States we use a vast array of devices and procedures. These
range from criminal penalities, to the possibility of fines and
injunctions, to administrative cease and desist orders, to licensing requirements, to systems of tax and other economic incentives, and beyond. Together, they constitute a broad range of the
possible degree of pressure that government may use to encourage
or coerce compliance with stated standards. Generally, as the
pressure becomes greater, the likelihood is that more of those who
otherwise might not comply will do so. However, the trade-offs
along the way are legion. For example, criminal penalties are
severe forms of coercion. Thus, most regulated firms will comply
with standards that are subject to such enforcement. However,
because society finds such sanctions to be so severe, administrators will be loathe to enforce isolated, minor infractions by
bringing criminal prosecutions. Therefore, if the only enforcement
device for a given standard is a criminal penalty, one can expect
that some deviation from the standard will be tolerated, and,
thus, the standard is not as confining as it appears on its face.

The result of these observations is that we must look at
regulatory regimes rather than particular regulations. Consider,
for example, a range of facts about OSHA (an example already referred to): the standards are meticulous, enforcement is required
if a violation is discovered, and inspections are unlikely unless
particular problems turn up. Therefore, there is a low probability
of enforcement for violations, but a high probability that the
agency will enforce against a violation that it does discover.
That is not the only incentive to comply with OSHA rules, however.
Insurance companies require inspections of the workplace to under-
write insurance, and serious noncompliance with OSHA standards
would probably raise doubts about the wisdom of insuring the
facility. Further, employers rely on insurance investigators to
tell them areas in which they are not complying with OSHA standards, and one can assume that many employers will voluntarily
comply with the standards upon discovering they are not. Finally,
employees are protected from disciplinary sanctions or dismissal
for blowing the whistle on their employers to OSHA, thus stimulating special inspections for important problems. It may be that
a random inspection is likely for ordinary employers only once in
28 years, but the whole regime to this regulation encourages the
employer to comply with OSHA's standards regardless.

Conclusion

Most regulations probably have some good in them. It is unlikely that any stay around very long if they serve no public purpose. On the other hand, all regulations have some bad. They
would not be worth having unless they constrain some people who
do not want to be constrained. And, they do that in ways that,
inevitably, can be shown to be inadequate. The only sensible
approach to the problem of improving regulation is to gain a

comprehension of the inherent inadequacies of regulation, to learn the range of alternative methods to set and enforce standards and the trade-offs among alternatives, and then to set about an inductive minimizing/maximizing game to search for the best alternative within the limits of what is possible.

RECEIVED March 8, 1979.

What Do We Really Know About the Impact of Regulation on Innovation?

JAMES W. LEENHOUTS

Dow Chemical U.S.A., 566 Building, Midland, MI 48640

Others so much more eloquent than I have extolled the value of innovation that I would do little good to join that competition. In reality, there isn't much sense, anyway, discussing what we agree on - innovation has priceless value. But before you get comfortable, be reminded that there are two substantial, and growing, philosophical cores that firmly disagree with us that innovation has value. For these thinkers, the answer to our problems is either the conservative position of stopping progress because it causes problems, or the radical position that even the progress we have witnessed is so slow we should demolish what we have built.

I am trying to find agreement on the subject of the impact of government regulation on innovation, while I'm not sure that the conservative and radical philosophies, like taxes, are not squeezing those of us progressives in the middle more than we want. I have to admit that, the more I observe attitudes today, the less confident I become that innovation is seen as universally desirable.

Innovation is the complex, successful combination of invention; a need; production, which is labor and capital; marketing and management. As such, many things impact innovation, and of these many things, government regulation has been universally indicted as an important factor. Since the rate of innovation in the U.S. is declining, and this is deemed unsatisfactory, we should be examining this important factor. (1, 2, 3) From what others have seen and reported, we might find a means to regain a more satisfactory progress rate. (4, 5, 6) Therefore, in the construction of this paper, I dedicated myself to the perspective of a review, a classification of the substantive studies available and a classification of the regulation types.

In my quest, I concentrated primarily on studies in which the author dealt with a data base or developed a carefully constructed model. I did this to avoid a number of references where data was skimpy or the author was more inclined to offer just his theory. These authors may be absolutely correct and remarkably

0-8412-0511-6/79/47-109-029$05.00/0
© 1979 American Chemical Society

eloquent, but I feel that some evidence is required.

I was pleased that, contrary to the feeling of others who have reviewed it, the literature is reasonably ample. Innovation and government regulation are popular things to talk about. Such was not the case in the 1920's and 1930's when Ludwig Von Mises and Joseph Schumpeter discussed bureaucracy, innovation and the failure of capitalism.

Types of Studies

It seems to me that there are four types of studies available in the literature; mathematical model studies, cost added studies, empirical studies and case studies. The distinction between each and their value to our subject is worth noting.

Model Studies. The spectrum of writing on the subject is broad as typified by Takayama, Professor of Economics at Purdue, who, in his Behavior of the Firm Under Regulatory Control, (7) reduced and modeled the problem to 26 equations. Model studies, unfortunately are not convincing. Those who labor to produce them do so in a lonely world at the present time. As yet, the complex question of human nature, emerging technology, economic cycles and national security mitigates against the modeler's credibility.

Cost Added Studies. Cost added studies are typified by, for example, those of Dr. Paul Chenea, Vice President of Research at General Motors, who, in his paper, The Costs and Effects of Regulation, (8) documents very well the costs of regulation in his company. He concludes that we need "reasonable regulation" and that "research is hobbled by excessive regulation".

Dr. Chenea, as many authors do, leaves us with the problem of what is "excessive" and what is "reasonable". One has a strong feeling that "excessive" is what does not make sense to General Motors. But suppose it is not seen as excessive to the regulator, a senator, Ralph Nader, or car drivers? I am reminded of one of those cute, catchy signs you see on peoples' desks - BE REASONABLE, DO IT MY WAY. While that may be humorous, the problem of distinguishing between "reasonable" and "excessive" is a very serious one. The literature is silent.

Therefore, without picking on an excellent piece of work - and I chose it just because it is - these types of studies, which I call "added cost studies", provide us with additional cost information due to regulation, but nothing we can really get our hands on with respect to innovation.

Many U.S. companies will be participating in a very ambitious, well documented, inter-company, Arthur Anderson study of the cost of regulation, to be completed in the spring of 1979. It will define the cost of regulation across 200 top companies. It will not enlighten us on the impact on innovation, although it will address itself to added research costs.

Without any question, regulation adds burdensome costs. Americans have been battling costs with a passion that would suggest, in a Darwinian sense, that regulation is a natural enemy of cost efficiency, and vice versa. We might wander off the subject by wondering why we have a plague of regulation, but that might be carrying Darwin too far. Cost added studies may be of inestimable aid in battling inflation, but the case has not been made that there is a particular connection with innovation.

Empirical Studies. The greatest value in understanding the impact of regulation on innovation should come with empirical studies. Furthermore, one specific series of empirical studies which involves drug innovations is particularly interesting. There have been several studies in this area and, while I specifically refer to the Henry Grabowski work, Drug Regulation and Innovation, (9) there are others, also. This is a detailed piece of work that deserves to be a major part of our thinking on the subject.

With drugs, authors in this area have had an unusual situation that has allowed them a unique opportunity to study the impact of regulations on an innovative industry with plenty of historical information and comparative data. Because drugs have been regulated for many years and have been systematically registered for safety purposes, and because drugs were specifically impacted by the 1962 Drug Amendments, Grabowski was able to document the disasterous consequences on innovation. In addition, because other countries also require registration but did not install new regulations at the time the U.S. Congress did, comparative national information is also available.

There are not many empirical studies. In fact, I can find only a few. Obviously, such studies are not easy to come by and they are expensive to research. Furthermore, very few have the situation so well set up for research as drugs. The real question is the applicability of drug innovation studies to other areas of technological innovation. Since I understand the Grabowski work has encountered this problem, empirical studies with any lesser foundation may be next to useless.

Case Studies. The last area of our spectrum is the case studies which, although numerous in the literature, are, like a developing mosaic, each too specific to present a broad picture of innovation and regulation. However, the mosaic is taking some form and the increasing weight of the case study literature is of real value while also helping us understand how a specific regulation did impact on a specific innovation. Case studies are numerous enough that a single month will bring plenty of examples. The real value of case study literature is to firmly fix the fact that regulations and innovation are related.

A good example of a case study is the Paul Oreffice, Let's

Stop Dumping U.S. Jobs, (10) in which he points out how The Dow
Chemical Company employed an innovative sulfur dioxide control
system in Michigan in which a complex, computer based weather
analysis program is fed meteorological data constantly to determine the balance of coal and oil to be burned in the various plant
boilers each day. In the many years this has operated, Dow has
been able to burn a maximum of U.S. produced coal, a minimum of
oil, thus reducing imports, all without a single excursion from
the EPA guidelines. The EPA does not intend to extend the Dow
permit an additional two years while a new power plant, now under
construction, can be completed. The new power plant has been
partly delayed, interestingly enough, by regulation. A failure
to permit would force Dow to use some $44 million more oil for no
purpose whatsoever.

Cost Versus Innovation Accounting

Both cost added and case studies represent the bulk of the
literature available. This is no surprise since it is a testimony to the American business system, which is much more accurate
in keeping track of what something costs to make rather than the
need it solves. In fact, probably only due to the slowly awaken-
ing American corporation's sensitivity to defend the social value
of its products, is the American corporation now dedicating a
larger and larger portion of its time to evaluate the good things
it has done as well as what it cost to do it. I surely think
this is a solid step in the right direction, because I really
don't think we would be having this symposium if the American
chemical business, or all business, had had an innovation
accounting system that approximates our cost accounting system.

Is Regulation A Spur To Innovation?

What has been said about regulation being a spur to innovation has been particularly intriguing to me, and I hoped this
review would shed some light. My problem is philosophical in that
government regulation - or any regulation, even inside a business
for that matter, is designed to make events and behavior "regular"
or "controlled". Innovation, which is successfully doing something for the first time, is change. Change and control are as
opposite as they can be, in my mind. Thus, in this review, I was
particularly sensitive to any documentation of regulation being a
spur to innovation.
Gerstenfeld's empirical studies of 107 successful and unsuccessful companies in Government Regulation Effects on the
Direction of Innovation: A Focus on Performance Standards, (11)
could only find that performance standards regulations have a
secondary, but positive, impact on the direction of successful
innovations. Lessing comes to the conclusion in Why the U.S.
Lags in Technology. (12) that government programs related to

technology continue to be dominated by short-term considerations
instead of basic technologies. Both of these studies, at best,
show a rather weak relationship.

The Washington University "CAPI Project", A State of the Art
Review of the Effects of Regulation on Technological Innovation
in the Chemical and Allied Products Industries, (13) states that
"other regulations stimulate innovations by setting performance
standards which current technology is unable to meet". I believe
that the authors would agree that this statement is more speculation than documentation as the "CAPI Report" conclusion does not
refer again to such an important conclusion. In fact, the "CAPI
Report" conclusions are not at all definitive, cautioning that
the literature only suggests that some relationship exists but
that the positive or negative and primary or secondary impacts of
regulation on innovation are not known.

It is possible that an innovation may come from or be spurred
by regulation, but it is equally probable that the innovation and
the regulation come independently from the same cause. Since
logic tells us that both innovation and regulation are expected
responses to a problem, it's interesting why we persist in developing the logic sequence that it is the problem that begets
regulation that begets innovation. With a few exceptions, which
are turning sour, we all know that by the time a regulation is
written, the technology for compliance exists. The result can
easily be the famous regulated cowboy. Now many of you have seen
this horse with the roll bars, turn signals and so forth. The
humorous aspect of this is that it is all too true. This is
exactly what a horse would look like simply because a horse is
inherently inefficient, dangerous and is a notorious pollutor.
The horse could be improved by such "innovations". However, the
automobile, which represents a vast improvement in all those
areas, would not have come into being because of such regulation.

As with turn signals on a horse, to order, by law, that a
certain new condition must be met and then count the installation
of that technology as an innovation, regardless of the economic
impact, desirability, or even the need, is to also grossly mis-
understand innovation. Do we spur innovation by the political
decision to ordain that a certain mix of automobiles manufactured
by a company should average 25 miles per gallon? I'm not con-
versant with the problems of getting 25 miles per gallon, but I
don't see how that regulation will bring on the battery powered
car - or gasoline from coal or corn stalks, or convenient urban
transportation, or a host of other innovations that might have
come to solve our fuel problems.

The premise that a problem begets both regulation and innovation is a significant new thought that explains much of the
confusion in the existing literature about what constitutes a spur
to innovation. Based on my review, we have a long way to go before regulation, no matter what other good it does, can be
possibly justified as a spur to innovation.

Types of Regulation Affecting Innovation

A review of the literature also yields relatively little
agreement or suggestions that there are various categorizations
of regulation and innovation. This is unfortunate for one who
would wish to study the subject. As a result, we read, repeat-
edly, that "reasonable regulation is good", "some regulation is a
spur to innovation", "regulation is essential to protect the public", or, "excessive regulation is bad". The same thing is true
for innovation. There are innovations that are claimed to come
from regulation, there are innovations that come from the action
of the free marketplace, and there are innovations that come from
government purchasing for defense, large scale projects and so
forth. No attempt has been made to identify these. As a result,
everybody who wants to talk about government and regulation is
right. He simply selects the innovations or regulatory actions
that suit him, and away we go.
    While regulatory categorization has not been attempted,
there is enough in the literature to suggest that agreement can
be found for the following listing, which I submit, not as my
idea, but as a distillation of better students of this subject.
    I have three categories of regulation, Anti-trust, Economic,
and Product or Process Standards. The latter category requires a
further sub-division into specifications and judgmental standards.
This, of course, is not meant to be a complete list of all the
types of regulations we have. This categorization is simply those
major regulation types that have been reported to have an impact
on innovation.

    Anti-Trust Regulations. Surprisingly, I found so little
literature on this important subject that I think it's my fault,
and I am tempted to go back with a finer net. The Kamien and
Schwartz work, Market Structure and Innovation, (14) discusses the
anti-trust monopoly question. Another paper by Foster and Gluck,
Impact of Anti-Trust and Regulatory Actions on Progress of Technology, (15) is excellent. The paper deals with the increasing
involvement of the government in technology-intensive industries.
It does not address itself, unfortunately, to innovations, limiting
itself only to the thesis that the technology based industries are
receiving more than their share of regulatory anti-trust activity.
Since these are the innovative growth companies, whose market
share is rapidly changing, such regulatory activity is not a
surprise.
    In view of the energy crisis, the need for energy innovation
and the moves to limit the oil companies, it is too bad we do not
understand this area very well. Anti-trust actions do have profound effects on innovation. Foster and Gluck refer to government
moves to break up IBM and Bell without any thought of the impact
on these one billion dollar research organizations. It is interesting that the authors refer to a Senate Bill authored by the

late Michigan Senator Philip Hart, entitled, The Industrial
Reorganization Act. The opening sentences of the proposed Act
make interesting reading as Senator Hart wanted Congress to find
that..."The preservation of a private enterprise system, a free
market economy and a democratic society in the United States
(lies in the belief that competition spurs innovation and productivity and) requires legislation to supplement the policy of the
anti-trust laws through new enforcement mechanism designed to
responsibly restructure industries dominated by oligopoly or
monopoly power".

Obviously, other than there is a profound impact of anti-
trust legislation on regulation, there is little agreement. I
offer just the thought that competition among railroads was not
settled by breaking them up. As any student of Schumpeter knows,
Messrs. Henry Ford, Wilbur and Orville Wright, were more effective
than any government at restructuring the railroads. I give you
that reference free - it was in most of your history textbooks.

We might leave the subject of anti-trust regulation with the
thoughts of Joseph Schumpeter, who pointed out that our motivation
to prevent trusts from getting out of hand can be accomplished by
either regulation or by innovation, which goes back to my original
point that a need may beget both regulation and innovation.

Economic Regulation. In this area, I find the greatest
agreement. Once again, the cost and efficiency conscious American
business can easily see this problem. There is abundant information that government regulation of the economy adversely affects
innovation. Such regulation does much more than just the "added
cost" situation discussed earlier. The primary impact on innovation lies in the formation of risk capital and taxes on growth or
capital gains. Both of these penalties are most heavily borne by
the innovator who would seek to acquire capital.

Paul Kelly in Governmental Over-Regulation and the Capital
Crisis (16) looks at the problem from the money standpoint; and
while he is not concerned specifically with innovation, his
message and cases are clear to anyone who understands that an
innovation requires, almost by definition, risk capital.

Elmer Staats, former comptroller general, in his paper,
Improving the Climate for Innovation, What Government and Industry
Can Do (17) treats the economic problems and further points out
that the U.S. Government is substantially behind other governments
in understanding and supporting innovation and its innovative
businesses.

Schweitzer, in Regulations, Technological Progress and
Societal Interests, (18) concludes that with some added interviews
supplementing the Gellman Research Associates, Inc. report that
"a clear relationship exists between economic regulation and
technological innovation" with "profound implications for
entrepeneurs in regulated industries".

Perhaps the most disturbing statement on venture capital

comes from Howard Nason's <u>Perceptions of Barriers to Innovation</u>,
(<u>19</u>) when he reports, from a Commerce Technical Advisory Board
report, that "Small new public issues in the U.S....declined from
$1.1 billion in 1969 to only $16 million in 1974, with an even
greater proportional decline of investment in technically oriented
companies. Further, between March of 1974 and August of 1975
there were no public financings of small technical companies,
after a steady decline from some 200 in 1969". To calmly accept
this statistic without physical pain is downright alarming. As
Joseph Schumpeter stated, "The report that a given ship is sinking
is not defeatist, only the spirit in which this report is received
can be defeatist. The crew can sit down and drink. But it can
also rush to the pumps". (<u>20</u>)
  The conclusion that I reach after much information, <u>and
agreement</u>, is that our government is not and does not see itself
as an economic partner, (<u>21</u>) but an economic policeman. While our
government may, or may not, keep things safely moving along the
economic highway at controlled, reasonable speeds with their regulations, they sure make it tough to get on the highway. Those of
you who have ever tried to kick into a 75mph super-highway from a
standing start on your kids' tricycle right between two huge
semi's can understand what it's like to be an innovator today.
You can get small comfort from the fact that the world needs your
idea, but you, for sure, won't find anybody out there ready to
insure you, let alone help you pump for dear life. The fact that
an economic policeman spreads the traffic out so that it isn't
coming in bunches with a few holes now and then doesn't help your
cause, either.

  <u>Product and Process Performance Standards</u>. Performance
standards involve the broad area of product safety, workplace
standards and environmental quality. Here we find OSHA, EPA,
CPSC, FTC, DOT and many others. Most of us are so well acquainted
with these types of regulations that they have become a day-to-day
part of our activities. Because they are so familiar to us, we
may miss the very significant distinction in this classification,
the distinction between <u>standards</u> regulations and <u>pre-market
registration</u>.
  Performance standards regulations attack the problem with a
somewhat exact <u>specification</u> of "go" or "no go" acceptability.
In contrast, pre-market registration or permitting requires a
<u>judgment</u>. With a specification an innovator knows what to expect.
The regulation does exist, one can look at it and study it. It
may be that you have to run from home to second to first to third
to score a run, but at least you can find that route in the regulation. With pre-market registration and some permitting, the
only thing one knows for sure is there will be a trial, relatively
late in the life of the innovation, in which the defendant is the
applicant. This is a remarkable difference for the innovator.
Furthermore, a specific action of pre-market registration by a

regulatory group is <u>not</u>, per se, a regulation. A regulation cannot just come into being without some public comment. Such is not
the case with a pre-market registration judgment action against a
specific product or process.

After my review, I must conclude that performance standards,
at best, have only been weakly associated with innovation. The
conclusion that standards regulations are only weakly associated
with innovation isn't going to be a very popular conclusion with
business people, but I really feel they are naturally reacting
more to the heavy cost burden of this unbelievable maze of standards than the direct relationship on innovation. On the other
hand, it isn't going to be popular with the regulators who feel
regulations can force innovation. As I pointed out earlier,
innovation and regulation may well be the natural, independent
effects of the need that created both of them.

Pre-Market Registration

Regulation requiring pre-market registration of products has
been indicted in the literature as a major negative factor on
innovation. In addition, there is data that these regulations
have actually created safety and health problems.

There are three major pieces of legislation that are a modern
out-growth of minimum product standards which require pre-market
registration. These are, the 1962 Drug Amendments of the Food and
Drug Law covering drugs; FEPCA, regulating insecticides; and the
Toxic Substances Control Act, regulating chemicals. In each of
these, an agency, commission, or regulatory group of some sort
would meet, ponder and issue or deny a pre-market registration.
In all fairness to Congress, such legislation was an innovation
as specific standards did not need to be set. This would allow
the permitting group, using judgmental guidelines, to make the
best fit considering the specific situation. In concept, a product in the hands of the public should be an issue different from
the same product in the hands of skilled processors. Congress
may have had an idealistic model in mind based on the success of
the American jury system, our political system of checks and
balances, an education system that produces an exceptional liter-
acy rate and just plain good sense of who wears what color hat.
These factors should have made the innovative legislative concept
of pre-market registration work but, if the literature is meaningful, it has failed.

The Grabowski study mentioned earlier shows us the steep
decline in new drugs approved from an average of 56 per year to
17 per year since the 1962 Drug Amendments. Professor William
Wardell, whose studies contributed much to the Grabowski work,
even estimates in <u>Therapeutic Implications of the Drug Law</u> (22)
that a substantial number of Americans have died because of the
failure to register an innovative drug in the United States that
was <u>already</u> being marketed in Great Britain.

Documentation of innovation depression in pesticides, another area that requires pre-market registration is equally as dramatic. William Tucker, in his very recent Of Mites and Men, (23) discusses the frustration of several innovative companies trying to develop biological controls instead of target-specific toxic insecticides. Like Grabowski and drugs, Dr. Wendell Mullison reported in 1975 that since the enactment of FEPCA, the pesticide Act of 1971, the number of major pesticides introduced has fallen from two per year in the 1960 to 1970 decade to less than one per year for the period 1971 to 1975 (24).

Although the Toxic Substances Control Act is history, just the inventory accumulation has been such a mouthful for the EPA that pre-market registration has not started yet. Thus, there are no facts and, obviously, no references to innovation impact in the literature yet. By and large, people are waiting to see what action will be taken by the EPA in 1979 on the pre-market registration of new chemicals or significant new uses.

However, a very recent study prepared for the EPA by Arthur D. Little, Impact of TSCA Proposed Premanufacturing Notification Requirements, (25) makes three interesting findings on innovation.

"Based on the distribution of the sample of recently introduced chemicals, 50% of chemicals currently being introduced for commercial sales would not be introduced if the TSCA notification costs are $10,000 per chemical. At a unit notification cost of $40,000, 90% of the chemicals would not be introduced. This reduction in the rate of chemical innovation does not reflect the number of chemicals held off the market because of toxicity problems."

"Medium and small size chemical companies are likely to be more severely impacted by the notification requirements than larger companies. The reasons are that smaller companies are less likely to be willing to cope with the uncertainties and costs of the notification process and will be less able to take on the higher risks of R&D."

"The Impact of the TSCA Premanufacture Notice Requirements will vary among the segments of the chemical industry and the firms in any one segment. The role of innovation varies from segment to segment and differs from firm to firm within a segment. The segments potentially most highly impacted by TSCA are: Soaps and Detergents, Surface Acting Agents, and Industrial Organic Chemicals, n.e.c. Also potentially highly impacted are relatively small chemical producing firms throughout the chemical industry, but especially in the following segments: Industrial Inorganic Chemicals, n.e.c., Plastic Material and Resins, Synthetic Rubber, Toilet Preparations, Perfumes, and Cyclic Crudes and Intermediates."

In the way of retrospect on the subject, which may also be a forecast for chemical innovation, few, I think, would disagree with former FDA Commissioner Alexander Schmidt, a regulator himself, when he stated, "For example, in all of FDA's history, I am

unable to find a single instance where a Congressional committee
investigated the failure of FDA to approve a new drug. But, the
times when hearings have been held to criticize our approval of
new drugs have been so frequent that we aren't able to count them.
The message of FDA staff could not be clearer. Whenever a controversy over a new drug is resolved by its approval, the Agency and
the individuals involved likely will be investigated. Whenever
such a drug is disapproved, no inquiry will be made. The
Congressional pressure for our negative action on new drug applications is, therefore, intense. And it seems to be increasing, as
everyone is becoming a self-acclaimed expert on carcinogenesis and
drug testing." (9)

The abstract to the yet-to-be published paper of John DeKany,
Meeting the Challenge of TSCA with Technical Innovation, (26)
refers to eliminating the need for regulation with a positive,
innovative response. I've already given my thoughts on regulation
and innovation both being responses to a need. For DeKany to take
a further step that innovation could eliminate a regulation makes
me view him as a fellow progressive. As an example, in his
abstract, he specifically points to an innovative chemical plant
that might be designed at the outset to minimize toxic effluent
discharges. To be as charitable as possible, I would assume that
Dr. DeKany is not aware of a $500 million chemical complex that
was to be built adjacent to a Dow Chemical plant in Pittsburg,
California, that did not have a single drop of effluent. In fact,
some water was even needed for make-up. Further, air emission for
the multi-chemical complex would have equalled in quality and kind
the emission of only 14 automobiles, measured in the plant areas.
Even this would have been undetectable at the plant fence. The
entire complex project, after a Dow expense of $4 million, was
abandoned with only 4 of the 65 permits obtained and with EPA air
regulations providing the fatal blow. If Dr. DeKany suggests that
such a complex is desirable, Dow people would assume he is speak-
ing for the EPA of the future.

There is one remaining problem we might have with the drug
and pesticide regulation; that is, the applicability of these
studies to other fields such as chemicals. I hope that my suggested categorization of regulatory types to differentiate between
specification regulation and judgment regulation explains this
problem.

The literature is quite conclusive that where judgmental pre-
market registration regulation is invoked, innovation is markedly
crippled. If this is credible, and because we are in the process
of using pre-market registration in chemicals, logic and history
would not be on the side of the new chemical or plastic innovator
as he searches for support for his ideas.

Summary and Suggested Studies

We have a strong case that economic regulation affecting risk

capital and pre-market product registration have a substantial
and negative effect on innovation. As such, I do not feel com-
pelled to suggest topics for future studies. Such studies will
come, for sure, and will be welcome, but the problem is not know-
ing more, but communicating what we now know to those who would
cherish innovation.

Anti-trust regulation is a serious problem that must be
studied and treated better. There are vast differences of
opinion that we cannot afford to leave unresolved. Either the
late Senator Hart or the late Joseph A. Schumpeter was right.

The unbelievable numbers of product and process specification regulations are a whipping boy for innovation. In spite of
a great deal of references, the direct connection with innovation
has not been well made. Perhaps, as my boss would say, "there is
still some meat in this stew", but one must conclude that these
regulations are really "cost adders" and, while they certainly
affect our general business health and may well bleed us to death,
they do not stab right to the heart of innovation.

I have also discovered two new thoughts about the field of
government regulation and innovation as a result of my review.
They need some examination and critique.

First, I contend that regulation and innovation are both
primary responses to a need stimulus, but only rarely to each
other. Because we install the regulatory response so quickly,
we block out the slower innovative response as having the same
cause.

Second, product and process regulation must be divided into
two entirely different types - minimum performance specifications
and pre-market registration judgments. Failure to do so will
significantly reduce the all-important communication of the
results of studies already carried out that could help us improve
our sagging innovation rate.

Abstract

While many acknowledge and much has been written about the
effect of government regulation on chemical innovation, most
references only assume that there is a strong negative or positive relationship between government action and chemical innovation. Relatively few attempts have been made to study and
quantify the relationship and fewer publications have been made.
Because chemical innovation is an issue of national priority,
there is need to assemble and report what is known in order to
create a broader understanding of the problem, aid the developers
of new products, assist legislators and foster further studies.
Based on the existing literature, the paper categorizes the
various types of regulations by their influence on innovation,
reports the major studies undertaken, and concludes with the need
for future effort.

Selected Bibliographies

Adams, J. F., "Consumer Attitudes, Judicial Decision,
Government Regulation, and the Insurance Market", The
Journal of Risk and Insurance (1975) 501-512.

Ancker-Johnson, Betty, "Current Policies and Options for
the Future", Research Management (January 1977) 7-12.

Baltera, Lorraine, "Federal Curbs Inhibiting Growth, Says
Smithline", Advertising Age, Vol. 46, No. 19 (May 12, 1975)

Brooks, H., "Technology Assessment as a Process", Int. Soc.
Sci. J, Vol. 25, No. 3 (1973) 247-256.

Chemical and Engineering News, "NSF Gets Fresh Input on
Bars to Innovation", (October 29, 1973) 17.

Chemical and Engineering News, "FDA New Drug Rules Called
Too Strict", (August 18, 1975) 6.

Chemical and Engineering News, "New Spur Needed for U.S.
Innovation", (April 26, 1976) 6.

Clauser, H. R. Ed, "The Future for R&D Gloom but not Doom",
Research Management, (July 1977) 2-4.

Cohn, H. B., "The Rationale and Benefits of Regulation",
Public Utilities Fortnightly, (October 7, 1976) 71-74.

Drug, Cosmetics Industries, "Keeping Posted", (August 1975).

Gillette, D., "How Regulations Encourage and Discourage
Innovation", Research Management, (March 1977) 18-21.

Gilman, G., "Technological Innovation and Public Policy",
California Management Review, Vol. 13, No. 3 (Spring 1971)
13-24.

Grether, E. T. and Holloway, K. J., "Impact of Government
Upon the Market System", Journal of Marketing (April 1967)
1-7.

Hlavacek, J. D. and Thompson, V. A., "Bureaucracy and New
Product Innovation", Academy of Management Journal, Vol. 16,
No. 3 (September 1973) 361-372.

Karber, J. W., "Competition and the Regulatory Process",
Chuart. Review of Economy and Business, Vol. 9, No. 3
Autumn 1969) 57-64.

Kleinman, H. S., "A Case Study of Innovation", Business Horizons, Vol. 9 (Winter 1966) 63-70.

Kohlmeier, L. M., "Federal Regulation in Industry Seen as Inefficiency Verging on Comedy", NAII Convention Special Issue (November 30, 1970) 30-31.

Laubach, G. D., "Dr. Laubach Dispels Myths About Status of U.S. Research", Pharmaceutical Manufacturers Association (PMA) Bulletin, (July 1978) 5.

Lehner, U. C., "Work-Safety and Anti-inflation Agencies Split over Drive to Cut Regulatory Costs", Wall Street Journal (August 3, 1978).

Levy, L., "National Science and Technology Policy-Needed: Institutional Breakthroughs", Research Management (January 1977) 21-24.

Nieburg, H. L., "Social Control of Innovation", The American Economic Review, (May 1968) 666-677.

Oster, S. M. and Quigley, J. M., "Regulatory Barriers to the Diffusion of Innovation: Some Evidence from Building Codes", Bell Journal of Economics, Vol. 8, No. 2 (Autumn 1977) 361-377.

Reinhardt, C. F., "Upgrading Testing and Evaluation for Regulatory Standards", Research Management (March 1977) 27-28.

Schultze, C. L., "The Public Use of Private Interest", Harper's (May 1977).

Schweitzer, G. E., "Regulation and Innovation-The Case of Environmental Chemicals", Abstract (February 1978)

Simon, W. E., "Restoring Competition to the American Marketplace", Treasury Papers (March 1976) 3-6.

Sommer, C. H., Interview "Government Interference", Nation's Business (February 1962) 34-35, 80-83.

Swearingen, J. E., "Complex Regulatory Process Poses Threat to our Economic Strength", The Commercial and Financial Chronicle (March 8, 1962).

Vanderslice, T. A., "Technology and Jobs: The Vital Link is Weakening", Dun's Review, Vol. 110, No. 1 (July 1977) 25.

Weidenbaum, M. L., "The High Cost of Government Regulation",
Business Horizons, (August 1975) 43-51.

Williams, D. N., "Economic Concentration in Industry Stifles
Innovation", Iron Age (July 24, 1969) 48.

Literature Cited

1. "Breakdown of U.S. Innovation", Business Week,
    (February 16, 1976) 56-58.

2. "Vanishing Innovation", Business Week, (July 3, 1978).

3. Lepkowsi, W., "Innovation and National Security: A
    Complex Relationship", Chemical and Engineering News,
    (July 17, 1978) 24-29.

4. Weidenbaum, M. L., "Where Overregulation Can Lead",
    Nation's Business (June 1975) 26-32.

5. Lewis, J. D., "National Science and Technology Policy-
    Its Impact on Technological Change", Research Management
    (January 1977) 13-16.

6. Leenhouts, J. W., "Inflation vs. Innovation", Chemtech
    (January 1976) Vol. 6, 30-31.

7. Takayama, Akira, "Behavior of the Firm Under Regulatory
    Constraint", American Economic Review (1969) Vol. 59,
    No. 3, 255-260.

8. Chenea, Paul F., "The Costs and Effects of Regulations",
    Research Management (March 1977) 22-26.

9. Grabowski, H. G., "Drug Regulation and Innovation",
    American Enterprise Institute for Public Policy Research,
    Library of Congress Catalog Card No. 76-25709 (1976).

10. Oreffice, P. F., "Let's Stop Dumping U.S. Jobs",
    Commonwealth Club of California (January 27, 1978).

11. Gerstenfeld, Arthur, "Government Regulation Effects on
    the Direction of Innovation: A Focus on Performance
    Standards", Transactions on Engineering Management,
    Vol. EM-24, No. 3 (August 1977) 82-86.

12. Lessing, L., "Why the U.S. Lags in Technology", Fortune,
    (April 1972) No. 85, 68-73.

13. Hill, C. T., Greenberg, E., Newburger, D. J., et al,
    "A State of the Art Review of the Effects of Regulation
    on Technological Innovation in the Chemical and Allied
    Products Industries", Center for Development Technology
    for National R&D Assessment Program, St. Louis, Mo:
    Washington University (February 1975), Three Volumes.

14. Kamien and Schwartz, "Market Structure and Innovation",
    J. Economic Literature (March 1975).

15. Foster, R. N. and Gluck, F. W., "Impact of Antitrust and Regulatory Actions on Progress of Technology", Research Management (July 1975) 7-10.

16. Kelly, P. K., "Governmental Overregulation and the Capital Crisis", Financial Executive (November 1976) 12-18.

17. Staats, E. B., "Improving the Climate for Innovation-What Government and Industry Can Do", Research Management (September 1976) 9-13.

18. Schweitzer, G. E., "Regulations, Technological Progress, and Societal Interests", Research Management (March 1977) 13-17.

19. Nason, H. K., "National Science and Technology Policy-Perceptions of Barriers to Innovation", Research Management (January 1977) 17-20.

20. Rogge, B. A., "Will Capitalism Survive?", Imprimis (May 1974) Vol. 3, No. 5, Hillsdale College, Hillsdale, Michigan.

21. Kawase, Takeshi and Rubenstein, A. H., "Reactions of Japanese Industrial Managers to Government Incentives to Innovation - An Empirical Study", Transaction on Engineering Management (August 1977) 93-101.

22. Wardell, William M., "Therapeutic Implications of the Drug Lag", Clinical Pharmacology and Therapeutics (January 1974) Vol. 15, No. 1, 83.

23. Tucker, W., "Of Mites and Men", Harper's (August 1978).

24. Lewert, H., "Silent Autumn", The Dow Chemical Company.

25. Little, Arthur D., Inc., "Impact of TSCA Proposed Pre-Manufacturing Notification Requirements", Office of Planning and Evaluation, U.S. Environmental Protection Agency (December 1978).

26. DeKany, J., "Meeting the Challenge of TSCA with Technical Innovation", In Print This Volume.

RECEIVED March 8, 1979.

The Effects of Health and Environmental Regulation on Technological Change in the Chemical Industry: Theory and Evidence

NICHOLAS A. ASHFORD and GEORGE R. HEATON

Center for Policy Alternatives, Massachusetts Institute of Technology, Cambridge, MA 02139

This paper presents the final results of a research effort which investigated the effects of environmental/safety regulation on technological change in the U.S. chemical industry. (1) The term environmental/safety regulation is used to include the legislation, regulations, and other related actions which attempt to control environmental pollution, protect worker health and safety, or ensure the safety of consumer products. Technological changes arising from regulation encompass both the immediate modifications in manufactured products or industrial processes which may be necessary in order to comply with regulation and the more indirect, or ancillary, effects regulation can have on technological change for non-regulatory, "main business" purposes. The major emphasis in this work is on technological change for compliance purposes.

We distinguish technological change from innovation. Innovation means new product or process technology actually brought by a firm into first commercial use. The term technological change has a broader scope and includes "non-innovative" changes such as the adoption of an existing technology.

The study's focus was on the regulations and chemical technologies pertaining to:
- lead
- mercury
- polychlorinated biphenyls (PCB's)
- vinyl chloride.

These are typical of substances that are in wide use and which are highly regulated. The choice was made to have a diversity of regulations and industrial contexts in our sample and to keep the study within manageable proportions.

The study involved both the construction of a model of the effects of regulation on compliance technology and the testing of certain relationships, suggested by the model, concerning the characteristics of the regulation, the nature of the technology employed by the regulated/responding firms, and the ultimate

0-8412-0511-6/79/47-109-045$05.50/0

technological response. Data about these relationships were
obtained from two series of interviews with firms subjected to
the principal regulations on lead, mercury, PCB's, and vinyl
chloride.

   *Other Work on the Regulation-Technological Change Rela-
tionship.* A 1975 literature survey of the chemical and allied
products industries concluded:
   Unfortunately, almost no work has appeared in the literature
   which has attempted to measure or even to model in a rigorous way the impacts of environmental regulation on technological innovation. (2)
Since that time, some important work has been concluded. In
early 1979, as part of the Domestic Policy Review on Industrial
Innovation undertaken by the U.S. Department of Commerce, the MIT
Center for Policy Alternatives (CPA) undertook a systematic
structuring of the effects of environmental/ safety regulation on
innovation, citing support for different effects from the existing work. (3)
   Although there are some broad, general studies and others
specific to particular industries, within the chemical industry
the most extensive literature concerns pharmaceutical innovation. Several researchers have argued that regulation has unduly
slowed the introduction of new drugs in the U.S. and has resulted
in a net health disbenefit to consumers. (4,5,6) However, a
recent analysis of the literature presented at the 1977 HEW Panel
on New Drug Regulation (the Dorsen Panel) has concluded that the
available data are not sufficient to support such an assertion.
(7)
   Several new analyses have recently been offered concerning
the general effects of regulation on innovation in chemicals.
All stress the idea that the regulatory framework now applicable
to the chemical industry has created a fundamental change in the
business environment which will have important long-term impacts
on the nature of innovation. Many of these impacts will be felt
through the level and nature of R&D support. One study based on
industry interviews has found a decline in real R&D spending in
general but a large increase in R&D devoted to environmental
control. (8) Others see the regulations as having a very uneven
impact across the industry, providing some firms with a lucrative
market opportunity and penalizing others. (9) Another study
(10), based on unstructured chemical industry interviews and
concerned mostly with the R&D effects, found considerable innovation in control technology arising from the research devoted to
environmental amelioration but a general "dampening influence" on
other new product and process development in large chemical companies. Changes in corporate organizational structure are consistently cited in all the studies.
   Taken as a whole, the existing studies are useful in provid-

ing some general insights into the nature of the impacts regulation can have upon technological change and in sometimes providing documentation of those impacts in specific industries. However, they can only be characterized as a beginning exploration
of the regulation-technological change relationship. A fundamental failing which pervades most of the studies is that they do
not pose or rest upon any articulated model of the relationship
between regulation and innovation. Many of the studies are
broad, general overviews. On the other hand, the few industry
studies which exist have only limited generalizability. What
results from this lack of conceptual framework is that the previous work lacks both precision and subtlety. The regulatory
stimulus is typically considered as a single, uniform event or
signal; in reality, different regulations are vastly different in
purpose and form and therefore can be expected to have significantly different effects. Similarly, innovation tends to be
treated as a simple phenomenon. Little attempt is made to distinguish between innovation for compliance purposes and innovation for general corporate purposes. Lastly, the studies are
rarely rigorously constructed to yield valid statistical results. Rather, they are typically surveys of a general nature
which try to make a beginning exploration in an ill-defined
research area.

   *A General View of the Regulation-Technological Change Rela-
tionship.* It is essential to distinguish between two separate
effects of regulation on technological change -- the technological changes necessary for compliance purposes and the other,
ancillary changes in technology which may also result. This
distinction highlights an important premise of this research --
that it is unwise to attempt to draw general conclusions about
the regulation-technological change relationship. Too much
depends on the characteristics of individual cases -- in particular, the form of the regulation, the kind of industry, and the
peculiar character of the firm affected. Thus, one of the few
certainties in this area is that there are no simple, general
answers. Most of the answers lie in particular cases.
   When one considers the technology developed for compliance
purposes, it is clear that regulation encourages technological
change. Indeed, this is almost a tautology since regulation is
intended to ameliorate the adverse consequences of technology by
changing technology itself. Certainly, the existence of a vigor-
ous pollution control industry attests to the fact that the regulations have an important expansive effect. In these instances
regulation creates a new market opportunity, which can be met
very profitably by some firms. In some cases, the regulated firm
markets the compliance technology.
   On the other hand, regulation, imposes a direct constraint
upon technological change. Certain regulatory systems are in-

tended to discourage some innovations in the sense that the regulators must refuse to allow the introduction of certain unsafe products. Moreover, all regulation forecloses or discourages certain technical options and therefore constrains to some degree the innovation process.

Another regulatory constraint to innovation, but one which is indirect, may occur as a result of the cost of environmental control. To the extent that the costs of environmental control divert resources away from other corporate activities, like R&D, and to the extent that innovation is directly related to the level of these resources, regulation is likely to penalize innovative activity.

Regulation may also indirectly stimulate innovation. Often, firms respond creatively to crises, and to the extent that regulation poses crisis conditions it may foster innovative responses. This appears to be the case particularly in older, non-innovative firms which, prior to regulation, felt no need to innovate.

A last kind of effect may result from a basic change in the nature of the business environment created by the "new regulation". This is a systemic effect which will significantly affect the skill mix of chemical firms, their R&D processes, and their general business strategy. These effects in turn have important, though still largely unpredictable, effects on the nature (as well as the outcome) of the innovation process in the chemical industry.

A Conceptual Model of Regulation-Induced Technological Responses

In its simplest terms, our model of the regulation-technological change relationship consists of three basic elements:
- the regulatory stimulus
- the responding industrial unit
- the technological response

Regulation may impinge on a regulated firm and, as a result, a response of some kind is elicited. A responding industrial unit to that regulation may not be the regulated firm. It might be a supplier; it might be a new entrant to the field. It is important to identify the unit that sees a market signal or a constraint and responds in some measure. Depending on the kind of regulation and the characteristics of the responding unit or the regulated unit, different responses can result.

The Regulatory Stimulus. The term regulation brings to mind a governmental edict, such as a piece of legislation, an agency rule, or a guideline. Similarly, the concept of a regulatory stimulus to technological change suggests that such change occurs as a result of a regulation. After completing this research, we have concluded that both of these commonly held conceptions are too simple.

In the environmental/safety context, "regulation" should be given a broad meaning. It should include all forces (both governmental and non-governmental) that are related to the governmental effort to ameliorate environmental or safety problems. The reason for adopting this broad definition of regulation is that any narrower concept (e.g. one limited to legislation and Federal agency rules) is not realistic and would impute more causality to a single government action than is in fact the case. In short, the regulatory process is complex, and should be viewed as such.

There are many "regulatory" stimuli faced by the firm. Some regulations appear to pose little, if any, stimulus because they are based upon industry consensus and thus simply ratify into law the existing practice of the majority of firms. Similarly, to the extent that regulations are based upon concepts like "feasibility" or "best available technology", they may be rooted closely to the technological status quo as it exists in at least some firms. Accordingly, regulation often stimulates change in only part of the industry. Moreover, the regulatory stimulus is often not responsible for (i.e., does not require) all of the technological changes which occur. Indeed, regulation often gives firms the opportunity to make needed modernizations. Although these changes would not have occurred but for the regulatory stimulus, it is not proper to relate them to that stimulus alone. Not only is the regulatory stimulus complex, but it also interacts in a complex way with other economic, technological and social stimuli.

A first important aspect of the regulatory stimulus is what part of the technology the regulation focuses on. There are three principal classes of regulation important for the regulation-technological change relationship:
- product regulation -- focusing on product characteristics
- pollutant regulation -- focusing on unwanted side products from production processes
- component regulation -- focusing on individual elements of the production process

A second important aspect of the regulatory stimulus is its purpose or kind. Obviously, it is to be expected that occupational safety and health regulation, for example, will produce different kinds of changes from water pollution control or pesticide regulation. Similarly, it is important to distinguish among differing operational mechanisms or modes of regulation, such as performance vs. specification standards, or tax incentives vs. mandatory standards.

Other characteristics of regulation appear to have an impor-

tant influence on the nature of technological changes. The
stringency of regulation, measured by its cost or by the degree
of change it requires, is obviously a major determinant of the
kinds of changes which result. Similarly, when there are a
multiplicity of regulatory stimuli rather than a single event,
the resulting change may be greater, other things being equal.
    Characteristics of the regulatory process may also be impor-
tant in determining the resulting technological changes. For
example, close participation of industrial representatives with
government officials in drafting standards often appears to
result in regulating at a level which is clearly feasible with
existing technology, thus requiring little change. The length of
time within which the regulatory scenario takes place also is
important in allowing for appropriate responses, as is time-
phasing of the regulation. Contrastingly, too much uncertainty
is often seen as inhibiting the most efficient compliance efforts. Also, it is clear that most regulations tend to change
over time and that the form of their changing requirements is
closely linked to the evolution of compliance technology.

The Responding Unit or Units. The person who has the legal
duty to comply with regulation is called the legally bound
party. However, the legally bound party may not be the responder
to regulation because the legal obligation does not always provide the most important stimulus to respond. For example, there
may be joint responses to regulation by more than one firm or
industry.
    A productive unit is the smallest production element employ-
ing a particular technology that could conceivably stand alone as
an individual firm. It may be a firm or only part of a firm.
For example, a single PVC polymerization plant (or part of a
larger plant) would constitute a productive unit.
    The group of firms or units within firms that employ a par-
ticular technology can be termed a productive segment. For example, all the firms that polymerize vinyl chloride would constitute a productive segment.
    The productive segment whose technology is the target of a
regulation is called the regulated segment. This concept includes productive segments not legally bound to comply but which
are nevertheless so commonly and closely related economically to
the legally bound segment that they can legitimately be included
within the regulated segment. (For example, the lead-in-gasoline
regulations technically apply primarily to marketers of gasoline;
however, the lead additive manufacturers are so closely linked
that both would be considered regulated segments.) Non-regulated
segments are defined as productive segments not within the regulated segment that is responding to the regulation.
    Regulation may be seen as imposing requirements on techno-
logies used in industry. We have attempted in this research to

categorize these technologies. The most important aspect of a
technology for this categorization is the concept of technological rigidity. This is defined as a continuum that has at one
extreme evolving (fluid) product lines and uncoordinated production technologies, and at the other extreme, mature, commodity-
like products and highly integrated, cost-effective production
technologies. Productive segments may be placed along the continuum of rigidity according to a set of objective criteria which
describe their technology.
  To simplify the analysis, we have separated the continuum of
rigidity into three distinct stages: fluid , segmented and
rigid segments. The concept of rigidity used in this work is
related to, but not identical with, that of Abernathy and Utterback. (11,12) They visualize an evolutionary process whereby
product and process technology develop together from an initial
stage in which the product is poorly defined and rapidly changing
and the process is uncoordinated and based on general purpose
equipment, through an intermediate stage in which the product
begins to standardize and portions of the process are automated
and optimized, to a final stage in which the product is a highly
standardized commodity and the process is automated, integrated
and large scale. Utterback and Abernathy's work suggests that
the likely future pattern of change can be predicted based on the
recent past. If units respond to regulation in the same way that
other technological changes are undertaken, then this work would
suggest that the particular kind of compliance response might be
determined by the technological rigidity of the responding segment.

  The Technological Response. In analysis of regulation-
induced technological change, we distinguish between (1) responses which are primarily for compliance purposes ("compliance
responses"), and (2) responses which primarily affect the development of technology for "main business" purposes ("ancillary
responses"). The compliance response consists of those technical
modifications to a firm's products or processes that are necessary for it to comply with a regulatory mandate. They also include non-hardware changes, such as changes in R&D, that are
related to the development of compliance technology, as well as
unsuccessful technological changes.
  The important characteristics of the compliance response
chosen for investigation in this study were:
  ●   whether the response is principally a product or pro-
      cess change
  ●   the "stage of development" of the response
  ●   the "novelty" of the response
  ●   the "comprehensiveness" of the response
  The "ancillary" responses are the technological changes that
occur in firms as a result of regulation that are not required

for compliance with regulatory requirements. They are the developments that would not have occurred in the absence of regulation. They include the development of innovations within a company's "main business." There are two basic kinds of ancillary
responses. One we have called "product- or process-specific" because it includes new or existing industrial products or processes directly traceable to a compliance response; the other we
have termed "systemic," because it results from changes in the
corporate structure or environment within which innovation occurs.

Relationships Within the Model. As discussed above, the
concept of a productive segment is fundamentally a characterization of a **technology**. A basic postulate of this research is that
the characteristics of a productive segment's technology are
important determinants of its technological response to regulation, along with the characteristics of the regulatory stimulus.
    The model constructed during the course of this research,
relating the regulatory stimulus, the regulated/responding unit,
and the technological response, is presented in Figure 1. In the
figure, the elements of the model that are connected with solid
lines are those which were the main focus of the research. The
elements connected by dashed lines are those about which less
information was collected. Hypotheses were developed concerning
those elements connected only with solid lines. Figure 2 is a
schematic of the specific relationships which were investigated.
The hypotheses tested in this research were as follows:
- Responses to regulation from the **regulated segment** will
  be predominantly product or process in a proportion
  corresponding to the expected pattern of innovation in
  the segment in the absence of regulation.
- All responses to regulation (whether or not from the
  regulated segment) will be predominantly product or
  process in a proportion corresponding to the expected
  pattern of innovation in the **regulated segment** in the
  absence of regulation.
- A large proportion of responses to regulation will
  arise from inside the regulated segment and inside the
  legally bound firm.
- A greater percentage of product responses than process
  responses will arise from outside the regulated segment.
- A much greater percentage of product responses than
  process responses will arise from outside the legally
  bound segment.
- Most responses to regulation are in a late stage of
  development and require only moderate development.
- Product responses will tend to be in somewhat earlier
  stages of development than process responses.
- Almost all responses will be in the "least novel" cate-

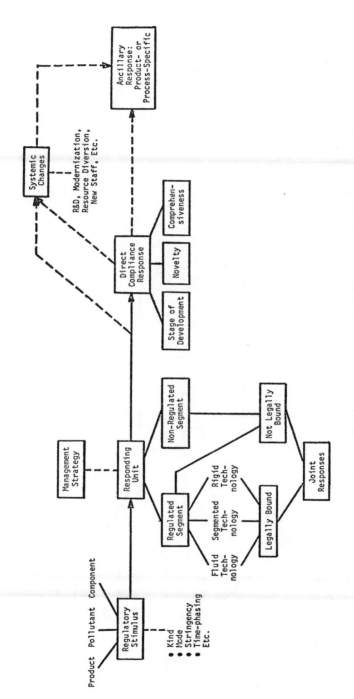

Figure 1.   Conceptual model of the regulation–technological change relationship

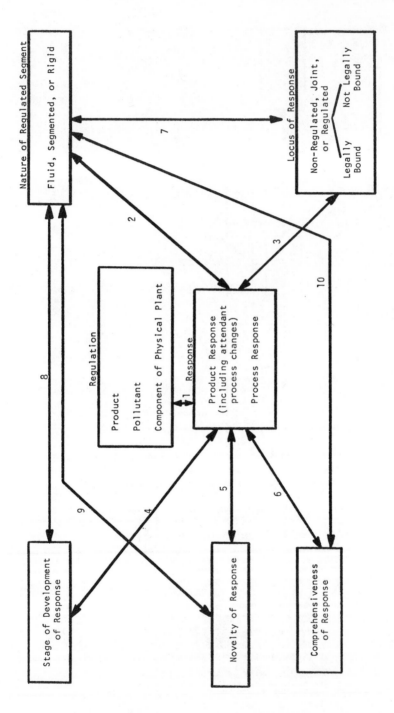

Figure 2.   Schematic of relationships investigated

gory, with occasional moderately novel responses and very few novel responses.
- Novelty will be equally as likely for product and process responses.
- In fluid segments, the response to regulation is more likely to come from an earlier stage of development than in rigid segments.
- The responses to regulation will be less novel, the more rigid the segment.
- Responses will tend to be more comprehensive, the more rigid the segment.

Description of Empirical Procedures

The research was divided into three phases:
- Phase I: An initial taxonomic exercise in which basic concepts of the regulation-technological change relationship were developed from first principles and existing literature
- Phase II: Pilot in-depth in-person interviews with a small number of leading companies believed to have made important technological responses to regulations on four extensively regulated chemical hazards
- Phase III: Focused telephone interviews with randomly-selected companies in the same industries studied during Phase II.

The Phase I survey of the diverse legislative mandates applicable to the chemical and allied products industry revealed that almost all of the individual environmental/safety regulations are substance-specific. Accordingly, we organized the study around a series of candidate hazard regulations which would provide case studies of how the productive segments concerned with the selected hazards responded technologically to regulation.

A search of the regulations promulgated in each of the major legislative areas yielded a large list of chemicals which had been the subject of at least some governmental action. This list was reduced in several stages to a final group of four hazards -- lead, mercury, PCB's, and vinyl chloride -- which were (1) subject to a diversity of regulatory actions of different kinds and modes which significantly restricted production or methods of use, (2) used in a number of different productive segments within the chemical industry, and (3) economically important in a number of uses.

In Phase II, the goal of our interviews was to develop hypotheses about the factors important in shaping technological responses to regulation and about the characteristics of the actual responses. To facilitate this task, the sample of firms for the pilot interviews was deliberately enriched with firms that were known to have made relatively innovative technical responses to the regulation(s) in question and by firms that were relatively easy to study because they were receptive to interviews and located in convenient geographic areas. The sample of firms was drawn from 12 productive segments where the four subject hazards were principally in use.

Interviews were conducted with 10 firms. (Because some firms spanned more than one productive segment, we were able to gain information about all twelve productive segments.) Interviews of about two hours' duration were conducted by two members of the study team with one to four people from the firm. The discussions were informal and flexible in order to allow the interviewees ample latitude to enlighten us about the aspects of the regulations covered, the industry, and the technical responses which they considered particularly significant. In all cases, the interviewees performed one (or both) of the following functions in the firm:

(i)   management of the details of the compliance response (i.e., the product or process change needed for compliance)

(ii) management of the overall firm response to regulation, including contact with the agencies, securing clearance for expenditures from corporate management, providing directions to the technical group, etc.

Phase III contained the major part of our empirical work. Its goal was to ascertain whether or not the hypotheses developed from the Phase II interviews and our model of the regulation-technological change relationship would be reinforced or altered by information derived from a more representative sampling of companies within productive segments. To construct the interview sample, we first arranged ten of the original twelve productive segments that had been directly subject to regulatory action in a matrix according to: (i) the characteristics of the segment's technology (i.e., rigidity/fluidity) and (ii) the primary type of regulation (i.e., product/pollutant), affecting the segment.

Next, lists of companies in each productive segment were compiled, and up to 16 companies per productive segment were randomly selected and arranged in a priority order for interviews. These ordered lists were then used to call companies; roughly equal numbers of usable interviews were obtained in each cell of the matrix. This procedure resulted in a sample that was stratified according to the two major foci of our investigation (i.e., technology and regulatory characteristics).

Forty Phase III interviews were conducted by telephone. The Phase III interviews were much shorter and more focused than those in Phase II, generally lasting less than thirty minutes. In addition they proceeded according to a rather specific questionnaire. In some cases it was possible to combine information from Phase II and Phase III interviews for analytical purposes.

The survey instrument consisted of a set of ten questions

which resulted in ten specific replies out of 33 possible replies in an interview. For example, one question which was used to determine the nature of the productive segment of the respondents resulted in one of three replies -- fluid, segmented, or rigid. In Phase II and III of the project there were 50 interviews and these interviews provided 121 sets of ten replies. Each set of replies is focused on a firm's <u>response</u> to regulation. A response was a particular set of actions directed toward meeting the requirements of the regulation. On the average, firms exhibited three responses to regulation and industrial segments exhibited twelve responses. The analysis presented here describes inter-relationships among variables related to the 33 possible replies -- drawn from appropriately aggregated responses of the industrial segments. The nature of the data collected led to a number of complexities for analysis. The interested reader is referred to the final report of the project for a detailed discussion. (<u>1</u>)

Summary of Major Findings and Conclusions

The conceptual framework developed for this research was valuable as a structuring device and seems to be an accurate description of compliance behavior. We feel that the model articulates most of the important aspects of the regulation-technological change relationship on an individual firm level and should serve as a basis for further empirical research.

The Regulatory Stimulus. The regulatory stimulus is a very <u>complex, time-dependent and variable</u> signal. Regulation is not a simple, single point-in-time phenomenon that elicits an industrial response. Various "regulatory" signals -- research findings, advance notice of rule-making, informal agency-industry contacts, etc. -- all influence firm behavior. Moreover, regulatory demands often change substantially over time, particularly as compliance technology changes. The way regulatory signals are perceived by the firm is also very important. These perceptions may sometimes differ quite substantially from those in the agencies and may even be incorrect as to the regulatory requirements. <u>Informal "regulatory" stimuli are as important, or more so, than formalized rulemaking.</u> Informal stimuli include publicity, government scrutiny, non-regulatory legal mechanisms like tort and contract law, and customer (or supplier) pressure. These additional forces tend to multiply the effect of regulation, and sometimes even preclude the need for regulation. The example of PCB's best illustrates this point. Only government "scrutiny" had occurred by 1970 when Monsanto, the sole U.S. producer, began restricting production. Fear of tort suits and adverse publicity were major motivators for action by PCB users long before the passage of the Toxic Substances Control Act in 1976, which phased-in a ban on PCB production.

In part because of the extra-regulatory forces at work, it is clear that compliance with regulatory goals may sometimes substantially pre-date actual promulgation of a rule. In such cases, the actual regulation serves the function of ratifying action that has already occurred and provides a model for similar requirements which might be mandated in the future. Forces other than regulation are thus the major stimuli for technological change in these instances.

We have also seen consistently that agencies use substantial industry input in drafting regulations. This input results from industry participation in the formalized rule-making process as well as through informal contacts with agency personnel. Industry input appears to be dominated by the large firms (and trade associations) which employ a variety of full-time specialists to handle regulatory affairs. The agencies often adopt the suggestions offered in comment on their rules. For example, the CPSC's final rule on lead-in-paint was modified substantially (principally as to the breadth of its application) on the basis of hearing comments.

For the four hazardous materials surveyed, the actual standards which finally emerged from the regulatory process appear in most instances to be based largely on considerations of technological feasibility or best available technology. It was rare to observe a standard set to require technology not already in use by at least some firms, although we did observe this in one important instance. (The OSHA vinyl chloride regulations apparently required a series of innovative process modifications for virtually all firms in the VC polymerization industry.) This is not to say, however, that a standard cannot successfully bring about changes in technology. The change may either be the development of an entirely new product or process -- or the diffusion of a given technology throughout an industrial segment. More recent regulatory initiatives, relying on stringent health-based criteria, may well require technological responses which go beyond current capability.

There is, as expected, a very strong correlation between the type of regulation and the nature of the technological response. Thus, "product" regulation generally leads to a product response, and "pollutant" and "component" regulations generally lead to process responses. In a few cases, however, product regulation was seen to elicit primarily a process change. For example, the petroleum refiners' principal response to regulatory limits on the lead content in gasoline has been to increase catalytic reforming, a process change.

We suspect that other characteristics of the regulatory stimulus not investigated here in detail or systematically are also important for technological change. They include the stringency of the regulatory demands, the time period allowed for the com-

pliance response to develop, the mode of regulation (e.g. performance vs. specification standards), and the presence or absence
of several regulatory demands in combination.

The Responding Units. We conclude that the characteristics
of the technology in productive segments/units are major factors
determining the nature of the technological response to regulation. The technology in use before regulation tends to dominate
the compliance response to regulation. Variations among individual firms were found, but overall, responses were fairly predictable across a productive segment.

Other more specific findings supported this basic conclusion. First, we found that the kinds of technical changes that
firms within a productive segment made in order to comply with a
given regulation were highly uniform. This uniformity cannot be
attributed to regulatory signals which required a single compliance technology because most of the regulations investigated
were performance standards. Rather, the response uniformity
within productive segments suggests that the character of the
existing technology does indeed dominate the response.

Second, we found that the proportion of product and process
responses to regulation closely resembles the expected balance of
product/process innovations occurring in the segment in the absence of regulation. Thus, we saw that fluid industries tended
to respond to regulation with product modifications, and rigid
segments tended to have more process responses than product
changes. Segmented industries, in contrast, exhibited both
product and process changes and a greater overall amount of
change than fluid or rigid segments. These responses are highly
consistent with the usual pattern of innovation in the absence of
regulation.

Perhaps the most interesting result concerns the relationship between the novelty of the response and the rigidity of the
segment. Regulation of rigid segments often elicited responses
as novel as those in fluid segments. For example, highly innovative responses were attempted, but unsuccessfully, to deal with
the lead-in-gas regulations. These included the development of
an entirely new fuel, "gasohol," and efforts by the lead alkyl
manufacturers to develop new automobile engine designs capable of
using leaded gas. On the other hand, the response to lead-in-
paint regulations by paint manufacturers (a fluid industry) was
simply to utilize existing substitutes. This finding lends some
support to the idea that regulation can change the overall character of innovation in rigid industries. Creative responses to
regulation may occur especially when the regulation precipitates
"crisis" conditions for the industry.

Regulatory requirements are typically made applicable to a
specific industry or industries. Nevertheless, the response to
regulation need not arise from the regulated segment or the

legally-bound firm. Although we have found that a large prepon-
derance of responses will arise from inside the regulated segment, the responses from outside the regulated segment are also
significant. Several very important, innovative responses were
seen to have arisen from new entrants to the industry, whose
entry was made possible by regulation. For example, successful
PCB substitutes arose from large oil and chemical companies,
transformer/capacitor manufacturers, and foreign corporations --
none of whom had been in the PCB manufacturing business.

When responses do arise from outside of the regulated segment or the legally-bound firm, they still require some kind of
adaptation or modification by the firm undertaking compliance.
Thus, responses from outside the regulated segment or firm are
typically joint efforts.

Although there are examples of both product and process
responses arising outside of the regulated segment, a greater
percentage of process responses arose from outside efforts than
for product responses. There appears to be some tendency for
rigid firms that are legally bound to look elsewhere for the
compliance solution, and some tendency for fluid firms that are
legally bound to develop their own compliance solution. There
are several important examples of the suppliers to regulated
firms actually providing the technical solution to their customer's regulatory compliance problem. In one such case, the
worker exposure and emissions problems of PVC fabricators were
essentially solved by the PVC polymerizers, their suppliers. The
polymerizers' production of "clean resins" largely eliminated the
potential for emission of vinyl chloride monomer during fabrica-
tion.

The Characteristics of Compliance Responses. Most technological responses to regulation are in a late stage of development and require only moderate development in order to achieve
compliance. This means that when the response to regulation was
begun there was, in most cases, an existing technology which
could be adapted to the regulatory purpose without the need for
major research/development work. (For example, in the mercury
chloralkali industry there were two principal production processes in use, one of which was a significant mercury polluter.
Regulations on mercury have prompted a diffusion of the second
process.) Thus, one might say that most responses were drawn
from technology already "on the shelf".

Comparing product and process responses, it was found that
product responses tended to be in somewhat earlier stages of
development.

It appears equally likely that rigid and fluid segment responses will require substantial development, although we expected
that the responses of fluid segments would be drawn from an
earlier stage of development than the responses of rigid seg-

ments. After reconsideration of the original expectations, this finding appears to be consistent with the theory that regulation has the effect of disrupting established modes of operation in rigid segments, and thereby elicits creative responses.

We found that almost all responses to regulation fell into the "least novel" category. This finding is consistent with the earlier finding that responses tended to be drawn from a late stage of development. It was also found that product and process responses were approximately equally novel (or non-novel).

Tests of the relationship between novelty and technological rigidity provided especially interesting results. The most novel responses seem to come from segmented firms, although we had expected that responses would be most novel in fluid segments. Moreover, it appears clear that rigid firms do not have less novel responses than fluid firms. Again, this finding supports the idea that rigid firms are prompted to develop creative solutions to severe regulatory problems. (Perhaps the principal example of segmented firm innovation comes from the vinyl chloride polymerizers, who modified their process in several important ways in responding to OSHA and EPA regulations. This response, especially the unique combination of responses, was perceived as remarkable by many in the industry, which had feared that the regulatory demands could not be met.)

No general relationship appears evident between comprehensiveness and product versus process change. It was found, however, that responses tended to be more comprehensive in more fluid segments. This finding appears consistent with the idea that fluid technologies, being relatively undefined (as opposed to rigid segments) are able to make a greater degree of change with more ease.

Qualitatively, the data show only a very few examples of radically new technologies arising in response to regulation. These few arose outside of the regulated segment and were in most cases, ultimately unsuccessful. (As mentioned above, "gasohol" has not succeeded nor have automotive design changes like "lead traps," etc.) However, successful responses did in some instances show a creative adaptation of existing techniques. For example, the development of MMT, a manganese-based fuel additive that now has been in commercial use for several years (although it recently was denied continued use by EPA) built creatively upon the research which had taken place several decades ago.

Most responses were developed over a relatively short time period. This perception is consistent with the finding that most responses were relatively non-novel and drawn from a rather late stage of development.

Systemic Changes. Although this study did not attempt to measure systemic changes in any rigorous way, we nevertheless were impressed by the assertion of many interviewees that the character of their business had changed as a result of environmental regulation.

An important phenomenon reported in several instances is the ability of new entrants to capitalize upon opportunities created by regulatory demands. This may occur, for example, when products are banned or when an existing process technology is severely restricted. (For example, mercury has long been the most important biocide for paint uses. The regulations on this use have elicited several new non-mercurial products, sometimes from companies not previously in the industry.) New entrants may thus be competitively advantaged by the opportunity to comply with regulations.

Systemic changes were investigated quantitatively via questions about environmental affairs groups in the firms. About 65% of interviewed firms had such groups. Although the primary purpose of environmental affairs units appears to be to aid the direct compliance effort, their new capabilities may have important long-term implications for the pattern of innovation in the primary lines of business.

Most of the environmental affairs groups had as their primary purpose a liaison function between the regulators and their company. They participated regularly in the regulatory process, often indicating to the regulatory agencies the technical limits of existing compliance capability. Inside the firm, the environmental affairs unit often functioned in a manner very similar to a regulatory agency. Specifically, environmental review procedures were often established, with the environmental affairs unit able to "pass" on the acceptability of various products or processes, particularly in their early stages of development. Thus, these groups are likely to be an important force for the production of safer products and process technologies.

Environmental affairs units appear to be more common in larger corporations. They are typically located in the central corporate headquarters rather than in production facilities. They may be staffed with young environmental scientists rather than engineers. As such, it appears they often do not play a major role in the development of new compliance technology or in the engineering aspects of compliance. These latter functions are more typically within the realm of the plant-level engineers or R&D personnel.

Another widely reported phenomenon was a change in the skill-mix in firms in order to give them the new capabilities and expertise to comply with regulation. One change, widely reported, is the improvement in analytical chemistry capability. This was made necessary by regulation but, of course, aids companies generally in establishing better the properties of their products and finding new uses for them. The effect of interjecting new technical skills into regulated firms is difficult to assess. To the extent that these new personnel are concentrated in environmental affairs units, their impact on abatement technologies is likely to be no different from that discussed above. However, we are also left with the impression that new skills and a new environmental awareness are being absorbed by engineers and that this may have a profound impact both on abatement technology and other innovations. Many interviewees at the plant level indicated that their jobs were very different since environmental regulation. Some said this begrudgingly, but others said they now found the work more "challenging and exciting."

Ancillary Changes. "Ancillary responses" to regulation are technological changes that occur as a result of regulation but which are not necessary in order to bring those firms into compliance with regulatory requirements.

Ancillary changes were investigated by a simple direct question to the interviewees. Approximately 20% stated that there had been ancillary innovations resulting from regulation. These innovations benefitted the company in areas not related to compliance. Ancillary responses included: development of a new catalyst for petroleum refining; initial development of a new chlorine manufacturing process; increased yields of PVC resin; better process monitoring techniques for PVC polymerization; and new paint formulations.

More work needs to be done in the investigation of ancillary responses. However, we do feel that their existence is beyond doubt. One of the problems in investigating ancillary responses arises from the fact that they are very diffuse and indirect and not likely to be appreciated fully by any single individual in the firm. Indeed this fact was cited often by interviewees in response to our questions.

Other Conclusions. Although no systematic attempt was made to assess the level of compliance with regulatory requirements, the interviewers were left with a very strong feeling that firms are substantially in compliance with regulatory mandates for lead, mercury, PCB's and vinyl chloride. By this, we do not mean that companies are simply on a legally sanctioned compliance schedule; but rather, that they have reached or surpassed the goals of the regulation in question. Thus, regulation did not, in any instance we investigated, present an insurmountable technical problem.

At least for the four hazards investigated, the level of controversy concerning regulatory demands appears to have abated considerably, and industry has accepted the necessity of compliance.

Within the 50 firms interviewed, the interviewees were remarkably candid, open and willing to discuss in detail the effects of regulation on the technology in use in their companies. Only a very small number of companies refused to be interviewed.

The vast majority felt that the research topic was worthwhile and thus were glad to contribute to our effort.
The encouraging attitude of the firms interviewed suggests that further empirical work to investigate the systemic and ancillary responses to regulation may be worthwhile.

Implications for Regulatory Policy

The model of the relationship between regulation and technological change developed in this research appears to be successful in analyzing past responses of the chemical industry to environmental and health regulation. Moreover, this conceptual framework may be useful both in the design of future regulations and in planning corporate strategy for responding to these requirements.

In the past, the chemical industry has been resilient in its response to significant regulatory efforts. It has reached or surpassed the technological requirements of regulation. In part, this is because the previous standards imposed appear to have been based on present technological feasibility or best available technology. But, in addition, the industry has been able to accelerate the development of new process technology which was needed for compliance. There is strong evidence that regulation can change the overall character of product and process innovation in the industry, providing the regulations are stringent enough and of the right kind.

The industry might well be viewed as being in a transition period between a past history of little emphasis on environmental and health concern and a future pattern of much greater activity. This is evidenced by increasing managerial attention to these issues via both the formal establishment of environmental affairs units and shifting emphasis in the nature of chemical product design and production. Direct regulation of specific hazards must be seen within the context of a more general need to restructure the nature of chemical production technology over the next decade or more, if real improvements in environmental quality and public health are to be made. The newer regulatory efforts, especially those concerned with workplace hazards, consumer products, and new activities by EPA under the Toxic Substances Control Act, may be particularly important for innovation both in compliance technology and in process or product redesign. This is to be contrasted with past efforts at air and water quality control which focused on single pollutants as emissions or effluents at the end of the production process.

In order to succeed in achieving a more general shift in the nature of chemical production, regulations must be designed to elicit the best possible technological response from the industry. Regulation must be "technology forcing". The past pattern of basing standards on existing technology must be altered. In addition, the overall stimulus for change must be strong enough to effect a shift in the general management approach to all possible hazards associated with production. The adoption of generic regulations or regulation of classes of chemicals would provide a stronger impetus for change than a substance-by-substance approach.

Our model of the regulation-technological change response implies that care must be taken in deciding whether to regulate the product or the process in a specific case. The technological response may be different. OSHA, CPSC, and EPA under their respective legislative mandates can bring about radically different responses to a particular hazard. For example, a product safety regulation controlling the permissible concentration of benzene in industrial solvents is much more likely to change the nature and production technology of those solvents than regulating workplace exposure. In addition, worker protection might more assuredly be achieved. This example illustrates the importance of selecting an appropriate regulatory strategy. This can be accomplished most effectively by coordination among the agencies, for example, through the recently-formed Interagency Regulatory Liaison Group.

In the past, one of the impediments to the design of "technology forcing" regulations has been the fact that the agencies have relied on the regulated industries as the source of their information about the potential for technological change. Accordingly, compliance has been largely the adoption of "off the shelf" technology and has resulted in less protection of health and the environment than might have actually been possible. Our research suggests that important changes in technology can be encouraged by regulation. This will be the case especially if, in the future, both the agencies and the industry develop an appreciation for the complexities of the regulation-technological change relationship. The regulatory agencies should be aware of the fact that it is possible to design regulations to stimulate the development of new technologies whose performance exceeds the expectations of both industry and government. This work is intended to help develop that awareness.

Acknowledgment

This paper, in part, reports preliminary findings of a major study of the effects of environmental/safety regulation in the U.S. chemical industry, undertaken for the National Science Foundation (Grant No. PRA76-21368) by the Center for Policy Alternatives at the Massachusetts Institute of Technology. Interested readers may wish to consult the full report. (1)

Literature Cited

1. See N.A. Ashford, D. Hattis, G.R. Heaton, A. Jaffe, S. Owen, and W.C. Priest, Environmental/Safety Regulation and Technological Change in the U.S. Chemical Industry, Report to the National Science Foundation by the Center for Policy Alternatives, MIT, March 1979.

2. C.T. Hill, et al., A State of the Art Review of the Effects of Regulation on Technological Innovation in the Chemical and Allied Products Industries, Vols. 1, 2 & 3, NTIS, PB 243728, Springfield, VA 1975.

3. N.A. Ashford, G.R. Heaton, W.C. Priest and H. Lutz, The Implications of Health, Safety and Environmental Regulations for Technological Change, Center for Policy Alternatives, MIT, January 15, 1979.

4. S. Peltzman, Journal of Political Economy, Vol. 81, Sept./Oct. 1973.

5. W. Wardell and L. Lasagna, "Regulation and Drug Development", American Enterprise Institute, 1975.

6. H. Grabowski, "Drug Regulation and Innovation", American Enterprise Institute, 1976.

7. N.A. Ashford, S.E. Butler and E.M. Zolt, "Comment on Drug Regulation and Innovation in the Pharmaceutical Industry" (prepared for the National Institute of Environmental Health Sciences), February 1977.

8. J.C. Iverstine, The Impact of Environmental Protection Regulations on Research and Development in the Industrial Chemical Industry, National Science Foundation, May 1978., May 1978.

9. George Eads, "Chemicals as a Regulated Industry: Implications for Research and Product Development", draft paper presented at the American Chemical Society Meeting, Symposium on The Effects of Government Regulation on Chemical Innovation, Miami Beach, FL, September 14, 1978.

10. G. Schweitzer, "Regulation and Innovation: The Case of Environmental Chemicals", Cornell University Program on Science and Technology, and Society, Ithaca, N.Y., February 1978.

11. W.J. Abernathy and P.L. Townsend, "Technology, Productivity and Process Change", Technological Forecasting and Social Change 7, 379 (1975).

12. J.M. Utterback and W.J. Abernathy, "A Dynamic Model of Process and Product Innovation," Omega 3, 639 (1975).

RECEIVED May 1, 1979.

The Impact of Environmental Protection Regulations on Research and Development in the Industrial Chemical Industry

JOE C. IVERSTINE and JERRY L. KINARD

Southeastern Louisiana University, Hammond, LA 70401

The Clean Air Amendments to the Air Quality Act and the Federal Water Pollution Control Act Amendments were enacted to protect the environment. They have directly affected the operations of chemical firms, particularly those of research and development.

In June, 1976, the National Science Foundation approved a proposal submitted by Southeastern Louisiana University to assess the impact of environmental protection regulations on research and development in the industrial chemical industry. Phase 1 of the study began July 1, 1976, and concluded January 31, 1977. Phase 11 of the study began April 1, 1977, and concluded April 30, 1978.

Objectives of the Study

During the first six years of the existence of the Environmental Protection Agency, over 19,000 formal enforcement actions were taken for air, water, and pesticide pollution. Between January, 1976, and September, 1976, the EPA initiated 6,613 actions, resulting in fines and penalties in excess of $1.5 million. (1) A significant number of enforcement actions have been taken against chemical firms.

Legislation passed to curtail environmental pollution has been successful in reducing emission/effluents into the air and waterways throughout the country. More stringent regulations, such as best practical technology requirements of 1977 and best available technology requirements of 1983, will result in further reductions in effluents/emissions. As a result of the implementation of regulation designed to control and alleviate pollution, operations of chemical firms have been directly affected. As evidenced by the findings of "The CAPI Project, (2)" however, the total effect of such regulations on the industrial chemical industry is undetermined. In order to assess the exact impact of environmental protection regulations on research and development in the industrial chemical industry, we explored the following areas:

0-8412-0511-6/79/47-109-067$05.00/0

1. The manner in which environmental protection regulations have changed or influenced traditional R&D activity. These influences include (a) changes, if any, in levels of R&D expenditures (as measured by the ratio of R&D expenditures to sales) from pre-regulation periods to the current period; (b) diversion, if any, of R&D funds from traditional R&D goals-product development and process improvement (excluding marketable pollution control treating agents and abatement equipment)-to projects specifically designed to abate pollution; (c) diversion, if any, of technical manpower to R&D activities specifically designed to abate pollution; (d) changes, if any, in product development and process improvement lead times caused by environmental protection regulations; (e) the utilization of R&D facilities (laboratories, pilot plants, computer time, etc.) for environmental protection projects; (f) the priority given R&D projects for environmental protection as compared to traditional R&D projects; (g) the extent of reliance on external (outside the firm) sources of innovation (universities, private research and consulting firms, etc.) to solve environmental protection problems; and (h) the allocation of various R&D efforts among the following: controlling existing pollution, developing analytical methods, eliminating sources of pollution, developing new products, and other such endeavors.

2. The effect of changes in R&D activity brought about by environmental protection regulations. This effect included (a) the extent to which treating agents and/or abatement equipment and technology have been developed as marketable products or services; (b) the degree of success of R&D activity in solving environmental protection problems (eliminating sources, controlling existing pollution, developing new products to replace harmful ones, etc.); (c) an assessment of the impact of redirected R&D efforts on new product development and process improvements; (d) a measurement of the tangible, but unexpected, benefits not specifically related to environmental protection which have occurred as a result of R&D efforts directed toward environmental protection; (e) an assessment of the perceived effectiveness of R&D activity in solving environmental protection problems if best practical technology and best available technology requirements are imposed in 1977 and 1983 respectively; and (f) an overall assessment from the firm's viewpoint of the benefits (marketable products or services, unexpected benefits, more efficient processes, and a cleaner environment) versus the costs (direct expenses and opportunity costs) of R&D activity for environmental protection.

3. An examination of the underlying bases for the above changes in R&D activity brought about by environmental protection regulations and an explanation of the effect of such changes.

Methodology

In order to satisfy the objectives of the study, a combina-

tion of structured and non-structured personal interviews with
R&D officers of firms in the industrial chemical industry was
used as a primary research instrument.

The research team sampled only "large" chemical companies
(sales over $200 million) because of large firm domination of
industry R&D. Fifteen firms were selected from the 36 companies
whose primary business activity is related to chemicals and which
have chemical sales over $200 million. This sample constitutes
71.6 percent of 1976 industry R&D spending. The research sample
includes: Rohm & Haas, Dow, Allied, Dexter, Celanese, DuPont,
Stauffer, Vulcan, W.R. Grace, Ethyl, Cabot, American Cyanamid,
Monsanto, BASF Wyandotte, and Ciba Geigy.

Findings And Conclusions

The following is a summary of the major findings and the
resulting conclusions from this study. Details of the methodology, analytical methods, and data are available in "The Impact
of Environmental Protection Regulations on Research and Development in the Industrial Chemical Industry" (3).

Overall Assessment of R&D for Environmental Protection. It
is recognized by the researchers that a total analysis of the
societal cost versus societal benefits of R&D for environmental
protection research is well beyond the scope of this study.

For example, the benefit of a cleaner environment was not
examined and, moreover, would be very difficult to measure. However, an objective of this study is to contribute to the on-going
process of evaluation of costs versus benefits of governmental
regulation of business. Hence, the following is a summary assessment of the costs versus benefits of environmental research in the
chemical industry.

Costs. It has been established that chemical firms are allo-
cating R&D resources to solve environmental protection problems.
Even though this research may be highly desirable from a societal
posture, it does represent a diversion of R&D resources from
traditional goals of product development and process improvement.
This diversion represents "opportunity costs" or the loss that the
firms sustain by foregoing the benefits that are provided by traditional research projects.

One way to minimize the impact of these opportunity costs is
to supplement R&D spending to off-set the funds allocated to environmental protection research. Hence, it was expected that
R&D spending as a per cent of sales would increase from pre-
regulation periods because of the necessity to conduct environmental protection research. However, the ratio of R&D spending
to sales has actually declined from .0424 in 1970 to .0297 in
1976. One possible explanation is that the inflation in chemical
prices has exceeded the inflation in R&D costs. Over this period,

it is possible that the level of R&D activity has been maintained
or has not decreased proportionally to the decline in R&D to
sales ratio.

   Another possible explanation for the decline in the R&D/sales
ratio was offered by Dr. Theodore Cairns, Director of DuPont's
massive central R&D organization. Dr. Cairns cited the fact that
duPont's current ratio of R&D to sales is approximately four per
cent compared to 6.5 per cent in 1970. He suggests that DuPont
adopted the policy of diversification and aggressive pursuit of
new products in the 1960's. Dr. Cairns notes that DuPont's
policy has recently changed to development of existing product
lines. He further suggests that a good industry research program will have a declining budget relative to sales, as at some
point, the industry must develop what has been researched.

   Both of the above explanations have some merit. In response,
however, to the first explanation, R&D costs are "managed." The
growth of these costs is dependent upon management decisions
with regard to number of scientists employed, purchase of equipment and facilities, etc. It is likely that increases in R&D
costs were below increases in chemical prices because of managerial decisions in the chemical industry to restrict the growth
of R&D spending relative to sales. This contention is supported
by the fact that the number of chemical R&D scientists and engineers dropped from 22,000 in 1970 to less than 20,000 in 1973.
In 1976, the number of chemical R&D scientists and engineers
returned to the 1970 level of 22,000. Hence, this decline in the
R&D to sales ratio during the 1970 to 1976 period is partially
due to fewer R&D personnel employed.

   Moreover, R&D spending in 1976 by the industry in terms of
constant dollars is at the 1968 level of $800 million, whereas,
sales have increased 28.6 per cent in terms of constant dollars
during this period. So, the growth of R&D in the chemical industry has definitely not matched the growth of the industry in
terms of sales.

   In response to the second explanation for this decline, the
researchers were not able to verify the contention that current
R&D efforts are capitalizing on important discoveries made during
the last decade. It may be that the industry experiences a
cycle of discovery and then development with corresponding increases in the sales to R&D ratio followed by decreases in this
ratio. However, the researchers found that the industry is currently spending approximately 44.6 per cent of its R&D on "new"
product/process development and approximately 37.5 per cent of
its R&D on "existing" product/process improvement. It appears
that the R&D effort is balanced between new developments and improvement of existing products/processes.

   From the evidence collected in this research study, it is
noted that approximately 13.5 per cent of chemical R&D is allocated to environmental protection projects (see Table I). This
represents an outlay of approximately $198.7 million by the indus-

try. It is also noted that there has not been an increase in the growth of R&D to off-set the necessity of having to conduct environmental protection research. In fact, total chemical R&D has remained unchanged from pre-regulation periods to the present in terms of constant dollar sales. Hence, it can be concluded that the necessity of having to conduct environmental protection research does represent a diversion from traditional innovative activities of product/process development and product/process improvement. Moreover, the inclusion of environmental protection regulations in risk models may further restrict R&D activities in the chemical industry due to the decision to forego numerous product development projects. These actions represent opportunity costs for the industry.

Table I

Summary of R&D Spending By The Chemical Industry

Category	Percentage of R&D Spending
Environmental Protection	13.521
Process Improvement	18.784
New Process Development	22.786
Product Improvement	18.867
New Product Development	21.978
Other (not included in above)	4.064
	100.000

Benefits

Success in Solving Environmental Protection Problems. The EPA reported that 1303 chemical plants out of 1371 were in compliance with the 1970 Clean Air Act. This represents a 95 per cent compliance rate. Also, 89 per cent of the chemical plants were in compliance with the 1977 deadline of "best practicable control" specified in the 1972 Federal Water Quality Act Amendments. (4) Hence, the chemical industry has been somewhat successful in utilizing its technology to meet environmental protection standards. Officers from twelve of the fifteen responding firms indicated that R&D effort to meet these deadlines represented efficient and effective solutions to pollution control problems.

Screening of Potentially Harmful Products. An EPA research director suggested that the inclusion of environmental protection regulations in risk models has screened out numerous products that may have been environmentally harmful. R&D officers readily agree that numerous product ventures have been dropped due to uncertainty in meeting environmental protection regulations. While these decisions may partially explain the failure of chemical R&D to match the growth of the industry, it is likely that they have succeeded in preventing environmental protection problems.

Marketable Products or Services Related to Environmental
Protection. As indicated earlier, R&D officers from two-thirds
of the responding firms reported marketable products or services
created by environmental protection regulations. R&D officers
from these responding firms quickly observe that revenues from
these products or services do not come close to off-setting costs
associated with meeting environmental protection regulations.
Nevertheless, these chemical firms are required to comply with
these regulations, and any recovery of costs from these newly
created revenue centers represent a benefit for these firms.

Unexpected Benefits. Of the fifteen responding firms, R&D
officers from only five firms report tangible benefits that are
not directly related to environmental protection. These benefits
include: better analytical chemists; closed system philosophy
of plant operation; improved knowledge of molecular structure of
products; and better process instrumentation.

Other Factors

Uniformity of Impact. It was expected that environmental
protection regulations would affect chemical R&D uniformly
throughout the industry. Even though there is variation in the
size and product lines of chemical producers, it was believed
that the impact of these regulations on R&D would be somewhat
uniform. The impact was assessed by per cent of R&D spent on
environmental protection. The researchers conclude that the
dispersion of R&D spending for environmental protection is no
greater than the dispersion of R&D spending for other categories.
Hence, the impact does appear to be uniform throughout the
industry.

Size of the Firm. Related to the above factor, the researchers suspected that small chemical producers may experience a
greater impact on their R&D function than larger chemical producers. Even though the research design eliminated firms having
sales less than $200 million, the sample did include a range of
sales from approximately $200 million to $8.4 billion. Within
this range, the researchers note that there is no correlation between sales and per cent of R&D spent on environmental protection.
A negative correlation of sales to per cent of R&D spent on environmental protection was expected if these regulations more
severely affected smaller firms. This was not the case.

Relationship with the EPA. When the researchers asked R&D
officers about their relationship with the EPA with regard to
environmental protection research, fifteen different reactions
were received from the fifteen responding firms. In describing

this relationship, the adjectives ranged from: "good, productive, on-going, some, guarded, little, arm's length, none, poor, and lousy." Perhaps the same reactions may be received from the EPA if asked about their relationship with the respective chemical firms. While these attitudes definitely do not represent "hard data," they, nonetheless, are important in policy formation for future environmental protection research. If relationships on the whole were "better", the result would be clearer communications, better standards through more input, better defined goals, and more efficient research. However, the researchers recognize the necessary distance that must be maintained between regulator and "regulatee."

Offensive Versus Defensive Posture. Almost all of the R&D officers noted a change in recent years from a defensive to an offensive posture with respect to the regulations. A number of these firms aggressively challenge the EPA if they believe that the regulatory agencies are misinterpreting the law, setting unreasonable standards, or over-stepping their authority as prescribed by the regulations. Several of these firms have spent millions of dollars in defense of products under attack because of environmental considerations. This "offensive" philosophy represents a shift from a more "defensive" posture when the regulations were first promulgated.

Direction of Future Regulations. All R&D officers unanimously agreed that the regulations will become more restrictive. They portrayed efforts to meet the standards as trying to hit a "moving target." The R&D officers expressed the hope that future regulations will not obviate R&D efforts in developing existing environmental protection technology. One reason cited for more restrictive regulations is the advances in analytical chemistry. In a number of cases, standards were based on the level of detection demonstrated by analytical methods. However, some methods have advanced from parts per million concentrations to parts per billion. Several R&D officers believe that the standards will become more restrictive as detection becomes more sophisticated. R&D officers from one firm exhibited an exponential increase in costs as the standard became more restrictive for one product.

Methodology Problems

In the course of the above research project, several methodological problems were encountered. The following is a discussion of these problems and the manner in which they affected the study.

Variations in Accounting. Although public accounting procedures and practices are basically standardized, the specific techniques employed by individual firms vary. Consequently, these differences present some problems in both external and internal analysis. External analysis is the comparison of one company to other companies in the industry and internal analysis is the historical comparison of different periods within a single company.

In analyzing the R&D activities of those firms included in this study, a determination of R&D expenditures as a percent of Sales and R&D as a percent of Sales minus Profit was made. Differences in depreciation methods, inventory methods, etc. will affect the Sales and Profit figures for a firm, thus making comparisons between firms using different methods difficult. Further, a change in technique by a single company necessitates adjustments in prior years to get comparable figures. Extra-ordinary items or experiences in a given year (i.e., a large write off) are reflected in the Sales and/or Profit figures for the firm, thereby possibly giving a distorted indication of the normal activity for the company.

However, despite these variations in accounting, the financial data presented in the annual reports of the sample firms provided a basis for establishing R&D expenditure patterns. No attempt was made to compare one firm to another. Instead, the data were used to access the pattern of R&D expenditures for each individual firm for the years 1970-1976 and for the sample firms as a whole.

Definition of Research and Development. The major purpose of this research project was to access the impact of environmental protection regulations on R&D in the industrial chemical industry. Therefore, it was necessary to identify the industrial chemical industry and to determine what constitutes a "chemical firm." To resolve this problem, the researchers used those firms classified in SIC Codes 2800 to 2899. Further, the industrial chemical industry is oligopolistic in nature; consequently, a select group of large companies constitute the bulk of all industry activity. A recent survey by Chemical and Engineering News noted that 19 companies account for about 80% of the chemical industry's sales and more than 90% of the entire industry's R&D dollars. Therefore, fifteen firms were taken from a universe of 36 large industrial chemical firms. (See section on methodology.) In 1976, these fifteen firms accounted for 71.6% of R&D expenditures. Finally, it should be noted that many of these companies are diversified and are engaged in various activities other than chemicals. Financial data presented in annual reports are often aggregate data and, consequently, it is difficult to determine the impact on R&D related only to chemical activities. Although many companies have chemicals as one of their products, the companies selected for this project are predominantly involved in the manufacture and sale of industrial chemicals.

Processing of Subjective Data. The research instrument used in this study combined both structured and unstructured questions. Analysis of the objective data from the structured portion of the

interviews was performed by the application of the appropriate
statistical tests. However, processing the subjective data presented an analytical problem as such data were not readily quanti-
fiable and, therefore, could not be evaluated by the use of empirical testing techniques. But despite this limitation, the
subjective data gathered provided meaningful and necessary information about the significance of environmental protection regulations on the R&D activities and plans of those companies visited.
The responses by those persons interviewed provided data on (1)
environmental protection philosophy (approach to pollution control ; i.e., "contain" vs. "eliminate source"; offensive vs.
defensive posture, etc.), (2) opportunity cost of environmental
protection projects,, (3) relationship with regulatory agencies,
(4) influence of energy conservation on environmental protection
projects, (5) the extent to which pollution control innovation
is freely shared among firms within the industry, (6) influence
of potential land use regulation on R&D projects associated with
new plant construction and plant expansions, (7) qualifications
of R&D personnel assigned to environmental protection projects,
and (8) future direction of regulation (as viewed by R&D officers.)
        In analyzing the subjective data, the researchers compared
the responses by the officials of the different companies in the
sample to detect consistencies and/or differences. This comparison was made to differentiate between responses that were unique
and those that appeared representative of the sample as a whole.
The attitudes, philosophies, and predictions of the upper-level
R&D officials interviewed in this study will, in large part, determine the future R&D policies and plans of these companies and,
therefore, are highly significant in accessing the impact of environmental protection regulation and its future ramifications.

        Problem of Verification. Much of the data used in this study
were gathered by interviews with R&D personnel from the sample
firms. These individuals provided both subjective and objective
information about their companies and the manner in which environmental protection regulations impact their R&D activities. Given
the size and complexity of these sample firms, this data were
difficult to verify. However, to help substantiate the validity
of the data provided, the researchers analyzed the responses for
consistencies or possible contradictions. Comparisons were made
between individual responses and data gathered from trade journals, annual reports, and other secondary data sources. Further,
in selected instances, the researchers made plant tours to personally observe the manner in which the companies had been affected.

        Financial Analysis. One objective of this research project
was to determine if, in the last several years, there have been
any changes in the R&D expenditure patterns by the firms in the

industrial chemical industry. To provide some insight into this matter, research was conducted to determine changes in the amount of dollars being spent on R&D activities by individual firms and by the sample firms as a whole.

A change in total dollars spent on R&D from one period to another does not, in itself, have much significance as variations can be caused by price changes, inflation, and other variables. However, the objective of this study was not to determine total dollars spent, but to measure relative changes in the R&D expenditures of the firms studied. To measure these changes, R&D as a percent of Sales and R&D as a percent of Sales-Profits were determined for individual firms for the years 1970-1976. Calculation of these percentages gives an indicator of the proportionate R&D expenditure level for a firm in a given year and permits a comparison of these proportions over time to access relative changes.

Acknowledgements

This material is based upon research supported by the National Science Foundation under Grant No. PRA 76-21321. Any opinions, findings, and conclusions or recommendations expressed in this publication are those of the authors and do not necessarily reflect the views of the National Science Foundation.

Literature Cited

1. EPA Enforcement - A Progress Report for 1976: Air, Noise, Water, Pesticides; Environmental Protection Agency, Washington, D.C.; (January, 1977), p. 1.

2. Hill, Christopher T., et al., A State of the Art Review of the Effects of Regulation on Technological Innovation in the Chemical and Allied Products Industries (CAPI Project), Volume I, Executive Summary, (February, 1975), p. 5.

3. Iverstine, Joe C., Jerry L. Kinard, and William S. Slaughter, The Impact of Environmental Protection Regulations on Research and Development in the Industrial Chemical Industry, (May, 1978).

4. Compliance Status of Major Air Pollution Facilities, U.S. Environmental Protection Agency, Office of General Enforcement, Washington, D.C. (November, 1977).

RECEIVED March 8, 1979.

Case Studies on Chemical Flue Gas Treatment as a Means of Meeting Particulate Emission Regulations

MURRAY S. COHEN and ROBERT P. BENNETT

Apollo Chemical Corp., Whippany, NJ 07981

Although the regulatory process is frequently cited as the responsible element in stifling creativity and the development of new products, Federal air pollution legislation enacted over the past 13 years is shown in this paper to have been responsible for the creation of a new and vital business. One industry, the utility industry, felt the impact of these regulations most severely. To respond to the needs of this industry, an innovative chemical company perceived an opportunity for a new system of chemical products. The development and marketing of these products and their performance in helping utilities meet national air emission goals is discussed.

Legislation Affecting Emission Control

Changing national priorities have generated Federal government regulations which, if separated out of the context of time, would appear highly contradictory. However, the process of Federal regulation becomes clearer if the reasons why these regulations were enacted is presented. Table I is a chronological listing of pertinent legislation.

The roots of current Federal involvement in air quality dates back to the Research & Technical Assistance Act of 1955 which provided a mechanism for the Federal government to make grants supporting research in air quality. There was no enforcement authority built into this legislation so that control of air quality standards remained a patchwork of state by state legislation. The first attempt at introducing Federal enforcement dates from the Clean Air Act of 1963 (1). This complicated piece of legislation extended the authority of the Health, Education and Welfare (HEW) Department to interstate disagreements on air quality. Intrastate intervention was allowed only if HEW was invited to intercede by the governor of a state. Authority was limited to calling conferences, public hearings and making recommendations. Court action was possible, but in the single instance of such action, it took five years to reach a court decision. Amendments were

0-8412-0511-6/79/47-109-077$06.25/0

TABLE I

REGULATORY LEGISLATION AFFECTING THE USE
OF AIR POLLUTION CONTROL SYSTEMS

1955   Research and Technical Assistance
        Act

1963   Clean Air Act of HEW

1965   Clean Air Act as Amended

1966   Clean Air Act as Amended

1967   Clean Air Act as Amended

1970   Clean Air Act as Amended (EPA)

1974   Energy Supply and Environmental
        Coordination Act (ESECA)

1977   Clean Air Act as Amended

1978   Powerplant and Industrial
        Fuel Use Act (PIFUA)

made to the act in 1965 (2) and 1966 (3). The 1967 (4) amendments were of some significance since it empowered HEW to recommend air quality standards and called for the states to prepare
plans for implementation. The amendments, however, contained
neither deadlines nor sanctions.
The 1970 amendments represent landmark legislation (5). Not
only did the law create the Environmental Protection Administration (EPA) as a separate agency reporting directly to the President, but it established schedules and a regulatory mechanism to
treat air quality on a national basis. No longer could an industry find pockets of laxity from state environmental controls. Air
quality was defined in legal tests and emerged as a new concept,
i.e., prevention of significant deterioration (PSD) and national
ambient air quality standards (NAAQS).
The legislation, which resulted in the 1970 amendments, must
be considered as an expression of the national will to achieve
clean air. As such, it was a determination on the part of Congress to halt deteriorating air quality by whatever means were
available. The legislation impacted most heavily on the large
stationary sources, the electrical utilities. At the time, utilities burned the cheapest, but dirtiest fuel, coal. Coal combustion
gives rise to high levels of particulates and, in the case of
Eastern coal, high SO_2 levels as well. To meet the requirements
of the 1970 amendments, a swing took place away from coal to low
sulfur oil. It must be remembered that economic incentives to do
this were readily available. Oil was plentiful and cheap. Large
capital investment in fuel oil desulfurization plants could be
rationalized by the predicted growth in demand for low sulfur oil.
However, this process of conversion from coal to oil was
abruptly interrupted by the Arab-led oil embargo of 1973. Prices
rose dramatically and the nation was shocked into recognizing its
vulnerability to the flow of imported oil. This recognition
found legislative expression in the Energy Supply and Environmental Coordination Act of 1974 (ESECA) (6), a regulation, in
effect, which prohibits the combustion of oil and gas by large
stationary sources. Utilities which are incapable of burning
coal are excepted, but all large sources which were designed
originally for coal,but had converted to oil under pressure of
the 1970 Clean Air Act, were required to reconvert. Also, those
stations which never burned coal,but could be retrofitted to do
so,had to convert as well. To resolve what were essentially
conflicting demands of environmentalists and those responsible
for energy independence, the ESECA laws require an environmental
impact statement to be made. This had to be approved by the EPA
for the reconverted facility to operate.
The final efflorescence of the Clean Air Act were the amendments of 1977 (7). Regulations stemming from these amendments
took recognition of the desirability of coal combustion. It
eliminated where possible the choice of low sulfur oil as a fuel,
and forced utilities to burn coal by requiring that air standards

be met through the use of best available control technology (BACT). Political considerations could not be neglected. The protection of the eastern coal economy was assured when regulations to reduce sulfur emissions were made by specifying reductions as a percentage of the sulfur in the fuel. This made is difficult for western low sulfur coal to compete with local coals in the east.

Because of limitations of SO_2 emissions, the large stationary sources were faced with unexpected capital expenditures for both SO_2 and particulate controls. Existing sources had to meet emission limitations set forth in their state implementation plans. New sources will be regulated under the stricter new source performance standards (NSPS). Best available control technology was required for emission controls. This meant that sources not meeting compliance had to retrofit existing facilities with costly control devices. New sources were restricted further. They could not get construction permits without incorporating into their plans the control equipment capable of achieving NSPS.

The intent of Congress to more stringently restrict oil imports appears in the Powerplant and Industrial Fuel Use Act (FUA) (3), now part of the National Energy Act (NEA). The new legislation removes the burden of proof from the government in justifying conversion from oil and gas to coal. Instead, it is now incumbent upon the stationary source to demonstrate why it cannot make the conversion.

Controls For Particulates

To a great extent, it was the emphasis on both dirty fuel combustion and environmental safeguards which created the opportunity for the new technology to be described in this paper to find its application and growth.

The pollutants which increased dramatically in converting from oil/gas to coal combustion are particulate matter and sulfur dioxide. State laws, especially those governing emissions in urban areas, specify limits for both species. They could be met when low sulfur fuel oil or gas was burned, but coal combustion required new or upgraded pollution control devices. To understand the problem of coping with both of these emissions, it is simpler to treat the response to particulate control separate from that of SO_2 control.

Pollution control devices for particulates do not depend upon new technology whereas SO_2 control does. Since the first decade of this century, as a result of Cottrell's original work (9), the electrostatic precipitator had been used to collect fly ash particulates. These devices were used on many of the older coal burning plants which had converted to oil. On the reconversion to coal, they were put back in operation or else new ESP units were put in the place occupied by the older ones. The performance of these systems, when designed for a specific coal, was excellent. However, allowable levels of particulate emissions in many cases had become more stringent so that original equipment could not perform at the required efficiency levels. Furthermore, efficiency of an ESP device is a function of the chemical and physical properties of the design coal. Thus, ash content, sulfur content, heating value, moisture content, air to fuel ratio could change and therby reduce the efficiency of the ESP. The utility could improve its particulate emission performance by incorporating additional collection area to existing ESP units, but as will be shown, this requires large capital expenditures.

The second problem encountered in conversion from oil to coal was the dramatic increase in sulfur dioxide emissions. Whereas much of the oil burned in urban areas was desulfurized to 0.5% sulfur or less, the coal, especially that found in the eastern U.S., had a sulfur content of 2.5% or higher. Western coal has a lower sulfur content (0.5 to 1.0%), but these coal fields had to be developed and the coal had to be shipped long distances at considerable cost to the site at which it is burned (10). Furthermore, western coal was found to produce a fly ash which was poorly captured by the ESP.

The reason why this occurs is now well understood. Particulates to be captured efficiently, must pick up a negative charge as the particle passes through the corona or ionizing discharge of the ESP. The negatively charged particulate then migrates to the grounded collector plate. If the resistivity of the particle is excessively high, the charge does not leak to the plate. The failure to sustain a sufficient difference in potential across the air gap impedes the migration of charged particles.
impedes the migration of charged particles.

A second effect of high fly ash resistivity is observed when the difference in potential across the collected dust layer rises to too high a value. A back corona can form as the EMF differential breaks down due to sparking across the dust layer. High currents flow between the wire cathode and plate anode thereby destroying the ability of the ESP to charge particulates.

High fly ash resistivity may be overcome by introducing polar chemicals which adsorb themselves on the fly ash surface and reduce surface resistivity. Howard (11) had reported in 1918 that particulate capturability was excellent in those flue gases containing high concentrations of sulfur trioxide. This polar molecule was proven to be the species responsible for reducing surface resistivity. The unusual characteristic of western coal is its low sulfur content (approx. 0.5% S). When burned, sulfur is converted to sulfur dioxide and a portion of the dioxide is fully oxidized to the trioxide.

The degree of conversion to sulfur trioxide is influenced by three factors: 1) the amount of sulfur in fuel, b) the amount of excess air used in combustion and, c) the presence of oxidation catalysts. Figure 1 illustrates SO_3 formation for coal and oil as a function of excess air used in combustion. More pronounced

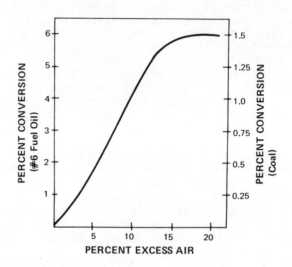

Figure 1. Conversion of sulfur to sulfur trioxide in combustion of #6 oil or coal with excess air

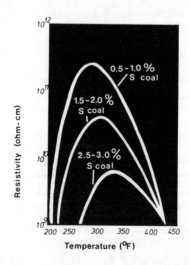

Environmental Science and Technology

Figure 2. Effects of temperature and sulfur content on fly ash resistivity (13)

catalytic effects are noted in oil combustion, probably as a result of the strong activity of vanadium found in oil but not, to any great extent, in coal (12).

The effect of sulfur trioxide on resistivity has been characterized and an illustration of this effect is shown in Figure 2 based upon data gathered by Research Cottrel, Inc. (13). It can be seen that resistivity also varies as a function of temperature, reaching a peak level at 300 to 350°F. This is approximately the temperature at which most cold side precipitators operate. Recent technology has shown that hot side precipitators, where collection occurs at temperatures higher than 600°F, do indeed avoid the resistivity problem. However, because of the higher temperatures, gas volumes are also significantly greater, which results in a need for larger collecting areas and, therefore, more expensive precipitators.

With the knowledge that the concentration of sulfur trioxide acts as a control on resistivity of fly ash, it is not surprising that precipitators not meeting design requirements made use of SO_3 addition to the flue gas. The injection takes place after the air heater, prior to entering the ESP unit for a cold side precipitator. In some cases, improvement in ESP performance was significant. In others, because of the nature of the fly ash, the improvement was marginal.

In cases in which the space charge across the electrical field was insufficiently intense for proper charge buildup, it was found that ammonia injection improved the capturability of the fly ash (14). Other studies confirmed the applicability of sulfuric acid, ammonium sulfate and ammonium bisulfate as useful conditioners (15).

Using much of this information as well as a knowledge of boiler operations, its geometry, chemistry, and thermal characteristics, it was now possible to develop formulations which could treat a wide variety of coals. In a series of patents issued to Apollo Chemical Corp., the combination of chemistry and its applicability to specific boiler characteristics was claimed for various ammonium sulfate salts (16) as well as other polar species (17).

As an outgrowth of this prior work, it was now possible to formulate flue gas conditioners in sophisticated combinations. Thus, regardless of what coal was used, each fly ash could be brought to the same chemical potential for capture by the ESP; fly ashes were, in essence, "democratized". As a result, by judicious selection of conditioners, both high and low resistivity fly ash can be optimally modified. Furthermore, through the use of agglomerating agents, the average particle size of the collected fly ash can be increased. This is of special importance since the small particulates (<1.0 micron) are suspect in health effects ranging from bronchial conditions to cancer (18,19). The range of treatment can also be extended to include several combinations of conditioner introduced through several ports of entry. Thus, in certain cases, we have found that dual injection

of two different additives or the same additive at different stations in the boiler was more effective than an equivalent dose by
a single injection (20). The points at which the conditioner can
be introduced into the boiler are shown diagramatically in Figure
3.

Case Studies On Flue Gas Conditioning

To illustrate how chemical flue gas conditioning works, the
following represents typical cases on how the technology was successfully used under actual operating conditions to reduce particulate emissions from a) low sulfur coal (high resistivity fly
ash), b) high sulfur coal (low resistivity fly ash), and c) fly
ash in a hot side precipitator. Moreover, the use of multiple
injection ports (d),(dual injection), is illustrated as is the
reduction of fine particulate emissions, (e).

a) Low Sulfur Coal. The original impetus to adopt flue gas
conditioning arose when utilities were forced to switch their
coal supply from high sulfur coal in order to meet SO_2 emission
levels. This gave rise to fly ash which had too high a resistivity to be efficiently captured by existing ESP units. The
results obtained on two typical low sulfur coal burning boilers
is described.
     In Table II, a former oil burning boiler that was converted
to burning low sulfur coal could not meet particulate compliance
levels. To continue to operate, the utility was forced to derate
from 650 Mw to 440 Mw. The LPA flue gas conditioner, however,
allowed operation at 582 Mw, well within particulate compliance
levels. (LPA and LAC are product series designations of Apollo
Chemical Corp.)
     In Table III, as a result of switching from high to low sul-
fur coal, the unit was out of opacity compliance and forced to
derate from 175 Mw to 148 Mw. Use of the flue gas conditioner
allowed the Mw load to be increased to 173 Mw and operate well
within compliance.

b) High Sulfur Coal. In a number of cases, units burning
design coal with high sulfur content still experience emission
problems. Assuming that the precipitator is in good mechanical
condition, there are several reasons possible for excessive emissions levels. One reason can be that of over-conditioning of the
fly ash. Too low a resistivity results in particles discharging
their acquired electrical charge too quickly so that they are
easily eroded and reentrained in the flue gas stream. A second
factor is that high exit gas temperatures must be maintained in
order to prevent condensation of excess SO_3 from the flue gas
which could result in corrosion and air heater pluggage. This
method of operation not only reduces boiler efficiency, but also
increases the gas volume and velocity through the precipitator,

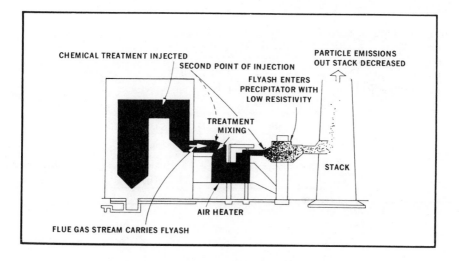

Figure 3.   Points at which chemical flue gas conditioner can be injected

TABLE II

LOW SULFUR COAL EXAMPLE

Description of Boiler

Boiler Manufacturer	Babcock & Wilcox
Capacity	650 Mw
Design Coal	Information not available
Current Coal	0.54 - 0.76% Sulfur; 6-10% Ash
Fuel Consumption	250 tons/hr.

Results at Increasing Loads

	LPA* Treatment Rate Gal./Ton Coal	Emissions lb/MM Btu	Percent Opacity
For compliance	-	0.05	20
At 440 Mw	0.0	0.057	10.7
At 570 Mw	0.2	0.012	9.5
At 575 Mw	0.2	0.011	6.5
At 582 Mw	0.25	0.006	3.5

*LPA and LAC are product series designations of Apollo Chemical Corp.

TABLE III

LOW SULFUR COAL EXAMPLE

Description of Unit

Boiler Manufacturer	Combustion Engineering
Size	175 Mw
Design Coal	1.2% S, 8.1% Ash
Current Coal	0.7 - 0.9% S, 8-10% Ash
Fuel Consumption	94.2 tons/hr
Precipitator Design	96% eff. at 175 Mw

Results at Increasing Loads

	LPA Treatment Rate Gal/Ton Coal	Emissions lb/MM Btu	Percent Opacity
For Compliance	–	0.25	40
At 148 Mw	0.00	0.25	40
At 158 Mw	0.07	0.11	18
At 163 Mw	0.11	0.18	15
At 173 Mw	0.11	0.16	18-19

thus reducing the precipitator efficiency.
In the case of high-sulfur coal, the resistivity of the ash is actually shifted toward higher values closer to the optimum by chemical treatment. In this case the effects of agglomeration of fly ash by the additive cannot be readily distinguished from electrical effects. The unit described in Table IV, burning design coal, was unable to meet particulate emissions compliance levels without additive treatment.

c) Hotside Precipitators. It was shown that resistivity, which has a major effect on the collectibility of fly ash, varies with temperature. An optimum range of resistivity exists in which fly ash is most readily collected. At approximately 220°F, fly ash resistivity is relatively insensitive to coal sulfur content; however, with increasing temperature the resistivity of fly ash from low-sulfur coal increases much more rapidly than that from high-sulfur coal. A maximum in resistivity occurs at about 300°F, and thereafter, the resistivity decreases steadily with increasing temperature. One technique,which is being used to take advantage of this aspect of low resistivity at high temperature,is to build a "hot precipitator" placed ahead of the air heater where the flue gas temperature will be in the 600-900°F range. In this temperature zone resistivity,generally,is within the optimum range for collection.
One unit firing low-sulfur western coal and utilizing a hot precipitator is described in Table V. This unit was unable to meet particulate emissions and opacity requirements consistently due to an excessive amount of fine particulate which was not being collected. The unit load had to be controlled so that the opacity limit was not exceeded. A chemical treatment program was established and several different chemical formulations were evaluated for their ability to reduce opacity since electrical response was not deemed to be the problem.
A dramatic reduction in opacity was obtained in a very short response time and at a relatively low additive treatment level.

d) Dual-Additive Injection. In discussions of mechanisms by which chemical conditioning can enhance the collectibility of fly ash (21,22), it has been noted that not all of these are equally effective. The predominant mechanism was found to vary in some cases with the temperature of injection. For example, it is possible to obtain dramatic, rapid reduction in opacity without necessarily seeing any change in precipitator power or fly ash resistivity if the additive or injection site is properly selected.
This discovery has led to a new technique of additive injection which takes advantage of this multiplicity of mechanisms. The technique involves the application of one additive into a hot section of the boiler, followed by injection of the same or a different additive into a relatively low-temperature zone, usually after the air heater. The combined treatment rate generally requires

TABLE IV

HIGH SULFUR COAL EXAMPLE

Description of Unit

Boiler Manufacturer	Foster-Wheeler, front-fired
Capacity	320 Mw
Precipitator	Buell
SCA	132 ft^2/1000 ACFM
Velocity	5.8 fps
Gas Rate	1.1 MM ACFM @ 268^{9}F
Design Coal	3.7% S; 8.5% Ash; 12,000 Btu/lb.
Current Coal	3.2-3.9% S, 9-13% Ash; approx. 12,000 Btu/lb.

Results at 320 Mw

	Emissions			Precipitator Efficiency
	#/hr	#/MMBtu	% Reduction from Baseline	%
For Compliance	350	0.100	-	99.1
Untreated, Baseline	488	0.139	-	98.8
LPA-treated (approx. 0.20 GPT) Average of all tests	180	0.055	68	99.5

TABLE V

HOT SIDE PRECIPITATOR AND LOW-SULFUR COAL EXAMPLE

Description of Unit

Boiler Manufacturer	Combustion Engineering
Capacity	280 Mw (1005°F/1950 psig)
Precipitator	Wheelabrator-Frye
SCA	347 ft^2/1000 ACFM
Velocity	5.16 fps
Gas Rate	1.664 MM ACFM at 695°F
Design Efficiency	99.5% (=0.01 grain/SCF outlet)
Design Coal	0.5% S; 11.5% Ash; 10,300 Btu/lb.
Current Coal	Approx. 0.5% S; 8-15% Ash; 10,500 Btu/lb.

Results at 280 Mw

	Emissions #/MM Btu	Opacity %
For Compliance	0.10	20
Untreated	0.10-0.14	22 - 30
LPA-40 treated (0.07 GPT)	0.02-0.03	12

less additive than a single injection. Additionally, this
technique gives greater flexibility for formulation in that different materials may be introduced to each injection zone. The
remaining discussion describes a unit which is currently being
successfully treated by this procedure.

The unit in Table VI had very low power and had emissions of
about three times the particulate compliance level. Application of
an LPA formulation produced increased power and reduced the ash
resistivity from 2 x 10^{11} to 5 x 10^{10} ohm-cm. Some reduction in
particulate emissions were obtained. This unit has a mechanical
collector ahead of the precipitator for the removal of large
particles. An LAC product was then applied to reduce reentrainment
with the result that emissions were reduced significantly below
the compliance level.

e) Fine Particulate Reduction. The relationship of exposure
to particulates vs health effects has not been explored in depth.
However, as explained in prior discussions (18, 19), the fine
particulate emissions, because they penetrate lung tissue most
easily and have shown certain mutagenic effects, are of greatest
concern. It was, therefore, of importance to determine whether
chemical flue gas conditioning has any effect upon the size distribution of particulates which escape the ESP.

This appears to be the case as is shown in a study of data
from two sources. Table VII and VIII describe a 480 Mw and a
575 Mw unit, which were treated subsequently with flue gas conditioning agent. Figure 4 & 5 are, respectively, the baseline and
treated bar graphs of particulate emissions from the unit of Table
VII collected by standard Anderson impactors. Similarly, Figure 6
and Figure 7 are the bar graphs (before and after treatment) from
the unit of Table VIII.

It can be seen in these cases that fine particulates were,
indeed,reduced on a percent basis and in addition, the total
particulates were also reduced.

Marketing Aspects of Chemical Flue Gas Conditioning

The chemical flue gas treatment business has required the
development of marketing skills not normally associated with
specialty chemical suppliers. Historically, the major customer,
the utility industry, had relied upon mechanical and electrical
devices for pollution control. Thus, cyclones, electrostatic
precipitators, and, more recently baghouses were the devices considered. The utility industry normally employs a technical staff
of skilled mechanical and electrical engineers who operate the
boilers and turbines. Thus, these personnel were available to
apply their skills to pollution control equipment as well.

When presented with the prospect of dealing with a chemical
system, there was a natural reluctance to accept this technology as
a normal part of the everyday operation. With the exception of

TABLE VI

DUAL INJECTION FLUE GAS CONDITIONING EXAMPLE

Description of Unit

Boiler Manufacturer	Combustion Engineering
Capacity	380 Mw (1005° F/2450 psig)
Precipitator	Buell
SCA	174 ft^2/1000 ACFM
Velocity	6.1 fps
Gas Rage	1.1 MM ACFM @ 260°F
Design Efficiency	Not determined after third field was put in.
Design Coal	0.6% S; 9.1% Ash; 13,370 Btu/lb.
Current Coal	0.8-1.5% (1.0% Av.) S; 13-17% Ash; 12,500 Btu/lb.

Results at 370-385 Mw

Emissions #/MM Btu

For Compliance   0.135

Treatment, GPT

LPA	LAC	
0	0	0.375
0.15	0	0.270
0.15	0.10	0.105

TABLE VII

SPECIFICATIONS FOR TWO UNITS (3 and 4)

480 Mw (Unit 4: 300 Mw)
B & W (3600 psig super-critical)
Research-Cottrell Precipitator
  98.5% Design Efficiency
  (2% sulfur, 6% ash)
  Using 1.0-1.5% sulfur, 10-15% ash
  1.48 MM ACFM at 272°F
7.02 Ft/Sec
  170 Ft^2/1000 ACFM

Compliance: 0.24#/MM Btu, 30% Opacity

TABLE VIII

SPECIFICATIONS FOR UNIT # 1

575 Mw. C.E. Boiler
Research-Cottrell Precipitator
97.3% Design Efficiency
  (Texas Lignite, 0.9% S, 12% Ash)

Compliance: 0.3#/MM Btu, 30% Opacity

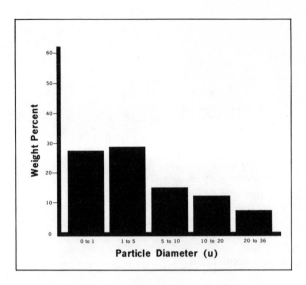

Figure 4.   Distribution of fly ash particle size in Unit #4 without fly ash conditioner (300 MW baseline)

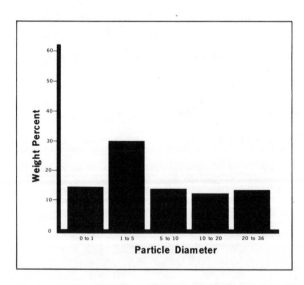

Figure 5.   Distribution of fly ash particle size in Unit #4 with fly ash conditioner (300 MW, 0.1 GPT LPA-40)

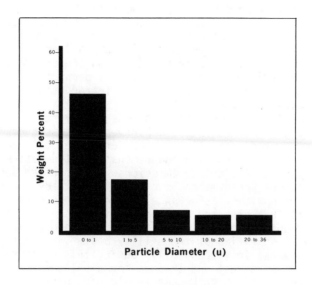

Figure 6. *Distribution of fly ash particle size in Unit #1 without fly ash conditioner (575 MW baseline)*

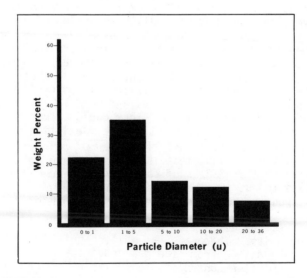

Figure 7. *Distribution of fly ash particle size in Unit #1 with fly ash conditioner (575 MW, 0.2 GTP LPA-410)*

a few utilities who,had built up a chemical engineering capability, most other utilities were inclined to rely upon us, as the chemical vendor, to handle the operation and maintenance of the chemical systems. It,thus,became necessary for our business to include the design, manufacture and operation of the entire delivery system. This included storage tankage, feed lines, proportioning pumps, automatic controls and injector for the introduction of our proprietary chemicals into the boiler.

The storage and feed equipment, when delivered on site, is assembled by our own mechanical department. It is checked out and tests are conducted over a 4 - 6 week period to optimize the additive type and composition and demonstrate the most effective means of reducing particulate emissions. A technical services engineer monitors performance as part of the steady state operation.

To assure optimum performance, it was also necessary for us to become expert in tuning and troubleshooting the electrostatic precipitator units, the coal preparation and feed equipment,as well as the general operation of the utility boiler. Such capabilities proved to be vital in successfully running this business. It required that we recruit and train a technical service department and mechanical staff,which became the largest organizational units within our company.

Economics Of Chemical Flue Gas Conditioning

The cost effectiveness of chemical flue gas conditioning has been presented by Kukin and Nelson (25). The technology was shown to fill a very real need for immediate reduction of particulate emissions at a very attractive cost. These advantages become apparent when one considers the alternatives available to a utility In the past, when particulate levels were above the permissible amounts, a utility had no recourse but to derate their unit and thereby lose income and profitability. This occurred because they sold less power at higher unit costs and were forced to purchase the make-up power at increased costs. They could reduce emissions without derating only by retrofitting their existing electrostatic precipitators or they could install baghouses, scrubbers, or cyclones. This type of equipment is capital intensive with a current estimated cost of $30/kw of capacity and would require two to three years to put in place. As shown in Table IX, this becomes an expensive recourse when compared to chemical conditioning.

Heretofore, the discussion has dealt with reducing emissions from existing units. There are, as well, significant economic advantages to be gained from flue gas conditioning in the design of a new plant's emission control system. Table X shows the capital savings realizable if flue gas conditioning is adopted in the original design of a 500 Mw unit. A 45% capital savings, which translates to over $0.73 MM in annualized savings, is possible.

TABLE IX

PARTICULATE EMISSION CONTROL ALTERNATIVES COMPARISON OF
"COALTROL" LPA WITH MECHANICAL SYSTEMS[1]

Unit Size	575 Mw
Coal HV (AR)	12,300 Btu/lb.
Heat Rate	9,200 Btu/Kwh
Coal Use, Max.	215 %/hr.
LPA Treatment	0.07 - 0.15 Gal/ton
	Coal Fired
Load Factor	70%

	"Coaltrol" LPA/LAC (Gemini)	Mechanical Systems at $30/Kw
Capital Investment Installed	$80,000	$17,250,000
Annual Fixed Charges	$60,000 (lease)	$3,105,000 (@ 18%)
Annual Variable Costs Including Maintenance	$250,000-$512,000	$862,000[2]
Total Annual Costs	$390,000-$652,000	$3,967,500
Mills/Kwh	0.11-0.19	1.13

[1]For example, Venturi scrubber, ESP's, cyclones, baghouses.

[2]At 5% of investment.

TABLE X

SAVINGS IN NEW PLANT PRECIPITATOR SYSTEMS

(Based on 500 Mw Unit)*

A. Precipitator without
    LPA Conditioning: $15,000,000
    (at $30 Kw x 500,000 Kw)
    Annual Fixed Charges at 18%   2,700,000
    Annual Variable Charges
        at 2.5%   375,000

            Total Annual Cost $ 3,075,000

B. Precipitator with LPA
    Conditioning - Total
    Equipment $ 9,000,000
    Annual Fixed Charges at 18%   1,620,000
    Annual Variable-Precipitator
        at 2.5%   225,000
    Annual Variable - LPA   250,000-500,000

            Total Annual Cost $2,095,000-2,345,000

        SAVINGS WITH LPA VS. NONCONDITIONED PRECIPITATORS

        Capital Saving, Equipment $ 6,000,000
        Annual Cost Saving $ 730,000-980,000

* (60% Capacity Factor
   (10,000 Btu/lb. Coal
   (10,000 Btu/Kwh Heat Rate

A comparison of costs for particulate control, made by Joy Manufacturing (25) for a typical 500-600 Mw boiler showed that the ESP, with conditioning, had the lowest annual cost vs. the use of a hot side ESP, a cold side ESP or a baghouse.

The Future Applications Of Chemical Flue Gas Conditioning

Until recently, the potential of chemical flue gas conditioning was not fully appreciated by regulatory agencies. Utilities would try to use chemical conditioning in order to reach compliance levels of emissions. If they failed to do so, they were required to invest in retrofit ESP units or baghouses. During the interim period, most units were allowed to operate under a compliance schedule. This could cover a period of two to three years or until the new equipment was in place and operating. Emissions were, in effect, allowed to continue in an uncontrolled manner.
Both Congress, in the actions of the Health and Environment Committee (25), as well as the EPA, have questioned the possibility of controlling these unnecessary interim emissions.
The situation is now being reviewed, especially in light of the ready availability and low capital cost of chemical flue gas conditioning. Thus, if chemical conditioning can reduce gross emissions significantly, it may be required as an interim control, even if it does not bring the unit into compliance.
A further incentive to consider gross reductions of particulates stems from the off-set policy. By reducing total emissions in areas in which it is not possible to exceed ambient air quality standards, room can be made to accomodate new industry.

Summary

This paper described the chronological development of two streams of Federal legislation, one regulating the emissions of particulates from large stationary sources and the other seeking to reduce our dependence upon foreign oil imports. It shows how these regulations offered an opportunity for the development and commercialization of a new technology called chemical flue gas conditioning.
To do this, the paper first explained the operation of existing particulate control devices, notably the electrostatic precipitator (ESP). It described how particulate capturability can be improved by chemical treatment and then illustrated how proprietary formulation has led to the treatment of a wide variety of fuels in both cold and hot side ESP units. Evidence was also presented showing fine particulate emissions, i.e., those implicated in health effects, could be significantly reduced. A description was made of the specific marketing problems that had to be solved when a chemical company sought to develop an industrial market where the customer has little or no chemical capability.

It justified the choice of chemical flue gas treatment by the potential user based upon its capability to bring emissions under control within a short time span at low cost. Both capital and operating costs were shown to be modest when compared to alternate methods, such as a new or retrofitted electrostatic precipitator or baghouse.

Finally, it predicted a significant expansion of applications for this technology because interim particulate control is now recognized as both inexpensive, rapid and highly feasible.

LITERATURE CITED

(1) Clean Air Act of 1963 - PL-88-206 (42 USC 1957 et seg.).

(2) Motor Vehicle Air Pollution Control Act of 1963 - PL-89-272 (October 20, 1978).

(3) Clean Air Act Amendments of 1966 - PL-89-675 (October 15, 1966).

(4) Air Quality Act of 1967 - PL-90-148 (November 21, 1967).

(5) Clean Air Act Amendments of 1970 PL-91-604 (December 21, 1978).

(6) Energy Supply and Environmental Coordination Act of 1974 - PL-93-319 (June 22, 1974).

(7) Clean Air Act of 1977 - PL-95-95 (August 7, 1977).

(8) Powerplant and Industrial Fuel Use Act (pending legislation).

(9) Cottrell, F.G., Journal, Ind. and Eng. Chem. 3, 632 (1911).

(10) Energy/Environment Fact Book, EPA 600/9-77-041, p. 41.

(11) Howard, W.H., Trans. Am. Inst. Mining Eng., 49, 540 (1918).

(12) Bennett, R.P. and Handlesman, B., Combustion (January 1977).

(13) Atkins, R.S. and Bubenik, D.V., Envir., Science and Tech,12 No. 6,657 (June 1978).

(14) Dismukes, E.B., APCA Journal, Vol. 25, No. 2, (February 1975).

(15) Dismukes, E.B., Southern Research Institute, EPA Contract 68-02-1303, ROAP 21ADJ-029, (October 1974).

(16) Bennett, P.P., O'Connor, M.J., Kober, A.E., Kukin, I., U.S. Patent 4,042,348, (August 16, 1977) and Bennett, R.P. and O'Connor, M.J., U.S. Patent 4,043,768, (August 1977).

(17) Kober, A.E., U.S. Patent 4,070,162, (January 24, 1978), and Bennett, R.P. and Kober, A.E., U.S. Patent 4,113,447, (September 12, 1978).

(18) Chrisp, C.E., Fischer, G.L., and Lammert, J.E., Science 199, 73 (1978).

(19) Oglesby, S. Jr., "A Survey of Technical Information Related to Fine Particle Control", Electric Power Research Institute, EPRI 259, PB 242-383, Section III, Health Effects of Fly Ash Inhalation, (April 1975).

(20) Bennett, R.P., Kober, A.E., "Chemical Enhancement of Electrostatic Precipitator Efficiency", Symposium on the Transfer and Utilization of Particulate Control Technology, U.S. EPA, Denver, Colorado (July 24-28, 1978).

(21) Oglesby, S. Jr., and Nickols, G.B., National Air Pollution Control Administration, 1970, Part I and Part II (NTIS - PB 19638041).

(22) Dismukes, E.B., A Study of Resistivity and Conditioning of Fly Ash, Environmental Protection Agency, EPA-R2-72-087, (NTIS-PB-212607).

(23) Kukin, I. and Nelson, H., Public Utilities Fortnightly, September 23, 1976.

(24) Harrison, M.E., Economic Evaluation of Precipitators and Bag Houses for Typical Power Plant Burning Low Sulfur Coal, American Power Conference, Chicago, Illinois, (April 24-28, 1978).

(25) Letter from Hon. Paul C. Rogers, Chairman, Subcommittee on Health and the Environment to Mr. D. Costle, Administrator, EPA (June 22, 1978).

RECEIVED March 9, 1979.

A Framework for Examination of the Impacts of Government Regulation and Input Prices on Process Innovation

EDWARD GREENBERG

Department of Economics, Washington University, St. Louis, MO 63130

Recent years have witnessed a considerable effort to determine the effect of government regulation on product innovation, but little has been done with respect to process innovation. In this paper, a framework for an analysis of this type is described and is applied to process change in the production of anhydrous ammonia. The ideas in the paper are more fully developed in (1).

In the context of chemical production, a process innovation may be defined as an addition to knowledge which allows some quantity of output to be produced by an input combination that could not previously be used to produce that output. For an innovation to be economically interesting, the innovation should result in a lower cost of production than other techniques at some combination of input prices. Whether the innovation is actually used in production will depend on a host of factors, including the patterns of input prices which producers face and the desirability of adding to capacity at the time that input prices favor the innovative technology. This last point assumes --often realistically, for chemical processes--that innovations frequently require changes in plant and equipment that would be undertaken only if justified by expected demand growth.

In principle, innovation should be distinguished from substitution, where the latter refers to a switch to a previously known production technique. Changes in relative input prices would be a reason for substitution, as would an increase in output sufficient to make it profitable to move to a more highly capital-intensive method of production. The distinction turns on the extent to which properties of the process to be used are already known. In practice, the distinction may not be clear-cut. Even simple substitution may involve some degree of uncertainty; some properties of the new process may remain unknown until it is physically implemented.

It is necessary to draw this distinction for the light it sheds on the effects of those government regulations that are concerned with workplace safety and health and with environmental

0-8412-0511-6/79/47-109-103$05.00/0
© 1979 American Chemical Society

protection. Changes in such regulations may induce substitution.
For example, a regulation designed to improve worker safety and
health may require a change to a more capital-intensive process
that both reduces the number of exposed workers and reduces the
probability of their exposure to a safety or health hazard.
Whether government regulation can have an impact on innovation
is another question. Since we have defined innovation as an
increase in knowledge, we must consider how regulation can affect
the behavior of those people engaged in the production of knowledge.

Determinants of Innovation

A first point to note is the implicit assumption that
activities of producers of knowledge can be affected by government regulations through their implications for the possibility
of using the knowledge in future production. In this view,
knowledge does not result solely from engineers and scientists
who indulge their own curiosities and scientific creativity;
rather, it assumes that at least some knowledge is gained from
a purposeful search for new methods of production that will be
consistent with government regulations. If the possibility is
granted that innovative activity is not the result of scientists'
and engineers' random activities, it becomes necessary to
identify factors other than government regulation that may influence innovation. This is so because empirical studies that
attempt to quantify the role of regulation in stimulating or
retarding innovation must control--statistically or in some
other way--for changes in such factors that happen to occur
concurrently with changes in regulatory activity.
In the standard economic model of the firm, business
decisions are generally explained by their effects on expected
profitability. Let us examine some ways in which innovative
activity and expected profitability interact:
   1. Expected demand increases: an industry that is expected to grow is likely to attract resources for the
   purpose of improving production processes, since cost
   savings will be greater at a greater volume of output (2,3).
   2. Cumulative output: an industry that has produced large
   quantities of a product may experience reductions in its
   required inputs. One explanation is "learning by doing" in
   plant operations; a second possible cause is "learning by
   doing" by firms that produce capital goods for the industry
   in question. That is, as capital goods producers supply a
   large number of units to an industry, they learn how to
   improve the performance of their products (2,4,5,6).
   3. Input prices: the literature on induced technical
   change takes the view that the direction of technical
   change--whether it is capital or energy saving, for example
   --may be influenced by input prices (7,8,9). In addition

to influencing the direction of technical change, changes
in input prices may increase the payoff to process-oriented
research in general, resulting in factor-saving innovation.
From this discussion it should be clear that there exist a
number of economic variables that could affect the overall
amount of innovative activity and its distribution across industries, and whether it emphasizes the saving of one or another
factor of production. A number of other economic factors affect
innovation, of which the most important is market structure.
Research in this area has recently been reviewed (10).

The preceding has emphasized what Rosenberg has termed the
demand for innovation (11). He points out that the supply of
scientific knowledge interacts with that demand to determine the
innovation actually achieved. However, supply and demand for
innovation are extremely difficult to disentangle in practice.
Thus, metallurgical and other types of knowledge were required
to produce tubes capable of withstanding the high pressures and
temperatures that are needed for the high pressure reforming
stage in ammonia production. But, to some degree, development
of such tubes was undertaken with an eye on the ammonia market.
In other cases, ammonia may have benefitted from attempts to
improve other processes.

Figure 1 presents a view of the main factors determining
process change. It depicts the exogenous influence on expected
future profitability of demand conditions, factor price changes,
and government regulation, with the latter two also influencing
the direction of innovation. Expected profitability helps
determine the amount of resources to allocate to process innovation and the amount of investment in new plant and equipment. In
turn, the latter stimulates process R&D through the "learning by
doing" route mentioned above.

A Production Model for Chemical Processes

Although innovation is an extremely complex activity, some
simplification can be achieved for purposes of empirical study
by delineating categories of innovation in the context of a
model of production. Production is assumed to take place within
a finite set of well-defined processes, rather than on a smooth
neoclassical production function. In this respect, the model is
a version of the "activity analysis" model. In contrast to the
usual activity analysis model, however, some of the inputs are
characterized by increasing returns to scale. Specifically,
engineers often assume that capital and labor (and perhaps other
inputs) may be increased at a slower rate than output, while raw
materials, energy, and other inputs are increased at the same
or nearly the same rate as output. The economics literature on
production functions discusses these points (12,13,14).

Assuming two inputs for simplicity, we designate the
"linear" input by N and the "nonlinear" input by K. A first

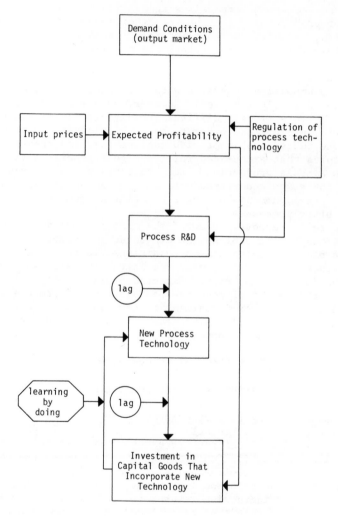

Figure 1.   Factors influencing process innovation

approximation to the production function for the ith process is:

$$Q_i = \min \left[\frac{N}{a_{ni}}, \left(\frac{K}{a_{ki}} \right)^{1/b_i} \right]$$

where Q_i is output from the ith process and $0 < b_i \leq 1$. The coefficients a_{ni}, a_{ki}, and b_i completely characterize the ith technology in economic terms. For a given input of N and K, this function states that output will be the smaller of N/a_{ni} and $[K/a_{ki}]^{1/b_i}$; it does not permit tradeoffs between these two inputs within a particular process. However, unless $b_i = 1$, the ratio of inputs varies with output. In particular, K/N decreases with output along a given process for $b_i < 1$. (Engineering production processes may be characterized in dimensions other than their primary inputs and outputs. They are associated with differences in at least the following: effluents, requirements for skilled labor, reliability, safety, adaptability to use of alternative feedstocks, and sensitivity of costs to less-than-full-capacity production.)

This model is displayed in Figure 2. The process lines represent combinations of N and K which satisfy $N/a_{ni} = (K/a_{ki})^{1/b_i}$. Since output is equal to the smaller of these two values, equality of the ratios implies no redundant inputs. Output is proportional to the vertical axis, since $Q_i = N/a_{ni}$, but the proportionality factor differs for each process. The exponent, b_i, is usually found to be approximately .6 or .7 if K represents plant and equipment measured in dollars. Because of the increasing returns to K when $b_i < 1$, it will generally not be profitable to produce output by using more than one process, so that many combinations of inputs will not be utilized when a small number of processes are available.

Subject to modification concerning substitution possibilities noted below, the model we have in mind is of the "putty-clay" variety. That is, although there is a choice of coefficients before a process is installed, the coefficients are fixed thereafter. This type of model has recently been examined by Myers and Nakamura (15). Their model permits a much wider scope for choice of coefficients than the limited set actually available for producing most chemical products.

Two modifications must be made to this model to make it conform more closely to engineering practice. First, there are upper and lower limits to the output possible from a given process at any point in time. Second, a certain amount of within-process substitution between inputs is possible. This type of substitution permits a degree of variation in a_{ni} and a_{ki}, but these variations are small relative to the differences in coefficients between processes.

The existence of upper and lower bounds on the scale of a particular process may be explained by a combination of technical

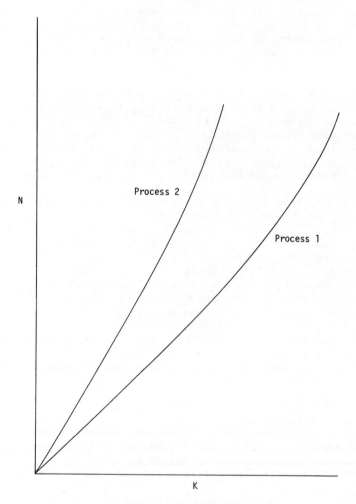

Figure 2. Process model

and economic reasons. To some extent the bounds are a simplified
method of indicating a sharp nonlinearity in the price of capital
equipment when nonstandardized units must be ordered. This may
make the cost of the resulting input combination so high that it
would not be used in the short run. In other cases, building
equipment at very small (or very large) scale is beyond the state
of engineering capability.

Upper bounds on process size are of particular interest
since, in the presence of increasing returns to scale, one might
expect that plant size would increase to the point that just one
plant produces all the output. A number of factors constrain
this growth. First is the high cost of using nonstandard sizes,
or indeed, the high cost of producing made-to-order equipment
much larger than that which is ordinarily produced. Costs of
production, shipping, and installation of such equipment may
rise faster than scale; we treat this as a constraint rather than
a nonlinearity in the price of the input. Second, there is the
problem of reliability. If a malfunction occurs in one of two
1500 t.p.d. (tons per day) plants, for example, only half of the
production is lost compared to the loss from the shutdown of a
single 3000 t.p.d. plant. A third consideration is the ability
to operate at less than full capacity and the sensitivity of
costs to less than full capacity operation, if it should become
desirable to produce at less than full capacity. Average costs
at less than full capacity are, of course, sensitive to the relationship between the fixed and variable costs of a process.

In practice, market size and transportation costs rather
than technical factors may set the most significant limits on
maximum plant size. Whereas the unit production costs implied
by the model decrease, the rate of decrease slows. The gains
from increasing scale, for a given process, becomes less and less
important. At the same time, if the plant's production will be a
large portion of the total market, or if customers will be very
large distances away from the plant, the net price received by
the producer may fall. Thus the marginal revenue may fall faster
than marginal cost, yielding an economic upper limit to production.

The second modification to the increasing returns activity
analysis model is the possibility of substitution among inputs
along a given process ray. For example, it may be possible to
use less feedstock and more fuel to produce the same output from
fixed capital equipment. The extent of this substitution is
limited by physical and chemical laws, as well as by legal restrictions and by equipment limits in the short run.

One kind of substitution between market inputs is what might
be called the "make or buy" decision. Depending upon local conditions, a firm may find it profitable to buy untreated water
for its boilers and do its own treatment, or to buy treated
water from a utility. Similarly, a firm may buy all of its
cooling water requirements from a utility, or it may recirculate

cooling water and buy only make-up water, supplying the cooling
towers and the electric power necessary to operate them. In both
cases the firm is buying inputs for the purpose of cooling; in
terms of market behavior, however, this activity may show up as
either large purchases of treated water or smaller purchases of
water and greater expenditures on capital and electricity. The
decision will be influenced by such conditions as local prices
and regulations.

A second type of substitution occurs in the form of substitutions of subprocesses within a particular process. For example, one step in the steam reforming process for ammonia production is the removal of carbon monoxide and carbon dioxide
from the synthesis gas. A number of processes, which differ
somewhat in energy and capital requirements, have been developed
for this purpose.

A third kind of substitution is the possibility of changing
operating conditions within a particular process, resulting in
moderate changes in coefficients. The most important example in
ammonia production is the choice of pressure at which the steam
system is operated; coefficients of capital, fuel, and cooling
water for producing one ton of ammonia depend on steam pressure.

Implications of the Production Model for Process Innovation

The production model just discussed permits the classification of innovations into four main categories. The most obvious
type of innovation is one which reduces the amount of one or
more inputs required for the ith process; that is, one which
reduces the a_{ni}, a_{ki}, or b_i. For example, such innovations may
result from improvements in catalysts, or from improvements in
the physical arrangements or efficiencies of equipment.

A second type of innovation is an increase in the substitution possibilities within a particular process; substitution of
energy for capital is an example. Whether an instance of such
substitution is an innovation or merely a substitution as the
term is used in the usual theory of production depends on the
extent of research and development necessary to implement it.

A third type of innovation is concerned with attempts to
weaken the capacity constraints at both upper and lower limits.
At the upper limit, weakening a constraint will reduce unit
costs on the assumption that the production relationship holds
at greater sizes with approximately the same coefficients that
characterized smaller outputs. Production beyond existing upper
limits, as noted above, may be associated with difficult engineering problems. Expansion of output by moving along a process
curve may not be possible because of additional stresses put on
equipment. In addition, attempts to reduce the minimum scale at
which a process may be operated may also be worthwhile because
of local conditions which both justify a smaller output than
may be produced by a given process and make a process attractive

because of relative input prices.

A fourth type of innovation is one which results in an entirely new process in the engineering sense. All the process coefficients may be very different; in fact, entirely different inputs may be used, or new physical or chemical principles may be employed. In contrast to production of ammonia from coal, steam reforming of natural gas was such an innovation, as was the shift from propellor to jet aircraft. Current research to produce nitrogen-fixing (ammonia-producing) bacteria that are symbiotic with corn through DNA manipulation is innovative activity of the fourth type.

The first two types of innovation noted above are similar to those utilized in the innovation models of Nelson and Winter (8) and Binswanger (9). These models are concerned with movements of input coefficients within a region close to their initial values. However, since these models neither incorporate constraints nor permit increasing returns to scale, there is no innovation along the lines of the third type discussed. See Levin (16) for a discussion of this type of innovation. The Nelson and Winter approach is based on alternative coefficients generated by a random process (perhaps because basic scientific discoveries are rather unpredictable) and employs a modified profitability test for their adaptation. Binswanger studies the generation of alternative processes in a deterministic model in which research expenditures may be allocated to change process coefficients in a desired direction. The Nelson and Winter model assures the generation of points near existing points by appropriate specification of the random process. If the R&D cost of changing coefficients in the Binswanger model generates relatively small period-to-period changes, the Nelson-Winter and Binswanger approaches would have very similar empirical implications.

Kamien and Schwartz (7) have put forth a variety of models which permit the introduction of innovations that either cause increases in output for the same inputs or expand input substitution possibilities. The returns from research are deterministic in their models, and fairly general R&D cost functions may be used. An attempt to model search activity for improving production processes has been made by Roth (17) who distinguishes between investigating known processes and spending resources to learn the properties of combinations of subprocesses not previously used. The existence of subjective probability distributions of returns to the various activities is assumed. It may be that engineering process data can provide information about the frequency distribution of changes in coefficients to be used in a Nelson-Winter type model. Although these data may be helpful for empirical implementation of such induced innovation models as those of Binswanger and Kamien and Schwartz, the absence of research and development expenditure data on a low enough level of aggregation is a serious obstacle. Furthermore, much of the R&D spending occurs outside the firm or industry in question.

None of these approaches seem suitable for modeling the development of new processes in the engineering sense. What makes new processes especially difficult to deal with is that they often require a considerable effort in basic science as well as in the overcoming of engineering problems. Basic science connotes an extremely risky activity in which payoffs are subject to high variance. Rosenberg (11), for example, points out that greatly improved knowledge of medicine took many centuries to develop despite the continuous flow of resources devoted to medical problems during that period. Detailed knowledge of a product will supply some a priori ideas about the portion of input space that could be fruitfully investigated, but this degree of detail may be more than is desirable for purposes of general economic modeling.

For several of the innovation types discussed above it is rather straightforward to determine the impacts of changes in relative and absolute prices. If all input prices were to increase proportionally, for example, the payoff to input-reducing innovation in general would increase. Changes in relative input prices would favor innovations that permit substitution against the relatively higher priced inputs and also stimulate the search for new processes that economize on those inputs. Implications of this nature follow from the models discussed earlier in this section. The effect of price changes on capacity-increasing innovations is more difficult to analyze: an increase in capacity leads to a lower average cost with constant input prices, but this will be offset to some extent by the higher costs associated with a price increase in the nonlinear inputs that constrained capacity--generally plant and equipment. Thus, it is not clear what effect a rise in the price of capital goods will have on capacity when such increases require additional capital goods; innovations that reduce capital intensity may become more attractive than those that increase capacity.

The effects of environmental and workplace regulations have not been explicitly included within this innovation model. Nevertheless, a few tentative generalizations might be offered. Some processes may be so harmful to the environment or worker safety and health that the development of a new process is necessary if continued production of the product is to take place. In other cases it may be necessary to substitute for an input which has deleterious effects on the environment or worker safety and health; for example, innovations designed to permit the use of fuels other than coal might be generated. Note that a change in fuel may not be a simple substitution because chemical process technology is highly integrated. For example, the same hot air or steam may be used for different purposes as it cools. Moreover, in steam reforming of natural gas, the same input is used both as fuel and feedstock, and purge gases are used as

supplementary fuel. In such cases an attempt to change any part
of the process may require changes throughout. Process modifications for control of regulated effluents may increase fixed
and operating costs in various ways and may thus stimulate a
search for factor-saving innovations in the absence of factor
price changes. Finally, capacity-increasing innovations may be
inhibited if an environmental regulation takes the form of limits
on total pollutant emissions at a given site. Of course, this
effect may be partially offset by reductions in input use or
substitutions for the offending input.

Issues in the Empirical Study of Innovation

The use of the above model as a framework for the study of
the effects of government regulation and other factors on innovation has a number of implications for empirical studies of
those effects. In particular, process innovation can be most
conveniently studied in an industry that: 1) has produced an
unchanging product; 2) has undertaken process change over a considerable period of time; 3) has made public data on input coefficients, capacity, input prices, and output prices; and 4) has
experienced a history of government regulation. With this information it should be possible to explore the relationship between
input coefficients and capacity on the one hand, and prices of
inputs and outputs and government regulation on the other.
Specifically, input coefficients and maximum plant capacity may
be treated as dependent variables in a multiple regression
analysis with input prices, output price, cumulative capacity,
and other variables as independent variables.

Input coefficients are of special interest because, as mentioned above, they describe the production technology. Although
input coefficients may be defined at various levels of aggregation, the most useful coefficients for studying innovation are
those that characterize the industry's leading commercial technology. Such coefficients will reflect innovative responses to
changes in input prices and government regulation far more
promptly than the average industry ratios of inputs to output
because an industry generally includes plants of various ages;
these embody technologies adapted for prices and regulations of
earlier periods. Coefficients for leading technologies are
available for many products in the open literature.

Several strategies are available for estimating the effects
of government regulation on input coefficients and capacity.
First, since a change to a new engineering process is generally
well documented and is widely discussed, it should be relatively
straightforward to identify the role, if any, of regulation in
causing the change. Input coefficient data are likely to be
available for both old and new processes so that costs could be
compared in an attempt to isolate the role of regulation in
bringing about the new process. Since the development of new

processes is extremely difficult to predict, this type of analysis would not be very useful for forecasting the engineering
nature or details of responses to government regulation.
The types of innovation that take place within a basic process could be examined statistically. Separate relationships
could be estimated for periods within which regulations were unchanged, and tests could be made for significant differences
between subperiods when regulations do change. If time periods
of unchanging regulation are too short, a set of dummy variables
representing regulatory modes might be included. In addition,
an effort should be made to determine the extent to which regulations were enforced, and variables representing the degree of
enforcement should be included in the regressions.

Application to Ammonia Production

The synthetic anhydrous ammonia industry satisfies several
of the criteria mentioned above. It was one of the first chemical products to be produced using modern techniques; its composition has remained constant over the years; it has been
produced with a variety of processes; input coefficients and
prices are available in the open literature; and parts of the
production process require considerable attention to workplace
safety and health and to protection of the environment.
Unfortunately--at least for the purpose of studying the
determinants of innovation--an intensive search of the legal and
technical literature revealed that ammonia production had not
been subject to restrictive government regulation over the relevant time period (1). Instead, sound engineering and business
practices resulted in reasonable levels of workplace safety and
environmental protection in the absence of regulation. Although
recent trends suggest increased government activity in this
industry, impacts on input coefficients have not yet appeared.
Empirical work was therefore restricted to the effects of
input prices and cumulative gross capacity on input coefficients
·and to the effects of output price, labor costs, capital costs,
and cumulative gross capacity on the maximum capacity of new
plants. Linear and log-linear equations were estimated. Input
coefficient data were obtained from engineering information
relating to newest plants. A search of engineering journals and
other publications uncovered numerous articles that present input
coefficients for the latest ammonia plants available at the time.
These were adjusted to improve comparability among plants with
respect to such items as which facilities are included in investment and whether steam is purchased or generated. Attention was
confined to plants that produced ammonia by steam reforming of
natural gas. The period studied, 1947-1972, witnessed the
switch from reciprocating to centrifugal compressors, which in
many respects may be regarded as a process innovation. Data on
plant capacity were estimated by compiling a history of U.S.

ammonia production facilities, and price data are available from government and industry publications. A detailed discussion of data, methods, and results may be found in (1).

The results from the input coefficient regressions were encouraging. They suggest that increases in the prices of natural gas, electricity, and capital result in a decreased use of the respective inputs with a lag of 6 years. A lag of this length suggests that more than simple substitution is taking place. The estimated coefficient of cumulative gross capacity implied that growth in installed capacity reduced inputs, but this relationship was not statistically significant.

Results with the capacity equations were not as clear-cut. Although variables affected capacity in the hypothesized directions, they were not generally statistically significant. One possible reason was the lack of a variable that measures transportation costs. Further research should attempt to rectify this problem.

Conclusions

Detailed conclusions and policy implications may be found in (1). Regarding the effects of government regulation on ammonia process technology, it was concluded that: 1) recent workplace and environmental regulation have not yet had a significant impact on ammonia production, but some proposed regulations may do so; 2) regulations concerned with the safety of pressure vessels, which have been in effect for many years at the state level, were consistent with, and possibly based on, standards devised by professional code-setting institutions; 3) certain aspects of EPA's policies lead to end-of-pipe treatment of pollutants rather than in-process treatment; and 4) OSHA's multi-tiered enforcement mechanism preserves some scope for process innovation.

The multiple regression analysis demonstrated that process technology responded to factor price changes in a manner consistent with the hypothesis that innovations tend to economize on relatively expensive inputs. If this phenomenon can be verified more generally, policy-makers may have greater confidence in the ability of the economy to adjust dynamically to changed availability and prices of inputs.

The approach described in this paper can be applied to other industries. It should be possible to identify chemicals that have been subject to government regulation for which input coefficients over a reasonably long period are available in the open literature. The finding that process innovation can be explained by movements in input prices should be subjected to further testing, and the study of other products may reveal more clearly the role of government regulations in determining process innovations.

Acknowledgment

Financial support was supplied by the National Science Foundation, Grant Number RDA 75-23266. Opinions and conclusions are those of the author.

Literature Cited

1. Greenberg, E., Hill, C. T., Newburger, D. J., "Regulation, Market Prices, and Process Innovation: The Case of the Ammonia Industry" Westview Press, Boulder, 1979.
2. Schmookler, J., "Invention and Economic Growth" Harvard University Press, Cambridge, 1966.
3. Nordhaus, W. D., Amer. Econ. Rev. (1969), 59, 18.
4. Asher, H., "Cost-Quantity Relationships in the Airframe Industry" RAND Corporation 12-291, Santa Monica, 1956.
5. Arrow, K., Rev. Econ. Stud. (1962), 29, 155.
6. Utterback, J. M., Abernathy, W. J., "A Test of a Conceptual Model Linking Stages in Firms' Process and Production Innovation," BH5 74-23, Graduate School of Business Administration, Harvard University, Boston, November 1974.
7. Kamien, M. I., Schwartz, N. L., Econometrica (1967), 36, 1.
8. Nelson, R. R., Winter, S. G., Amer. Econ. Rev. (1975), 65, 338.
9. Binswanger, H. P., Econ. J. (1974), 84, 940.
10. Kamien, M. I., Schwartz, N. L., J. Econ. Lit. (1975), 13, 1.
11. Rosenberg, N., Econ. J. (1974), 84, 90.
12. Moore, F. T., Quart. J. Econ. (1959), 73, 232.
13. Chenery, H. B., Quart. J. Econ. (1949), 63, 307.
14. Teitel, S., J. Common Market Studies (1975), 13, 92.
15. Myers, J. G., Nakamura, L., "Energy and Pollution Effects on Productivity: Putty-Clay Approach," National Bureau of Econmmic Research, N.Y., 1976 (Mimeo).
16. Levin, R. C., "Technical Change, Economies of Scale, and Market Structure" Yale University, New Haven, 1974 (Ph.D. dissertation).
17. Roth, T. P., Engineering Economist (1972), 17, 249.

RECEIVED March 8, 1979.

Economic Trends, Resource Scarcity, and Policymaking

RUSSELL G. THOMPSON

CBA Industry Studies, University of Houston, Houston, TX 77004

Modern man is becoming more and more aware that he is only one part of a very complex system. Energy problems are simultaneously environmental and economic problems. Issues cannot be compartmentalized. Nor are issues clearly good or bad for the nation. In solving complex national problems, policymakers must be aware of tradeoffs and costs of alternate actions. How these tradeoffs and actions are structured depends on the quality and breadth of knowledge of our nation's policymakers and their constituents.

Many worthwhile national goals are desired by Americans. Among these goals are reasonable energy independence, a clean environment, and low cost-of-living. How these goals are attained will affect the future of the United States as a leader of the free world. If, for example, the goal of reasonable energy independence is attained at the cost of a polluted environment or skyrocketing prices, then the attainment of that goal carries a price tag that the American consumer will not pay. Similarly, if the goal of a clean environmemt is sought by regimenting society with unnecessary costs, then the means of attaining that goal will be discarded.

Solutions to America's interrelated problems of scarce energy, clean environment, and price inflation require a comprehensive analysis of the economic consequences of policy alternatives before policy is changed. Major policy changes, in the face of resource scarcities, are greatly modifying the structure of the economy. Structural changes are resulting in totally new economic trends in supplies, demands, and prices.

For that reason, historical data are not sufficient to forecast future trends in a period of great policy change. As realized by President Carter in the National Energy Plan (1),

> The future availability of energy has
> significant economic implications that
> are not captured by current projections
> of the GNP or other economic indicators.

0-8412-0511-6/79/47-109-117$05.00/0
© 1979 American Chemical Society

Clearly, econometric models must be redeveloped to show how policy changes will transform the economic structure of the economy and how this structural transformation will result in new trends. The data base for these new econometric models must include not only management's historical responses to past policies and economic conditions, but management's anticipated responses to future policies and economic conditions.

Fulfilling these needs will require a comprehensive mathematical modeling capability for both industry and the economy. At a minimum, the modeling capability must encompass industry models to reflect the nation's heavy industry at the core of the fossil energy and materials sector (electric power, petroleum refining, basic chemicals). This industry core generates the nation's electricity, refines the nation's petroleum products, and transforms the nation's chemicals into useable endproducts. New trends in production costs, resource use, and environmental quality will generally be influenced significantly by what happens in this heavy industrial core.

Modeling Developments and Results

The foundation for evaluating how changes in policy will result in new economic trends has been laid by industry modeling work at the University of Houston (2-7). This industry modeling capability permits direct energy, environmental, capital, and selected tax constraints to be imposed in a mathematical model of the interrelated petroleum refining, electric power, and basic chemical industries of the economy. The integrated model of these three industries is interfaced with supply functions for raw fossil energies and demand functions for manufactured energy endproducts. This interface of supply, demand, and industry models gives the equilibrium price/quantity tradeoffs of different energy prices, environmental conditions, and capital availabilities. New input-output tables for the nation's economy are formed from the equilibrium results; see (6,7).

Brief Description of Models. The industry modeling capability includes detailed process economic models for the ten 4-digit Standard Industrial Classification industries shown in Figure 1. These process models are designed to evaluate the important substitution possibilities among the fundamental systems of production, process energy use, water use and waste water treatment, air emission control, and solid waste and brine management in the ten industries; see Figure 2. The ten industry models, which are identified in Figure 1, are combined into an integrated industry process model of the electric power, petroleum refining, and basic chemicals industries of the nation to account for interdependencies among these industries. The integrated industry model refines the nation's raw crude oil into refined petroleum fuels and refinery byproducts; the integrated industry model proc-

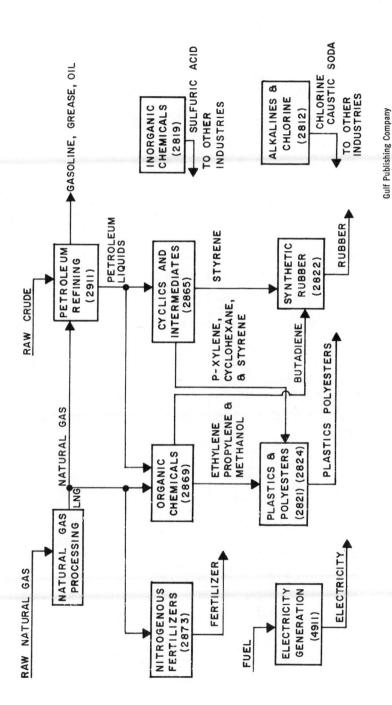

Gulf Publishing Company

Figure 1. General interrelationships among ten four-digit standard industrial classifications in the integrated industry model (5)

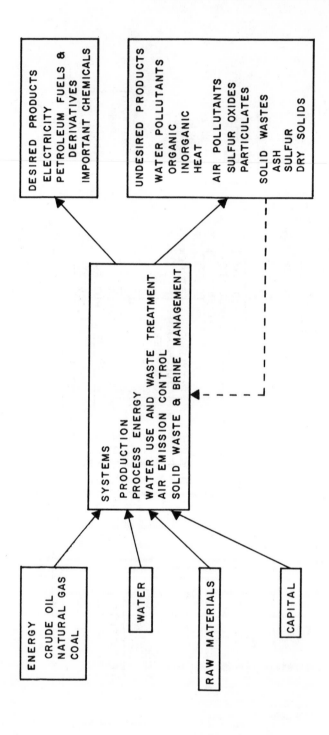

Figure 2.   Fundamental components of representative industry models (5)

esses the nation's petroleum refinery byproducts and natural gas
feedstocks into basic petrochemicals for use as inputs in the
plastics, polyesters, rubber, and fertilizers industries; and the
integrated industry model generates the nation's electricity for
use in the residential/commercial, industrial, and transportation
sectors of the economy. Additionally, complementary components
of this integrated model prepare the nation's coal and natural gas
for heating and cooling uses in the economy.

The integrated industry model evaluates the economic cost,
resource use, and technical configuration effects of possible policy decisions limiting or not limiting (1) the discharge of any
major water or air pollutant, and (2) the availability of any
scarce resource input (energy, water, raw materials, and capital).
This basis may be used to evaluate the economic, resource, and
technical effects of (a) increased or decreased requirements for
any of the endproducts in the model and (b) higher or lower prices
(including taxes) for resource inputs and product outputs. Simultaneously, the integrated industry model determines the economically efficient allocation and valuation of the resource inputs
used to produce the endproduct requirements of the ten industries
modeled. This economic allocation both minimizes the economic
costs of producing the desired endproducts and maximizes the economic value of the limited resources used by the industries modeled.

For each policy specification, the technology matrix of the
integrated industry model is transformed from the productive
structure existing before the policy change to the productive
structure existing after the policy change. This structural
transformation is the master key to identifying the economic demands and supplies of the industries modeled. Identification is
necessary to soundly estimate: (1) the economic demands for crude
oil, natural gas, coal, water, and capital; (2) the economic
costs of pollution control for major water and air pollutants;
and (3) the economic supplies of the endproducts in the model.
The integrated industry model includes detailed capital considerations for existing plants, modifications to existing plants, and
new grass-roots plants in the electric power, petroleum refining,
and organic chemical industries. Also, the integrated industry
model includes detailed regional fuel use/electricity generation
considerations for the nation's electric utilities. Also, extensions are underway to include additional industries, namely
iron and steel, pulp and paper, aluminum, cement, and food and
fiber processing. In addition, extensions are planned: (a) to
model advanced coal, nuclear, and solar technologies; and (b) to
evaluate substitutions between as well as within different time
periods.

The integrated industry model has been interfaced with economic supply functions for crude oil, natural gas, and coal (low,
medium, and high-sulfur) and with economic demand functions for
important energy products (gasoline, fuel oils, electricity,

natural gas, coal) to give an equilibrium model for the fossil
energy sector of the U. S. economy. This equilibrium model for
the free market case is an application of the Walras/Cassel theory
of competitive equilibrium to the fossil energy sector. Iterative
solutions to this model are computed until the definition of a
competitive equilibrium is fulfilled; the Leontief balance equa-
tion with the transactions table for the fossil energy microcosm
is derived from this equilibrium solution. With modifications in
the economic structure of the process models to reflect deviations
from a free market situation, iterative solutions are computed to
find a solution as close to the competitive equilibrium solution
for the revised model as the policy-imposed constraints will allow. The "equilibrium solutions" for the revised model are also
used to form transactions tables for the fossil energy microcosm.
See Dorfman et al. (8) and Intrilligator (9) for theoretical
developments.

Significant Uses of Models. Several significant uses of
this economic modeling capability have been made to date. Two
of these uses will be briefly described here to indicate the sub-
stantiveness of the implications. A significant implication of
current environmental policy is captured by one set of economic
indicators; and a significant implication of recent energy proposals is captured by another set of economic indicators.

Environmental Policy Analysis. In 1975, the Environmental
Protection Agency was estimating the costs of implementing uniform effluent standards by measuring the costs for each industry
independently and summing the independent estimates. This procedure was of concern to leading technicians in the Office of
Management and Budget because the cumulative demand, supply, and
price effects were ignored.
    The following argument illustrates the point. Uniform
technology standards for pollution control will simultaneously
expand the demands for all resources needed to implement the uniform technology standards. (Suppose for illustrative purposes
that all of these resource demands are completely insensitive to
price.) Increasingly costly resources will be required to fulfill
the expanded demands. Incentives to bring forth the additional
supplies will result in higher market prices for all the resources
used; see Figure 3. EPA was capturing the increased costs of the
additional resource use at constant resource prices (Area q_0 ABq_1);
however, EPA was failing to capture the increased costs of all the
resources used because of the higher market prices required to
bring forth the additional supplies (Area p_0 p_1 CB).
    Two different modeling cases were constructed for 1985 to
measure the significance of EPA's underestimate. In the one case,
the endproduct uses and resource prices were specified as parameters (engineering cost analysis); and in the other case, the
endproduct uses and resource prices were determined as solutions

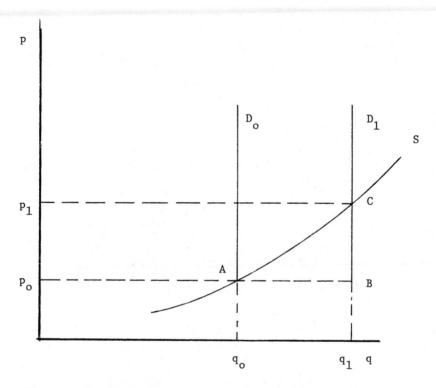

Figure 3. Illustrative graph of cost increasing effects of uniform effluent standards

to economic variables (economic pricing analysis). Significant
implications were captured by the modeling evaluations. Cost increases of the uniform technology standards were three to five-
fold greater in the economic pricing analysis than in the engineering cost analysis. Increasing supply costs of scarce resources, according to the model, will inflate significantly the
costs of achieving a clean environment; see Chapter 12 of Thompson
et al. (5).

Energy Policy Analysis. In 1977, President Carter proposed
a National Energy Plan (NEP) to the Congress for the nation's
future energy policy. This plan represented a significant de-
parture from current policy at that time; also, it stood in sharp
contrast to the market-pricing recommendations of the Texas Energy
Advisory Council.
    The Advisory Council contracted for an evaluation of the most
salient pricing, taxing, and environmental recommendations in the
President's Plan. Similar equilibrium evaluations were made of
the Advisory Council's recommendations and a Business-As-Usual
policy. All evaluations were made for 1985.
    Results of the NEP modeling analysis showed that market
prices and windfall profits taxes would accomplish the President's
1985 energy demand reduction goal (energy growth of less than 2%
per year) and would come closer to attaining the President's 1985
increased coal production goal (400 million tons per year) than
the program he proposed. However, full imposition of the President's proposed gasoline excise tax would be necessary in any
program to fulfill the 1985 gasoline consumption goal (10% reduction from 1977 level) and the 1985 oil import goal (6 million
barrels per day).
    Use of the equilibrium results to develop new transactions
tables for an energy/materials microcosm of the economy showed a
serious economic shortcoming of both policy alternatives. As
modeled, the President's policy and the Advisory Council's policy
would increase, rather than decrease, the direct plus indirect input requirements of the three basic conversion industries (petroleum refining, electric power, basic chemicals) from petroleum
mining sources. Also, both policy recommendations would decrease,
rather than increase, the direct plus indirect input requirements
of these three industries from the coal mining sector. This economic implications, which evidently was not captured by state-of-
the-art econometric models, means that neither policy recommenda-
tion is sufficient to transition the economy from petroleum to
alternate energy resources; see Thompson (7).

Important Messages

    The important messages to be gained from these two modeling
evaluations are: (1) significant economic implications of supply scarcities may be captured by models designed to evaluate the

structural consequences of major changes in energy and environmental policies; and (2) the cumulative hidden economic costs of
environmental and energy policy inadequacies seem to be at the
roots of the nation's stagflation interlock of low real economic
growth, continued high unemployment, rapidly inflating prices,
small capital investments, unfavorable trade balances, and depreciation of the dollar.

Serious consideration needs to be directed to revising the
nation's strategy for attaining a clean environment. Uniform
technology standards for pollution control impose unnecessarily
great economic stress throughout the economy because of inefficient resource use implications. Much more efficiency in resource use and much less inflation of market prices would result
from a balanced combination of economic instruments and technology
controls. Such a balanced combination could be designed to accomplish the economic efficiency considerations of importance to
economists as well as the physical interaction considerations of
importance to engineers. Both considerations are critical to
achieving publically acceptable tradeoffs for a desired balance
among economic growth, clean environment, and energy independence
goals.

If the goal of the United States energy policy is to transition the energy base of the nation from petroleum to alternate
energy sources, then serious consideration needs to be directed to
extending the forthcoming energy legislation to include an economically efficient, yet environmentally acceptable technology
development plan. This plan must be designed to decrease over
time the real resources of the economy going into petroleum mining sources and increase over time the real resources of the economy going into alternate energy sources. In addition to supporting the research and development of new technologies, the economics of this plan must come to grips with the increasing uncertainty of long-term investments in alternative energy resources.

This increasing uncertainty is being heavily influenced by
the steadily growing inventories of U. S. dollars in the hands of
a few oil-endowed nations. Modern day communications and banking
technology allow billions of these dollars to be transferred almost instantaneously from one money market to another for a wide
array of political and economic reasons. The fluidity of these
dollars and their concentrations in a few hands adds a whole new
dimension to investment and financial analysis. In this economic
arena, the fundamental premises of competitive markets are definitely questionable: large numbers of small players, free trade,
market-determined prices, and widely held information; see (10)
for requisites of competition. Today's investment and financial
markets seem better characterized as economic games of just a few
"high rollers". These economic games are largely outside the control of United States financial institutions (e.g., Federal Re-
serve); however, their outcomes significantly affect investments
and financial decisions in this country.

An effective transition of the nation's energy base from petroleum to alternate energy sources will require relatively large capital investments. Incentives to make these investments will be influenced by our nation's capability to control its money supply and execute a desired monetary policy. The United States faces the sobering task of designing a technology development plan and implementing it. Its development and implementation will require an effective United States monetary policy.

Literature Cited

1. Executive Office of the President, Energy Policy and Planning, The National Energy Plan, Supt. of Documents, U.S. Govt. Printing Office, Washington, D. C., 20402, April 27, 1977.

2. Kim, Y. Y., and Thompson, R. G., "An Economic Model of New Crude Oil and Natural Gas Supplies in the Lower 48 States," Gulf Publishing Company, Houston, 1978

3. Thompson, R. G., Calloway, J. A., and Nawalanic, L. A. (eds.), "The Cost of Clean Water in Ammonia, Chlor-Alkali, and Ethylene Production," Gulf Publishing Company, Houston, 1976.

4. Thompson, R. G., Calloway, J. A., and Nawalanic, L. A. (eds.), "The Cost of Electricity," Gulf Publishing Company, Houston, 1977.

5. Thompson, R. G., Calloway, J. A., and Nawalanic, L. A. (eds.), "The Cost of Energy and A Clean Environment," Gulf Publishing Company, Houston, 1978.

6. Thompson, R. G., Stone, J. C., Singleton, F. D., Jr., and Raghaven, S. "Predicting the Structural Economic Consequences of Different Interrelated Energy and Environmental Policies," technical report to the Electric Power Research Institute, July, 1978 (draft).

7. Thompson, R. G., "Forecasting New Economic Trends in the Energy and Materials Sector of the U. S. Economy," Review of Regional Economics and Business, Vol. 4, No. 1, Oct. 1978.

8. Dorfman, R., Samelson, P. A., and Solow, R. M. "Linear Programming and Economic Analysis," McGraw-Hill Book Company, Inc., New York, 1958.

9. Intrilligator, M. D., "Mathematical Optimization and Economic Theory," Prentice-Hall, Inc., Englewood Cliffs, 1971.

10. Stigler, G. J., "The Theory of Price," The MacMillan Company, New York, revised edition, 1952.

RECEIVED March 8, 1979.

Methodology for Measuring the Effects of Regulation on Pharmaceutical Innovation

Regulatory Disposition and National Origin of New Chemical Entities in the United States

JEAN DiRADDO and WILLIAM M. WARDELL

Center for the Study of Drug Development, Department of Pharmacology and Toxicology, University of Rochester Medical Center, Rochester, NY 14642

As long as any disease that is potentially treatable by drugs remains unconquered, there will be a need for pharmaceutical innovation. Among those disease areas that could benefit from pharmaceutical innovation are arthritis, cancer, the muscular dystrophies, and schizophrenia. Despite the advances in drug therapy that have occurred, there is still a pressing need for new and better medicines within many therapeutic areas. Valuable innovations in such areas would offer drugs that are more effective, have fewer or significantly different side effects, and/or are more convenient than existing therapies.

Although the aim of pharmaceutical regulation is to ensure the safety and efficacy of new drugs, regulatory criteria should not be so stringent that they inhibit innovation. In April 1976, the President's Biomedical Research Panel gave the following description of how the regulatory process may act as a roadblock to the development of new drugs.

"There is a clear impasse arising between society's desire for new and better drugs and the barriers society is erecting to their development and introduction. These barriers, based on a valid desire to improve the standards of safety and efficacy and to insure ethical control in clinical evaluation, increase developmental costs. There is a real danger of bringing the development process and access to clinical resources to a halt."[1]

It is important to balance the effects of drug regulation with the need for innovation. As the clinical pharmacologist Walter Modell has said, "Only progress is protection. Without progress we have no protection."[2]

This paper examines the impact of regulation on pharmaceutical innovation in the United States and the methodological problems involved when one attempts to measure pharmaceutical innovation. Data describing the rate and manner of passage of new chemical entities (NCEs) through the U.S. regulatory system and the national origin of NCEs marketed in the U.S. are presented.

0-8412-0511-6/79/47-109-127$06.00/0

Pharmaceutical Regulation in the United States

Legislation. The first major legislation concerning drugs
was the Pure Food and Drugs Act of 1906. This Act banned adul-
terated or misbranded foods and drugs from interstate commerce.
Although directed against both impure foods and drugs, its main
impact was on foods.

The Food, Drug and Cosmetic Act of 1938 was enacted following the Elixir Sulfanilamide tragedy (in which the untested use
of diethylene glycol as a solvent caused the deaths of about 100
people). The aim of this Act was to prevent the marketing of
untested, potentially harmful drugs. Its major provision was
that the manufacturer was required to demonstrate the safety of
a drug to the FDA (in a new drug application or NDA). Unless the
FDA determined within 60 days that safety was not established, a
drug could then be marketed. Exemptions to the prohibition
against interstate transfer were allowed for drugs intended
solely for investigational use by qualified scientific experts.

The next major legislation was also enacted after a
tragedy--that of thalidomide. The major provision of the Drug
Amendments of 1962 (the Kefauver-Harris Amendments) was that the
manufacturer must show substantial evidence of a drug's effectiveness (in addition to its safety) to obtain approval for marketing. Other changes were that positive FDA approval of a drug
was required instead of automatic clearance; FDA control over
the clinical testing stage was expanded; and the Secretary of
HEW could immediately suspend a drug's NDA approval if the drug
was found to represent an "imminent hazard" to the public
health. (3)

Regulation. The regulations promulgated by the FDA to
implement its responsibilities as defined by the legislation
have had, and continue to have, a significant impact on pharmaceutical R & D.

Examples of particularly important regulations include the
1970 regulations that defined what constitutes the "well-
controlled investigations" needed to provide substantial evidence
of effectiveness as required by the 1962 Amendments.

In 1975 regulations came into effect to enhance the
acceptance by the FDA of foreign data meeting certain requirements. The aims of these regulations were to eliminate duplicative clinical research and to expedite the availability of
important new drugs in the United States.

In July 1976, due to concerns over the findings of FDA inspections of certain research laboratories, the Bioresearch
Monitoring Program was initiated. Four components of this program relate to drugs: regulations regarding preclinical testing
(Good Laboratory Practices)(4), those proposed for sponsors and
monitors of clinical studies(5), those proposed for clinical
investigators(6), and the proposed regulations pertaining to in-

stitutional review boards or IRBs.(7) Proposed regulations may
be modified on the basis of comments submitted to FDA before
they appear in final form. Implementation of any of the proposed
regulations included within this program will raise the cost of
developing new drugs and may influence the process of drug
development in other ways as well. For example, British pharmaceutical firms have stated that they cannot meet the requirements of the proposed sponsor/monitor regulations in Britain(8),
so presumably clinical data from Britain (and probably from other
countries as well) will become unacceptable in support of an NDA
if these regulations are implemented as currently proposed. Universities will have severe difficulties in meeting the requirements of, for example, the proposed regulations on Good Laboratory Practices.(9)

Following the appearance of the Final Report of the HEW
Review Panel on New Drug Regulation in May 1977, considerable
attention was devoted by the FDA and by some members of Congress
to formulating legislation that would significantly revise pharmaceutical regulation in this country. The outcome was The Drug
Regulation Reform Act of 1978 (S.2755, H.R. 11611, H.R. 12980),
which was introduced in both houses in March 1978.

The Drug Regulation Reform Act (DRRA) represents a complete
revision of the Food, Drug and Cosmetic Act of 1938. Although
the FDA is currently practicing some of the procedures described
in the bill, and would be able to follow others by initiating
appropriate regulations, passage of this legislation would clarify and formalize the nature and extent of the authority that
Congress intends the FDA to have.

The bill is lengthy and complex. Even among legal and
scientific experts there is disagreement as to which aspects of
the drug development and approval processes should most appropriately be covered by legislation and which should best be dealt
with by regulations. Although this particular bill was not enacted in 1978, the issues raised during the hearings and debates
on it are extremely important and will undoubtedly reappear in
future bills.

Since both the 1938 Act and the 1962 Amendments were passed
in the wake of tragedies, they were oriented towards risk-
avoidance; the FDA is primarily required to prevent harm from
drugs and at present has no congressional mandate to promote the
improvement of health or to maximize the benefit obtainable from
drugs.

The DRRA recognizes the need to encourage innovation and
research and to get new drugs on the market faster. In practice,
however, many of its provisions would probably inhibit research
and innovation.(10) Significant aspects of the bill include the
following:

1. provisions for limited distribution of a drug;
2. required postmarketing surveillance of a new drug for
    five years (unless waived by the Secretary of HEW);

3. postmarketing studies of a drug's effectiveness for indications other than those for which approval is sought could be required for uses that are known or could reasonably be expected to occur;

4. continuation of the current requirement for "adequate and well-controlled investigations" as evidence of effectiveness (in contrast to the provision in the Medical Device Amendments of 1976 by which the Secretary may determine whether other valid scientific evidence is adequate to establish the effectiveness of a device);

5. a new definition of safety to mean that the health benefits of a drug must clearly outweigh its risks with regard to society and the public health;

6. provision for removal of a drug from the market if it represents a substantial risk of illness or injury (this would replace the current provision which requires that a drug be shown to represent an "imminent hazard");

7. provision for the accelerated approval of "breakthrough" drugs if certain requirements are met;

8. the disclosure of all safety and effectiveness data submitted to the FDA (some of which is currently considered as trade secret information);

9. provision for the export of drugs not approved for marketing in this country under certain conditions;

10. expansion of the FDA's jurisdiction to include all drugs (not only those involved in interstate commerce); and

11. provision for drug innovation investigations for the purpose of examining clinical pharmacology, making preliminary assessments of the risks or effectiveness of a drug, or studying the biological mechanisms in humans. The FDA review of such investigations would focus only on the protection of subjects, not on the adequacy of the scientific design. (The aim of this provision is to avoid interfering with the discovery and development of new drugs but the extent to which the provision would achieve this aim has been questioned.)

For estimating the impact and effects of proposed changes in the regulatory system, it would be essential to have a thorough evaluation of the present system. Ideally one would like to see a cost/benefit assessment of the current regulations—cost representing not only economic cost but also the cost of missed innovation, and benefit representing the improved health and safety of the public. One part of this task that our group has approached is a study of the effects of regulation on pharmaceutical innovation. The first problem that must be dealt with in such a study is how to measure innovation.

Nature of Innovation

The present predictive state of pharmacological science is such that the therapeutic or even pharmacologic value of an innovation usually cannot be foretold at the time of its discovery. Thus, a certain amount of innovative activity may never yield real breakthroughs, while certain innovations that may appear scientifically trivial can turn out to be useful contributions to medical progress.

Pharmaceutical innovations that lead to advances in medical therapy occur in a variety of ways. There are dramatic "breakthrough" innovations that depend on a single major concept or discovery, examples being penicillin, levodopa, the beta-blockers and the H_2-antagonists. In contrast to these, the cumulative results of several minor or incremental innovations may, when taken together over a period of years, constitute a major advance. The areas of antihypertensive therapy and combination chemotherapy for cancer illustrate this type of innovation. Important therapeutic advances may also come about through chance observations of the effects of drugs in man in those situations in which science and animal models are not yet capable of making reliable predictions, such as the use of chlorpromazine as a tranquilizer and of iproniazid and imipramine as antidepressants.

Mechanisms of Innovation

We shall assume, rather arbitrarily for the purpose of this discussion, that the starting point of pharmaceutical innovation is the development of a new biologic concept (or a new approach to an existing concept) that is potentially therapeutically exploitable. Moving from the earliest and most a priori to the later and more empirical methods of drug discovery, the following types of innovation can be distinguished.
1. Synthesis of a new molecular structure (new chemical entity or NCE) with possible biological significance.
2. Discovery of a new pharmacologic action (e.g., the beta-blockers and the H_2-antagonists).
3. Structural modification of an existing molecule to improve its therapeutic value, e.g., by making it more effective, less toxic, better absorbed, or longer acting (such modification can also lead to the discovery of a new pharmacologic action, as in point 2 above, or of new therapeutic effects in man, as in point 5 below). An instructive example of the major therapeutic advances that have been obtained by molecular modification is seen in the family of penicillins that followed benzyl penicillin, the original member of the series. In little more than a decade from its first characterization, the original benzyl penicillin molecule was

structurally modified to yield phenoxymethyl penicillin
(orally active), ampicillin (orally active against gram
negative organisms), the penicillinase-resistant penicillins (active against certain resistant organisms,
particularly staphylococci), and carbenicillin (active
against Pseudomonas organisms). These are all relatively trivial modifications of the original benzyl
penicillin molecule, the few successes out of competitive programs that synthesized literally thousands of
such modified molecules, but they are some of the major
therapeutic advances of the antibiotic era.

   Similar examples abound in most fields of therapeutics. For example, the major tranquilizer chlor-
promazine--the first drug found to have true anti-
psychotic properties--is a trivial modification of
phenothiazine, which was known for decades and used as
a de-wormer for livestock. The parent phenothiazine,
and many of its structural modifications, have no anti-
psychotic activity at all; it is only certain minor
structural modifications that have the essential pharmacologic and therapeutic properties. (Chlorpromazine
also happens to be a classic example of the serendipitous empirical-clinical method of discovery of a drug's
unique therapeutic value, a method described below.)

4. "Pharmaceutical" modifications of drugs to improve performance, e.g., the production of different formulations
   or delivery forms. On the overall scale of innovations,
   these pharmaceutical modifications are generally regarded as being of relatively minor innovative significance; however, some can be of disproportionately large
   medical value. For example, the simple concept of the
   depot (long-acting injectable forms of) phenothiazines
   has improved the long-term treatment of psychotic
   patients whose disease predisposes to noncompliance
   with the therapeutic regimen and resultant treatment
   failure; in some cases the depot form can avert the
   need for institutionalization. Depot preparations of
   injectable contraceptives similarly overcome the obvious
   problem that can result from noncompliance. The Ocusert
   and Progestasert systems, which deliver drugs locally
   into particular body compartments (the eye and uterus,
   respectively) reduce the total systemic burden of a
   drug, reduce side effects, and provide more uniform and
   reliable release; the inhaled form of steroids for
   asthma serves a similar purpose. These are a few of
   the many examples where pharmaceutical innovations of a
   relatively modest conceptual or technical nature have
   nevertheless led to substantial improvements in the
   quality of medical treatment.

5. Discovery of therapeutic effects in man that may not be

predictable from animal models, also known as serendipitous discovery or the "Oates Type II" method of discovery. Examples of major therapeutic advances that
have been made in this way include some of the most
important therapies of the past three decades: all the
major psychotherapeutic drugs (the major tranquilizers
and both classes of antidepressants); the thiazide
diuretics; the antiparkinsonian actions of levodopa and
amantadine; the anti-inflammatory actions of steroids
and of phenylbutazone; the antihypertensive actions of
beta-blockers and methyldopa; the antigout action of
allopurinol; and the protective effects of beta-blockers
and platelet modulators against coronary death and myocardial infarction, and against stroke.
   6. Discovery of new uses for existing drugs, including
      those uses discovered as in point 5 above.
When one examines the nature, sources, and funding of pharmaceutical innovation, certain principles become apparent. The
areas where federal support has been most prominent are in basic
research and in large-scale clinical trials. These happen to be
areas where the benefits--while very real--are long-term, not
immediately apparent ones.
   Conversely, the development of specific therapeutic drugs
has to a large extent (with the exception of some important areas
such as cancer chemotherapy) been achieved by the pharmaceutical
industry, without federal funding. For example, the original
basic work on beta-blockers, new beta-agonists, H_2-antagonists,
and cromolyn sodium was all done in laboratories of pharmaceutical firms (foreign laboratories, as it happens), and the most
important clinical development was also performed by firms
abroad. If one traces the research back still further, one can
usually find connections with research supported by public funding, but the connection is not an immediate one.
   An important trend appears to be developing. Basic research
knowledge, once produced, is an international commodity because
of the well-developed systems that exist for scientific publication and communication. It is ironic that while most publicly-
financed basic knowledge is probably generated by U.S. funding,
the U.S. pharmaceutical industry may not be proportionately as
prominent in making applied use of this knowledge. It is as if
foreign companies are getting "first crack" at these U.S.-
originated basic-knowledge opportunities. It is possible that
the facility to exploit basic knowledge for therapeutic purposes
is dependent on the regulatory environments in particular
countries.

Measures of Innovation

   There are several possible ways of measuring pharmaceutical
innovation, but all present technical problems. Two general

approaches are the use of absolute measures, using some absolute criterion to measure innovative output, and comparative measures, such as comparing the nature and extent of the output of two different countries. Among the possible absolute measures are the number of new molecular structures (NCEs) synthesized, the novelty of their molecular structure, the novelty of their pharmacologic action, the number of patents issued, the number of NCEs tested in man, the number of NCEs submitted for marketing, the number of NCEs marketed, and qualitative measures of the value of marketed NCEs.

Measures such as the number of compounds synthesized and the number of patents issued have been criticized on the grounds that they are more measures of R & D activity (input) rather than of output.(11) Novelty of molecular structure represents a technically difficult assessment which, if performed at the time of synthesis, involves molecules with unknown pharmacologic and therapeutic properties. Novelty of pharmacologic action represents a fundamental measure of at least the potential for therapeutic innovation. In practice, however, this represents a judgmental issue and the necessary data on untested or unmarketed drugs would be difficult to obtain.

The problem with using the numbers of NCEs, whether tested in man, submitted for marketing, or marketed, is that these measures consist of numbers alone without interpretation or assessment of therapeutic value. Furthermore, as measures of innovation, they are confounded by regulatory influence during the IND and NDA stages. The therapeutic value of marketed NCEs can be evaluated but the real assessment can only be made some years after a drug has been marketed and its properties fully ascertained (e.g., aspirin's prophylactic effects against myocardial infarction). Therapeutic assessments have been made by the FDA for example(12), but the methodology for such assessments has not been well-developed.

The measure we have recently developed in some detail is the number of NCEs taken into human testing. This is a valid and useful measure since it represents a firm's decision that a compound is worthy of further testing and investment. It also represents the first appearance of innovative output outside a firm, and in the U.S. it marks the entry of a compound into the regulatory pathway. Although, as described above, this measure of innovation is made before a compound's therapeutic properties are known, it is made at a point when the compound's pharmacologic and toxicologic properties are already defined.

A further reason for the importance of this measure is the seemingly paradoxical one that some of the most important therapeutic properties of a drug cannot be predicted at the time a drug is first taken into man. In the present rather primitive state of knowledge about structure-activity relationships, our ability to make a priori predictions using such relationships is poor. We therefore depend more than is generally realized on the

"Oates Type II" or serendipitous method of discovery, in which major new properties of drugs are discovered only after their introduction into human therapeutics. The more compounds that are studied in man, the more potential there is for this serendipitous method of discovery. Thus, the number of NCEs taken into man for study is one of the more important of the feasible indices of innovation.

The New Drug Approval Process in the United States

The upper portion of Figure 1 depicts the various stages through which a new drug must pass before it can be marketed in the United States. After the preclinical testing phase and initial toxicological studies, a manufacturer may file with the FDA for an investigational new drug exemption (IND) prior to initiating human testing. The clinical investigations are divided into three phases. During Phase I a drug is given to a small number of healthy human volunteers with the principal objectives of looking for evidence of toxicity and determining the basic properties of the drug in man. In Phase II the drug's effects on a small population of patients with the appropriate disease are examined to determine its therapeutic value and to detect any adverse effects or possible toxicity. Phase III consists of large-scale testing to uncover less common side effects and to approximate more closely the type of drug utilization (e.g., in patients of varying disease severity) that would occur in medical practice if the drug were marketed.

When a manufacturer believes he has adequate evidence to demonstrate the safety and effectiveness of a compound, an NDA is submitted to the FDA. After the NDA has been approved, the drug can be marketed in this country. The term Phase IV is used to denote postmarketing studies that are done to examine the properties of the drug in more widespread or long-term utilization.

Regulatory Disposition of NCEs in the United States

To measure innovation we examined the rate of flow of NCEs into human testing, the earliest point at which reliable information appears outside the pharmaceutical industry and the point at which NCEs enter the regulatory pathway. The rates at which these compounds pass the milestones of the U.S. regulatory pathway (the points of IND filing, NDA submission, and NDA approval) were defined. In addition to the overall analysis, the data were analyzed by individual therapeutic areas. The observed differences between categories of NCEs imply the existence of scientific, industrial, and/or administrative differences between these categories.

Data were obtained by an exhaustive survey of all pharmaceutical companies operating in the U.S. An NCE was defined as

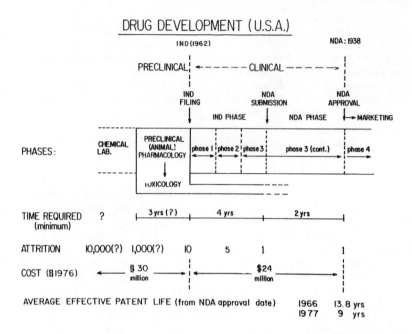

Figure 1. *The stages through which a new drug must pass before it can be marketed in the U.S. (32). The time and attrition data are described in the text; the cost data are described in Reference 13.*

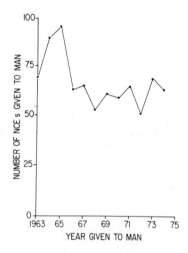

Figure 2. *Total number of NCEs given to man worldwide by U.S. companies by year first given to man (13)*

a compound of molecular structure not previously tested in man
(excluding new salts or esters, diagnostic agents, and vaccines).
For U.S.-owned companies, NCEs taken into man anywhere in the
world for the first time from January 1963 (the year the IND requirement was first implemented) to the time of the survey (September 1975) were included. In the case of foreign-owned
research-based firms operating in the U.S., we obtained complete
data on their U.S. experience with NCEs but not on their worldwide experience.

Information was obtained on a total of 1,103 NCEs, 859 from
36 U.S.-owned companies and 244 from 10 foreign-owned companies.
(A more detailed description of this study is in (13).) The
portion of the U.S. pharmaceutical industry responsible for the
NCEs was highly concentrated; seven companies accounted for one-
half of the NCEs and four of these companies accounted for one-
third.

The annual rate of NCEs tested in man by U.S. companies rose
from 70 in 1963 to a mean of 94 in 1964-1965, then declined
sharply to a lower plateau that has been relatively stable (with
a mean of 62 NCEs per year) from 1966-1974 (Figure 2).

The interpretation of this trend is not simple. The values
in 1964 and 1965 are relatively high whereas those in 1966-1974
are not very different from 1963. To interpret this, more information for 1963 and prior years is necessary. If 1963 was an
"ordinary" year, then the temporary upsurge in 1964 and 1965 needs
to be explained but the changes in the later 1960s and early
1970s have been small. If, however, 1963 represents an unusually
low year, the subsequent decline from the levels of 1964-1965 has
been substantial.

Our best interpretation of the present data, based on answers to questions asked of the firms, is that the 1963 values
are artificially low (because of the need then for companies to
divert their efforts toward compiling materials for the required
retrospective IND filings on drugs already in clinical research),
while the 1964-1965 values are artificially rather high (because
of a catching-up process).

Analysis by pharmacologic area showed that most NCEs tested
by U.S. companies were in the areas of anti-infective drugs
(19.4%), psychotropic/neurotropic drugs (14.3%), cardiovascular
drugs (14.3%), analgesic/anti-inflammatory drugs (13.0%), and
endocrine drugs (11.8%). The strongest time patterns were the
large rise and fall in the early years seen overall (as described
above) and particularly with anti-infective and cardiovascular
compounds, but not with psychotropic/neurotropic, endocrine, or
analgesic/anti-inflammatory drugs. After 1966 the trends were
not strong, but there was a perceptible decline in anti-infective
and a rise in endocrine compounds. Psychotropic/neurotropic compounds showed a marked fall between the early and later years
studied.

In recent years there has been a large shift in early U.S.

drug studies abroad (Figure 3). From 1963 to 1969, an average of
only 8% of U.S.-owned NCEs were first studied abroad by the 36
U.S. firms, but this rose to 34% in 1973. (It fell to 31% in
1974 but showed a continuing rise to 47% in our incomplete data
for 1975.) The increase in the number of drugs being initially
studied abroad was particularly marked within the larger companies; in 1973 the four largest companies first studied 50% of
their NCEs abroad. The proportion of drugs first studied abroad
also varied by therapeutic area, with gastrointestinal and endocrine drugs having the highest percentages.

The annual rate of IND filings by U.S. companies declined
from an average of 87 per year during the two first full years
(1964-1965) to a low of 42 in 1972, with a subsequent return to
the general levels prevailing in 1967-1970 (Figure 4). The
steepest decline occurred between 1965 and 1966; the interpretation of the magnitude of this decline is complicated by factors
previously discussed.

By constrast, the rate of foreign-owned NCE IND filings
showed no time-related trend and averaged 19.5 filings per year
from 1964 to 1974 (range 14-26). The decline in the rate of
total filings was thus due solely to the decline in the U.S.
portion. This is consistent with, but does not by itself prove,
the hypothesis that an inhibitory influence was acting on U.S.
companies but not on foreign companies during this period.

Of those NCEs that entered the U.S. regulatory system, 12.5%
of the INDs filed before 1970 (i.e., those which had at least
five years to be acted upon) had reached the stage of NDA submission by 1975. Of the NDAs submitted prior to 1970, 88% were
successful. The finding that decisions on most INDs that were
discontinued before the point of NDA submission were made primarily by the companies themselves has substantial implications
for the structure of the regulatory process. Of those compounds
that reached the NDA stage, where most of the regulatory assessment by the FDA is involved, only 12% failed to pass in five
years. Nevertheless, the NDA review phase occupies a substantial
fraction of the total IND-NDA time requirement; for many of the
drugs that were ultimately approved, the NDA phase exceeded the
length of the IND phase.

The total time required for clinical investigations and
approval of a successful NCE in the U.S. (IND and NDA stages)
rose from a mean of 31 months in 1966 (17 months IND plus 14
months NDA) to a peak mean of 71 months in 1969 (28 months IND
plus 43 months NDA), and has averaged 62 months over the last
two complete years (1973-1974; Figure 5). In the last but incomplete year, 1975, the mean time required rose sharply to 82
months (55 months IND plus 27 months NDA), mainly due to the
rise in the duration of the IND stage.

The most recent data available on the time requirements and
the attrition rates are shown in the bottom portion of Figure 1.
The cost estimates provided in the figure are from a study by

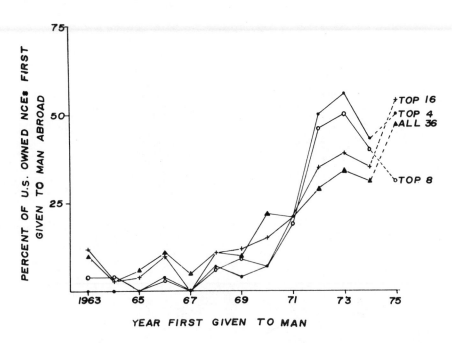

Clinical Pharmacology and Therapeutics

Figure 3.   Percent of U.S.-owned NCEs first given to man abroad by year first given to man. Data are shown for all 36 companies, the top 16, the top 8, and the top 4 companies, as determined by ranking the number of NCEs which each company took into man over the entire period (13).

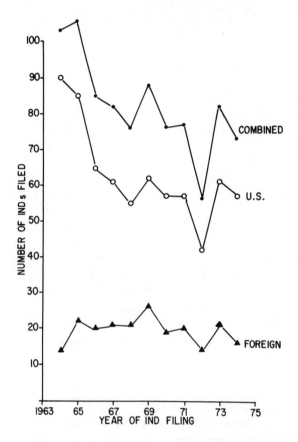

Clinical Pharmacology and Therapeutics

*Figure 4.   Number of INDs filed by year of filing. Data from U.S. and foreign
companies are shown separately and combined (13).*

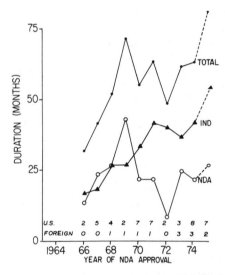

Clinical Pharmacology and Therapeutics

Figure 5.   Duration in months of IND (mean time from IND filing to NDA submission), NDA (mean time from NDA submission to NDA approval), and Total (mean time from IND filing to NDA approval) stages for approved NDAs by year of NDA approval. Data from U.S. and foreign companies are combined and the figures at the bottom indicate the number of NDAs approved each year for U.S. and foreign companies (13).

Hansen(14), who obtained economic data from U.S. firms on a sample of compounds that were included in the NCE study. He found
that, taking failures into account as well as successes, the
average cost for a U.S. firm to develop its own NCE to the point
of marketing in this country is $54 million in 1976 dollars.
This is higher than previous estimates, largely due to capitali-
zation of expenditure flows and exclusion of licensed compounds.
      A survival distribution analysis was performed to study the
success rates of NCEs in the IND and NDA phases and the amount of
time spent in each phase (residence time). There was a trend
toward increasing residence times and decreasing success rates
with time, but this trend was not significant with the statistical tests employed. The success rates and residence times of
U.S. and foreign companies were quite similar in each phase.
      The duration of the NDA phase varied significantly between
pharmacologic classes. An example from U.S.-owned NCEs was the
relatively quick approval of anticancer drugs in contrast to the
relatively long times for approval of cardiovascular drugs.
      The duration of the NDA phase for all NCE NDAs (i.e., not
just that subset represented by the cohort with new INDs) rose
from a mean of approximately 6 months through the latter half of
the 1950s to a mean of 44 months in 1969, and then fell rather
sharply to a mean of 17 months in 1972 (Figure 6). The reasons
for these large changes are not at present clear. Some actions
taken by the FDA may have contributed to this shortening of the
NDA phase, such as an increased number of Public Health Service
physicians assigned to the FDA, an increase in the number of
Advisory Committees, and the institution of new internal management systems at FDA. Since 1972, the duration of the NDA phase
has been rising again to a value of about two years. This pattern
needs further investigation since an understanding of what caused
it could help to elucidate the role of regulation versus other
factors in the causation of these changes.
      This is the first time a data base of this size and degree
of comprehensiveness has been compiled on the state of new drug
development in any country. We are currently obtaining further
information on investigational NCEs, which will include the
reasons for termination of clinical research by the firms and
full data on licensed compounds. These additional data will
clarify some of the trends that have been revealed by the present
study, and will allow further analyses to be performed of the
reasons behind the observed changes.

National Origin of NCEs Marketed in the United States   (15, 16)

      The national origin of NCEs introduced onto the U.S. market
is a key measure of the location of pharmaceutical innovation,
and of changes in location. The number and nature of drugs discovered or originated in each country are important because these
data reflect the scientific climate, as well as regulatory and

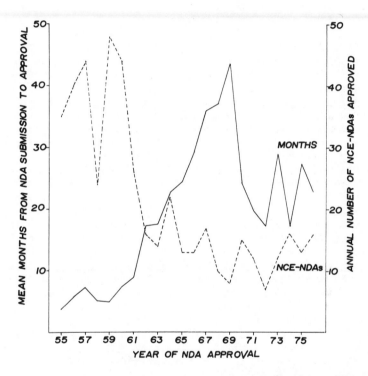

Clinical Pharmacology and Therapeutics

Figure 6. Number of NCE NDAs approved and mean duration of NDA stage (months from NDA submission to NDA approval) by year of NDA approval (13)

economic considerations, in that country. Cultural and geographic influences will also be seen if there is an emphasis on certain therapeutic areas or diseases in a particular country. An analysis using this type of measure can provide a useful picture of worldwide innovative activity; furthermore, the findings in one country can also serve as a control group for making comparisons with another country in assessing the influence of national regulations on innovation. Ideally the origin of new drugs introduced onto the entire world market should be assessed, but data are available only for certain countries; our study focused on the U.S. market.

Two analyses were performed based on data compiled by Paul deHaen (17, 18) and by Harold Clymer.(19) In one analysis the national origin of an NCE was defined as the location of the laboratory where the drug's pharmacologic activity was discovered and in the other the national origin was taken as the nationality of the parent company that owns the drug (i.e., the patent). According to both definitions of national origin, the percentage of U.S. NCE approvals that were accounted for by U.S.-originated drugs generally declined from the early 1950s through the early 1970s, but several transient fluctuations in this pattern were observed. Since there was considerable variability from year to year, three-year moving averages were used rather than yearly figures to represent general time-related trends. By laboratory of origin, the percentage of NCEs originated in the U.S. ranged from a high of 76% in the years centered around 1954 to a low of 47% around 1973 (Figure 7). By nationality of the parent company, for which data were available from 1963 to 1975, the percentage of U.S.-originated NCEs ranged from 63% in the years centered around 1964 and 1966 to 38% around 1972 (Figure 8). This decline has been followed by a recent rise in the portion of U.S.-originated NCEs, but the U.S. has not regained the prominence it had in the earlier years.

A similar pattern was observed in both analyses when the percentages of U.S.-originated "significant" NCEs (i.e., those rated by the FDA as representing important or modest therapeutic advances) over time were calculated.

The three major foreign contributors to the U.S. market by either definition of national origin have been Switzerland, Britain, and Germany; the order of their importance has varied over time however.

Since factors other than innovation, such as commercial considerations affecting foreign entry onto the U.S. market, influence the observed patterns, analysis of the national origin of NCEs using the definitions employed here is not a highly sensitive or specific measure of pharmaceutical innovation. However, the observed trends are consistent with the tightening of regulatory policies first in the U.S. and then subsequently abroad.

We are currently obtaining data that will improve and expand upon these national origin analyses. The new information includes,

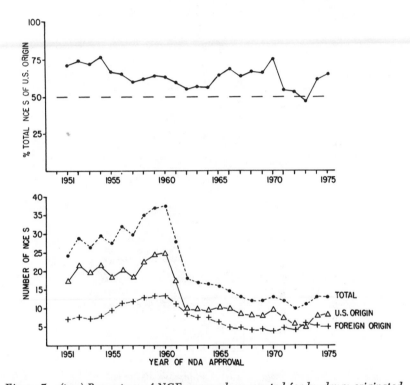

Figure 7. (top) Percentage of NCE approvals accounted for by drugs originated in U.S. Laboratories (three-year moving averages). The dashed line indicates the 50% level (an equal number of U.S. and foreign-originated drugs). (bottom) Number of NCEs originated in U.S. and in foreign laboratories (three-year moving averages).

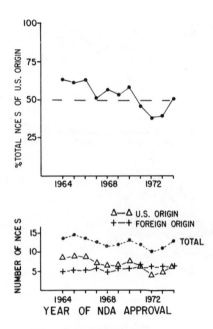

Figure 8. (top) *Percentage of NCE approvals accounted for by drugs originated in U.S. parent companies (three-year moving averages). The dashed line indicates the 50% level (an equal number of U.S. and foreign-originated drugs).* (bottom) *Number of NCEs originated in U.S. and in foreign parent companies (three-year moving averages).*

for each NCE marketed in the U.S. since 1963, the countries of its
first chemical synthesis, its first pharmacologic study, and its
first administration to man. Information on licensing patterns
and on international transfers of drugs at different stages within companies is also being obtained. These data will clarify the
observed patterns of national origin and will provide more sensitive measures of international shifts in world pharmaceutical
innovative activity.

Comparative Methods of Measuring Innovation: NCEs Marketed in
the United States and Great Britain

Since the techniques for measuring pharmaceutical innovation,
in particular its scientific and medical value, are not yet well
developed, alternative approaches to absolute measures of innovation should be explored. An obvious alternative is the international comparative approach, comparing the performance of drug
innovation under the U.S. regulatory system with the performance
of drug innovation systems in other countries having different
types and amounts of regulation.
    Clearly this type of comparison will be affected by inter-
national differences other than regulatory ones--in particular,
the different states of sophistication of pharmacological and
pharmaceutical science and technology between countries, and the
state of development and prominence of the industry in different
countries' economies. Nevertheless, although communication
channels from the U.S. National Institutes of Health to U.S. firms
are potentially shorter, basic knowledge is an international
commodity. Substantial information can therefore be obtained
from international comparisons, as in the case of the international comparison between the U.S. and Britain for the period
1962-1971 performed by one of the authors.(20, 21, 22)
    An update of the comparison of NCEs marketed in the U.S. and
Britain from January 1972 through December 1976 indicated that in
this five-year period 82 new drugs appeared for the first time in
one or both of the two countries.(23) Of these, only 29% became
mutually available in both countries--2.4 times as many becoming
available first in Britain as in the U.S. Of the 71% that became
exclusively available, 2.6 times as many became available in
Britain as in the U.S.
    More important than numerical data are the clinical impli-
cations of differences between the two countries. The largest
differences have narrowed since the previous study, but important
categories in which the U.S. still lagged behind Britain in
December 1976 included cardiovascular drugs, peptic ulcer treatment, and central nervous system drugs--including therapies for
depression, epilepsy, and migraine.

Conclusions

While the inhibitory influence of regulation on innovation
is clear, we have not been able to measure the precise extent of
this influence with our present data. The main problem lies in
separating the specific contributions of influences other than
regulation that are also acting to inhibit innovation. Factors
such as the generally increasing amount of scientific evidence
required to document safety or efficacy, together with economic
considerations, have no doubt contributed to the decline in innovation. The attribution of causal relationships for recent policy
changes is helped, however, by the fact that we have better data
on the timing and size of recent regulatory changes, by correla-
tions between the observed differences in innovation between different therapeutic areas and known differences in governmental
policies in these areas, by an international comparative
approach(20, 21, 22, 23), and by economic analyses.(14) The results from our studies, and those of others(24-31), are consistent
with the hypothesis that over the past 15 years increased regulation has reduced the amount of pharmaceutical innovation.

Acknowledgement

Acquisition of the new data described in this paper was
supported by a grant from the National Science Foundation (#75
19066-00). Any opinions, findings, conclusions, or recommendations expressed in this paper are those of the authors and do not
necessarily reflect the views of the National Science Foundation.

Literature Cited

1. Report of the President's Biomedical Research Panel,
    Appendix A, DHEW Publication No. (05) 76-501, p. 236, 1976.
2. Modell, W., Clin. Pharmacol. Ther., (1976) 19, 121.
3. Bresler, J.A., "A legislative history of the Federal Food,
    Drug and Cosmetic Act (Revised)," Congressional Research
    Service, Library of Congress, 77-98 SP, 1977.
4. "Non-clinical laboratory studies: Good laboratory practice
    regulations," Fedl. Reg., (1978) 43, 59986.
5. "Obligations of sponsors and monitors of clinical investi-
    gations," Fedl. Reg., (1977) 42, 49612.
6. "Obligations of clinical investigators of regulated articles,"
    Fedl. Reg. (1978) 43, 35210.
7. "Standards for institutional review boards for clinical
    investigations," Fedl. Reg., (1978) 43, 35186.
8. Association for the British Pharmaceutical Industry:
    Regarding sponsor/monitor regulations, Brit. Med., (1978,
    in press).

9. Blozan, C.F., "Results of the nonclinical toxicology laboratory Good Laboratory Practices pilot compliance program," Food and Drug Administration, OPE Study 42, (1977).
10. Wardell, W.M., Clin. Pharmacol. Ther., (1978) 24, 374.
11. Pharmaceuticals Working Party of the Chemicals EDC, "Innovative Activity in the Pharmaceutical Industry," National Economic Development Office, London, 1973.
12. U.S. Congress, Senate, Committee on Labor and Public Welfare and Committee on the Judiciary, "Examination of New Drug Research and Development by the Food and Drug Administration," 93rd Congress, 2nd Session, 25 and 27 September 1974, pp. 619-633.
13. Wardell, W.M., Hassar, M., Anavekar, S.N., and Lasagna, L., Clin. Pharmacol. Ther., (1978) 24, 133.
14. Hansen, R., Center for Research in Government Policy and Business, University of Rochester, GPB 77-10 (1977), "The pharmaceutical development process: Estimates of current developmental costs and times and the effects of regulatory changes."
15. Hassar, M., Clymer, H.A., Wardell, W.M., and Lasagna, L. (Abstract), Clin. Pharmacol. Ther., (1976) 19, 108.
16. Wardell, W.M., Hassar, M., and DiRaddo, J., "National origin as a measure of innovative output: The national origin of new chemical entities marketed in the U.S." in Lasagna, L., Wardell, W.M., and Hansen, R., "Technological Innovation and Government Regulation of Pharmaceuticals in the United States and Great Britain," final report submitted to the National Science Foundation, August 1978.
17. DeHaen, P., Pharmacy Times, (1976) 40.
18. DeHaen, P., "New Product Survey, 1976: Newly Synthesized Drugs Introduced in the United States," Paul deHaen, Inc., New York, 1977.
19. Clymer, H., Unpublished manuscript, (1975) "NDA approvals - new chemical entities, 1950-1974."
20. Wardell, W.M., Clin. Pharmacol. Ther., (1973) 14, 773.
21. Wardell, W.M., Clin. Pharmacol. Ther., (1973) 14, 1022.
22. Wardell, W.M., Clin. Pharmacol. Ther., (1974) 15, 73.
23. Wardell, W.M., Clin. Pharmacol. Ther., (1978) 24, 499.
24. Baily, M.N., J. Polit. Econ., (1972) 80, 70.
25. Grabowski, H.G., "Drug Regulation and Innovation: Empirical Evidence and Policy Options," American Enterprise Institute for Public Policy Research, Washington, D.C., 1976.
26. Grabowski, H.G., "Regulation and the International Diffusion of Pharmaceuticals," paper presented at the symposium on "The International Supply of Medicines," American Enterprise Institute for Public Policy Research, Washington, D.C., 1978.
27. Grabowski, H.G., Vernon, J.M., and Thomas, L.G., J. Law Econ., (1978) 23, 133.
28. Jadlow, J.M., Unpublished Ph.D. dissertation, "The economic effects of the 1962 Drug Amendments,", University of Virginia,

       1970.
29.   Peltzman, S., "The benefits and costs of new drug regula-
       tions," in "Regulating New Drugs," R. Landau, Ed., pp. 113-
       212, University of Chicago, Center for Political Study,
       Chicago, 1973.
30.   Peltzman, S., J. Polit. Econ., (1973) 81, 1067.
31.   Peltzman, S., "Regulation of Pharmaceutical Innovation: The
       1962 Amendments," American Enterprise Institute for Public
       Policy Research, Washington, D.C., 1974.
32.   Chien, Robert I., Ed., "Issues in Pharmaceutical Economics,"
       D. C. Heath and Company, Lexington, MA, 1978.

RECEIVED March 8, 1979.

Innovation in the Pharmaceutical Industry: Possible Effects of the Proposed Drug Regulation Reform Act of 1978

GAIL UPDEGRAFF

JRB Associates, Inc., McLean, VA 22102

This paper is a discussion of the impact of the proposed Drug Regulation Reform Act of 1978 (DRRA) on innovation in the pharmaceutical industry as assessed by examining the DRRA's economic impacts. (Before proceeding, the reader may want to refer to the brief overview of the DRRA at the beginning of the section on the Economic Analysis of the DRRA (See p. 9).) Although only a small segment of the paper will discuss the various forces that have led to proposing the DRRA, arguments made concerning U.S. drug laws, primarily since the 1962 Amendments to the Food, Drug and Cosmetic Act (FD&C), that are relevant to direct or indirect effects of this law on drug innovation will be discussed. (The 1962 Amendments required that drugs not only be safe, but also that they be effective.) Hence, a brief synopsis of the ongoing debates surrounding the drug law embodied in FD&C and also the way the Department of Health, Education, and Welfare's Food and Drug Administration (FDA) has administered this law will be presented.

Determining the impact of the DRRA on drug innovation involves recognizing several problematic steps in relating regulation and innovation. The first is the evaluation of the dollar costs to industry of the regulation. Second, a determination of the extent to which costs imposed on industry affect R and D expenditures must be made. Next, the extent to which changes in R and D expenditures affect innovation must be assessed. Then, one needs to categorize the innovations (say, therepeutically significant versus not significant) in order to determine whether those innovations that are most beneficial to society are the drug innovations affected. Finally, it is imperative to attempt to determine the effect of other regulatory and nonregulatory factors on drug innovation. Each of the above points are covered, some to a lesser degree than others, in this paper. However, no attempt is made to cover the potential benefits of the DRRA in terms of preventing "harmful" (ineffective and/or unsafe drugs) innovations from being marketed.

0-8412-0511-6/79/47-109-151$05.00/0

The analysis of the DRRA presented below demonstrates that it is possible to predict that the proposed Act, the DRRA, will have both positive and negative economic impacts (i.e., will impose savings as well as costs on the pharmaceutical industry), and, hence, impacts on innovation. The different sides in the ongoing debate concerning government regulation of the drug industry and its impact on pharmaceutical innovation usually appear to overlook this notion of effects in opposite or countering directions. In fact, the proponents and opponents, rather than searching for truth, appear to be searching for the most damning, most supportive case. The result is that effort is primarily expended not on reaching a fair and accurate conclusion, but instead searching for the winning argument. It will be possible to relate many of the "predicted" impacts of the DRRA on drug innovation to previous arguments on this topic.

This paper will primarily concentrate, as discussed above, on the economic aspects of the impacts of the DRRA as they interface with drug innovation. Economic aspects of the impacts means those aspects that directly influence the ability of firms to finance research and development (R&D) and, therefore, possible innovations. There are also indirect economic impacts such as the time it takes to obtain market approval for a drug and the possible health effects this has on consumers from having to forego an effective alternative treatment—this, of course, can have a multitude of monetary effects on the patient (lost employment, more expensive alternative treatment costs, etc.). Of course, the timing of market approval can have negative monetary impacts on the ability of drug firms to finance R&D because of lost or "untimely" sales (untimely in that R&D projects are curtailed because drugs that are approved were done so too late to generate revenue in time to support the projects).

The point made earlier concerning the relationship between R&D expenditures and drug innovation is an important one. Although U.S. introductions and discoveries in the drug field have exhibited a declining trend since the late 1950's, constant U.S. drug firm R&D dollar expenditures have continued to increase, as shown by Grabowski, et. al (1). Many have argued, as have Grabowski, et. al, that the decrease in drug introductions and discoveries is due in large part to government regulation, particularly that by FDA. Others have argued that there is a depletion in our knowledge of the drug field that has led to a declining trend in drug introductions and discoveries even though constant dollar R&D expenditures have continued to increase—the increase has been taking place at a decreasing rate in the past several years. This argument is often supported with reference to the boom years of innovation that came with the various vaccine, antibiotic and psychotherapeutic drug breakthroughs. In summary, there does not appear to be a readily identifiable relationship between marginal changes in

R&D expenditures and the discovery and introduction of new drugs. Nevertheless, the assumption will be made that a continuous and substantial erosion in R&D expenditures will have a negative impact on drug innovation.

This paper is organized into two main sections followed by a summary and conclusion section. The first section presents the definitions and assumptions necessary to bring about a cohesive and meaningful exposition on the possible impacts of the DRRA on drug innovation. This section also discusses the multitude of forces, besides the provisions of the DRRA, that influence the dollars available for R&D. Finally, this section gives a brief overview of the criticisms that have been made of FDA's regulatory authority and behavior, especially since the passage and promulgation of the 1962 Amendments to FD&C.

The second section begins with an overview of the DRRA, and then identifies the sections of it that are relevant to the economic aspects of drug regulation and innovation that are the focus of this paper. This section is really the heart of the paper, and for this reason, caveats are spelled out in essential detail. Traditionally, considerable latitude has been given to Federal agencies in implementing newly acquired as well as existing authority—this has changed some, however, because of court decisions over the past few years (2). Hence, it is desireable to explain underlying assumptions, thereby lessening the chance of misinterpretation.

Background and Supporting Material

It is necessary for an area such as the relationship between government regulation and drug innovation to set forth the assumptions, caveats, definitions, etc. that are to be used in a discussion of the topic. The reason for this is that this is a very difficult area in which to establish a supportable relationship. First, we have to establish what it is we mean by drug innovation. The definition of an innovative drug should include at least the following drugs: (1) a safer and perhaps even more effective (but at least as effective) drug as is on the market for a given disease; (2) a drug that is at least as safe (and perhaps safer) and yet is more effective in treatment than drugs already on the market; (3) a drug that meets the law's safety requirements and is effective in the treatment of a disease for which there was no previous treatment; or (4) a drug that is significantly less expensive but just as safe and effective as drugs already on the market.

Since there has been disagreement over the meaning of the terms safe and effective, this paper will use new chemical entities (NCE's) approved for marketing by FDA as the measure for drug innovation -- the more approved NCE's per R&D dollar, the more productive drug research is, if one accepts this definition. It appears to be a commonly accepted definition (1).

In addition, since this paper is discussing possible revisions to the U.S. drug laws, the definition is a logical as well as practical one to use. Nevertheless, it should be noted that the FDA and others distinguish between NCE's that are therapeutically significant and those that are not. In spite of the necessity of classifying innovations in this way as acknowledged at the beginning of the paper, no system acceptable to both government and industry presently exists.

A basic premise of this paper is that prescription (or ethical) drugs have been providing and will continue to provide a benefit to society. The important thing about drug innovation should be that it is a benefit to societal health, not that it possibly means the financial growth of drug firms.

There is support for the thesis that prescription drugs may be a societal benefit (3). At a time when health care costs are rising rapidly (4), drugs provide a relatively inexpensive form of treatment. Antibiotics have allowed the treatment of numerous infectious diseases with a consequent decrease or elimination of hospitalization in many cases. Psychotherapeutic drugs have cut the cost of both inpatient and outpatient care for mental traumas and illnesses, and probably increased a segment of the population's productivity. Drugs are now approved or in the pipeline for treatment of such illnesses as ulcers, gallstones and certain forms of cancer. These treatments are considerably less expensive than surgery in some cases, and they have far less negative social impact in some instances. Finally, vaccines have reduced the demand for health care through the prevention of several once widespread illnesses. Of course, there are also going to be drugs that are not therapeutically significant and which even may be harmful because they are unsafe, or effective treatment is foregone.

A point that merits discussion before proceeding is the behavioral and resource assumptions that must be considered in regard to how the DRRA might be implemented. When HEW Secretary Joseph A. Califano, Jr. first addressed FDA staff shortly after coming into office, he called FDA the most under-staffed, under-resourced agency in HEW. It is only logical that if any of the criticisms that have been made of FDA (these will be briefly discussed later in this paper) is true, and if one gives credence to Secretary Califano's statement, then the failures that FDA has been accused of will probably not be solved by a revision of the drug laws alone -- sufficient additional staff and resources must go along with the DRRA. If they are not provided, innovation may be slowed as a result of the market approval process being slow. Hence, one assumption I make is that the increase in resources is adequate to efficiently administer the drug laws if they are revised. This might even take a revision in the salary scale for physicians, as some have advocated, in order to attract more medical doctors into the FDA.

An important behavioral assumption with respect to the
individuals and teams (medical doctors, pharmacologists, toxicologists, chemists, etc.) which review applications for approval
to market a drug is that, for various reasons, they are not
adequately motivated. When an important discovery is made in the
drug field, and when the drug (or series of drugs) continues to
give evidence that it is safe and effective, then who gets the
credit -- the drug company, of course. The FDA reviewers may
receive some explicit or implicit credit with FDA, but most of
the public and private praise will go to the drug company (or
the company and the discover(s)). This negative impact on
innovation, along with low salary scales and other adverse
factors, such as the inability of these teams to do research
because of the present nature of their work, makes it difficult
to recruit the requisite staff.

However, if FDA reviewers approve a drug that turns out to
be unsafe or ineffective, particularly one that ends up being
unsafe, then FDA and these reviewers will take a major share
of the criticism -- this criticism will come from the public,
from Congress, and from the Executive Branch, including
criticism of the reviewers by fellow FDA staff. The result of
this situation is probably that FDA and its reviewers have
become conservative in their market approval policy -- the
negative incentives appear to be much stronger than the positive
incentives related to drug approval. Hence, to change the drug
laws without changing FDA staff incentives may be a futile
exercise, depending on what one is trying to accomplish. This
is not meant to be a criticism of the process of drug market
approval. It is meant to reveal what the author's thoughts are
with respect to changing the process of drug approval while
ignoring problems perhaps even more important than the process
itself (5).

Given the above discussed assumptions and definitions, the
next topic that is covered is the background or setting in
which the DRRA was introduced. Two areas are of importance
here. The first is the other influences, besides FDA regulation, that affect the ability of U.S. pharmaceutical firms to
carry out innovative research and, ultimately, develop new
drugs as a result of the discovery of NCE's. The second is the
numerous criticisms that have been leveled at FDA by the
pharmaceutical industry, Congress, academia, public interest
groups, etc.

One needs to be cognizant of the influences, discussed
immediately below, on the drug industry other than FDA regulation because these influences also effect (1) the amount of R&D
expenditures and (2) the proportion of these expenditures that
go into drug discovery research. The cost of discovery and
development of a new drug is a starting place for examining other
influences, since other things relate back to it regarding the
ability of firms to finance drug R&D. It has been estimated

recently that the cost of discovery and development for a new drug is now approximately $50 million (6). This estimate includes the cost of failures during research. Of this cost, about half is for discovery and half for clinical testing of the drug to determine its suitability for marketing -- i.e., is it safe and effective? FDA, until this year, was not involved in the discovery or innovative phase. They have now started to regulate animal toxicology laboratories, hence they have become involved in the innovative phase since it depends heavily on animal testing. FDA has estimated the cost of this involvement to industry, academia and the government at about $50 million (7), but industry claims it will be more. In fact, during informal discussions of the DRRA, one drug company executive asserted that it would cost his firm alone $20 million to comply with FDA's animal toxicology regulations. The point is that FDA is now involved in the discovery phase via a new regulation it has promulgated, but the impact of this involvement on R&D costs is still uncertain.

FDA's primary impact is on the other half of the costs of obtaining drug market approval -- the development phase. Accepting the estimate of $50 million and that half of this goes to the developmental phase, we have $25 million in cost that is split up in several ways. A part of the clinical testing would be done regardless of FDA's regulations on market approval. Drug firms would do this testing to decide which patients would benefit from the drug (i.e., what the market is); to prevent negligence suits; and to satisfy corporate ethics. Certainly the degree of testing might vary from company to company. The problem is estimating how much would be done and how well. The same goes for labeling, package inserts for physicians and other marketing functions. The view to date is that government must watch over the pharmaceutical industry to assure the public of safe and effective drugs. Thus, at least some proportion of development phase costs must be attributed to FDA regulation. To date, no one has been able or willing to estimate what this proportion is.

Whatever the proportion of development phase costs that can be attributed to FDA regulation is, it has been clearly demonstrated that the cost of drug research and development has been increasing significantly -- from $30 million in 1967 to $54 million in 1976 by one estimate (6). The cost of testing equipment and materials, scientific personnel, facilities, etc. needed to meet government regulation or due to other factors have all contributed. These are areas where the DRRA will have little if any impact. Yet the cost of R&D is very important because it determines how far an R&D dollar goes, just as food prices determine how far our food dollar goes.

Besides the market approval regulations of FDA, there are other FDA regulations that influence the cost of drugs. The most significant of these is the set of regulations for good

manufacturing practices (GMP's). The GMP's are presently being
revised, and there is considerable debate as to what the
economic impact of these revisions will be on the pharmaceutical
industry.

One important area of regulation outside FDA's regulatory
authority are cost containment policies and programs such as
maximum allowable cost (MAC). (MAC is a proposed HEW program
whose objective is to lower the cost of drugs purchased through
Medicare-Medicaid without sacrificing the quality of drugs
purchased). This program, which FDA is only a contributor to
through its expertise in such areas as bioequivalence, can be
expected to decrease the revenues of drug firms because the
indication is that the volume of drugs sold will stay the same
but the sales price will be the same or lower for drugs under
this program. The effect of a decrease in sales revenue is
quite likely to be a decrease in R&D expenditures (9).
Referring to what was said earlier, I cannot conclude that this
decrease in R&D expenditures will lead to a decrease in drug
innovation.

The international drug law and regulation situation
presents still another influence on the ability of U.S. drug
firms to generate sales and hence R&D dollars. Although many
U.S. pharmaceutical firms have argued that drug regulation in
this country is, in many instances, forcing them to invest
abroad, this is not to say that drug laws and regulations are
not also getting stricter in other countries. In fact, Wardell,
in his most recent work on the so-called "drug lag", says that
the U.S. is closing the gap between Great Britain and the U.S.
in new drugs approved; one of the reasons he gives is a relative
increase in drug regulation by Great Britain (10). Finally, on
the international side, we can expect foreign competition to
increase as scientific capabilities of other nations expand in
the pharmaceutical field. Productivity in other nations
relative to the U.S. is an increasingly important topic of
discussion, and there is no reason to believe that it will not
be just as important an issue in the drug area as it is in
other areas.

Although there are probably other relevant influences on
drug innovation besides the FDA's regulatory efforts, the last
influence I will mention is a potential one -- national health
insurance (NHI). Actually, NHI could lead to an expansion of
sales revenue and hence R&D dollars. The reason for this is
that NHI is expected to make health care (including, of course,
treatment by drugs) available to a larger population than is
now the case. Offsetting these expected revenue effects would
be regulatory programs such as MAC.

All of the above influences that impose costs on drug firms
do so only to a certain extent. That extent is the degree to
which the drug firms can raise their prices to cover cost
increases. The consumer then pays the cost and, in a sense,

helps to maintain R&D in the pharmaceutical field. Foreign
competition is one factor that would limit the ability of drug
firms to cover cost increases. Cost containment policies for
health care could emerge as another.

In addition to the non-FDA influences described above with
respect to their effect on the ability of U.S. pharmaceutical
firms to fund R&D, the background for the revision of the FD&C
Act includes the criticisms of FDA regulation that the DRRA is
attempting to address. One often advanced criticism has already
been discussed -- the cost of research and development for
discovery and marketing of a new drug. (No conclusion was drawn
by the author with respect to the magnitude of FDA's impact on
this cost). Another criticism of FDA and the statutory authority it operates under is that there is a "drug lag" (safe and
effective drugs are approved quicker in other countries than in
the U.S. as indicated earlier for Great Britain and the U.S.)
in the U.S. as a result of the FD&C Act, particularly the 1962
Amendments to the Act, and of the way in which FDA has implemented the drug laws. The consequences of this "drug lag" as
put forth by the proponents of the argument are that some drugs
that are therapeutically significant are not available to people
living in the U.S. as a result of FDA regulation (10). Attempts
have been made to quantify this loss (11), but even Peltzman's
well-known cost-benefit study has not escaped criticism (12).
The criticism appears to at least partially negate Peltzman's
conclusion that the costs of the 1962 Amendments exceed their
benefits -- costs in Peltzman's study refer to "effective"
drugs that do not reach the U.S. consumer and benefits refer to
"ineffective" drugs kept off the U.S. market. Nevertheless, the
speed at which drugs are granted market approval and the impact
of FDA and its authority on drug innovation (the two parameters
of the "drug lag") are still viable issues.

U.S. drug laws have also been criticized for not allowing
drug companies to export drugs that have not received FDA
approval for marketing in the U.S., but have a potential
market(s) outside the U.S. and are considered acceptable in
this market(s). Since requirements for obtaining market
approval vary by country, some drugs not yet acted on regarding
market approval or denied approval in the U.S. may still be
eligible for approval elsewhere in the world. Consequently,
U.S. drug firms are given the incentive to locate facilities
abroad (13).

A criticism advanced by many individuals and groups, but
not by the pharmaceutical industry, is that the FDA operates in
secrecy when it decides whether to grant market approval for a
drug. The argument is that since the safety and efficiency
data that drug firms submit to FDA in support of a drug are
proprietary, the public is not given sufficient information to
have meaningful input into the approval process. The argument
is then usually extended to say that drugs are being approved

that are either unsafe or ineffective as a result of pressure
from the pharmaceutical industry (14).

Finally, the rate of return (ROR) on R&D investment in the
drug industry and the possible effect of FDA regulation on ROR
has been examined. Schwartzman has argued that even though the
potential for discovering important drugs is significant, drug
companies will actually cut back their R&D programs (17). The
reason for this cutback, he argues, is that the expected ROR for
a drug firm with respect to its R&D activities has declined from
11.4 percent in 1960 to 3.3 percent in 1972. It is argued that
FDA regulation is one of the factors in this decrease. Opponents
have argued that if ROR on R&D were as low as 3.3 percent, then
drug companies would stop investing in drug R&D -- the critique
of Schwartzman's work is not this simple, of course, but this is
a major point.

Economic Analysis of the DRRA

The DRRA was submitted to Congress on March 16, 1978. The
proposed Act, if passed, would represent the first total revision of the drug portion of the F, D and C Act since its
passage in 1938 and the 1962 Amendments. The DRRA constitutes
a rewrite of all facets of the present U.S. drug laws—i.e.,
it revises statutory authority with respect to market approval,
manufacture, distribution, promotion and use of pharmaceuticals.
In addition, it provides the statutory authority to deal with
problems that arise after a drug is granted market approval.
This authority includes the right of FDA to ask for reports
on experience with a drug's use and provides for stiffer
enforcement mechanisms. The DRRA also authorizes the establishment of a National Center for Clinical Pharmacology (NCCP) as
part of HEW.

More specifically, it is proposed under Title I that the
present process of obtaining market approval for a new drug
(the New Drug Application (NDA) process) be replaced with one
that includes establishing a monograph for a drug entity first,
and then obtaining a license to market drug products made up of
one or more drug entities. The monograph represents the
innovator's submission of evidence to FDA that has the purpose
of establishing the conditions for safety and efficacy of the
drug entity. The basis of deciding whether a drug product
should be licensed is the compliance of the product with the
requisites of the monograph (see 16 and 17 for elaboration on
the monograph).

Title I of the DRRA also attempts to provide flexibility
in the investigational use of human drugs. It does so by
categorizing these drug investigations into three types for
the purposes of regulation—drug innovation, drug development,
and drug treatment—and gearing the regulations to the type of
investigation while still maintaining the goal of protecting

human subjects. In addition, Title I sets forth protective measures for those who use a drug once it has obtained market approval. These measures pertain to drug labeling and marketing techniques as well as to educational programs for consumers and health professionals.

The only other part of the proposed Act bearing a direct relationship to the discussion in this paper is the provision setting forth conditions under which a drug product not approved for marketing in the United States may be exported (see 16 and 17 for more detail on the DRRA).

The analysis of sections of the DRRA that follows expands on those parts of the Act that have consequences for drug innovation through their economic implications. Again, it should be emphasized that the impact of the proposed DRRA depends on how the proposed Act is implemented. The manner in which it is promulgated is crucial to estimating its consequences. For example, will the good manufacturing practices now in force be carried over under the new Act? And, what about the recently proposed revisions of the bio-research monitoring program for safety and efficacy testing of drug entities, as well as other drug research? Will they remain intact? These decisions will primarily be made when rules are promulgated based on a new drug law. When this occurs, the pharmaceutical industry, the public, and other governmental entities will have an opportunity to affect how the law is implemented. Of course, these same groups now have an opportunity to affect the proposed law, which is written in more general language then the implementing rules will be. This is the reason for the uncertainty as to what impacts a new law will have.

The sections of the DRRA to be discussed with respect to economic implications and, eventually, impact on R&D expenditures, can be divided into two categories -- (1) time and cost saving provisions, and (2) time and cost expending provisions.

There are four sections or provisions of the DRRA that are discussed in this paper that fall under the "time and cost saving" category:

   -- the "breakthrough" drug provisions;
   -- the export provision;
   -- the drug innovation provision;
   -- the batch certification provision.

The listing represents a subjective ranking of the four provisions (which may represent one or more sections of the DRRA) based on the author's perception of which provisions will have the larger time and cost savings.

The "breakthrough" drug provisions of the DRRA are expected by FDA to increase the availability of significant new drugs in the U.S. Drugs that are considered to be therapeutically significant advances (whether they are or not is usually

a point of disagreement between industry and government as stated
above) will, under this provision, be given the opportunity for
faster market approval. These provisions, therefore, would be
expected to decrease the "drug lag" in the United States. In
addition, drug companies would receive sales from these products
earlier, hence revenues available for R&D funding would be
expected to increase. Offsetting these revenues, however, will
be the costs of the post-marketing requirements for a "breakthrough" drug, including recordkeeping and reporting.

The export provision in the DRRA will allow, under certain
restrictions, drugs that contain an entity, or entities, for
which there is not an approved monograph(s) to be marketed outside the United States. This provision can be expected to slow,
to some extent, the shift of pharmaceutical firm investment
abroad. The extent, again, depends on how the Act is administered. There are other factors, however, affecting investment
abroad--investment and tax incentives, wage rates, availability
of scientific personnel, etc. These factors may swamp the
effect of the export provision.

Dividing, for purposes of analysis, the stages of drug
research and development into the innovative phase and the
developmental phase, the DRRA offers the possibility of less
restrictions in the innovation phase; i.e., the drug innovation
provision. This provision states that in the initial phase of
clinical trials for new drugs, only those aspects of the trials
that may adversely affect the health or rights of participants
will be regulated--scientific design and other technical aspects
will not be. If the Act were implemented to accomplish what its
stated objectives are, and if the intensity of review by FDA in
the developmental phase increased by shifting resources, the
cost to pharmaceutical companies of bringing a drug to market,
and the time it takes to bring a drug to market, should decrease.

The final cost and time saving to be discussed is the batch
certification provision. The important aspect of this provision
is that FDA, not industry as in the past, will now be responsible
for certifying the quality of batches of such drugs as antibiotics. Hence, given that FDA would be paying the bill and
would be responsible in part for an adequate supply of drugs such
as antibiotics, the certification process is expected to be
timely. Furthermore, under this provision, companies can establish a certification record that will allow them to be exempted
from this requirement--a time as well as cost savings.

Four provisions will be discussed in this paper under the
time and cost expending provisions. Subjectively ranked in
order of probable time and cost expenditures, they are:

-- the safety and efficacy data release provision,
-- the post-marketing study and monitoring provisions,
-- the patient package insert (PPI) provision, and
-- the unit of use packaging provision.

The impact of the safety and efficacy release provision is, at present, one of the few impacts for which publicly available, quantitative impact data exists. This provision permits the disclosure of safety and efficacy data submitted for a drug entity monograph. The degree to which data is made public depends on whether the monograph has been approved; portions of the data are available prior to monograph approval only to individuals or entities that take part in the hearing on the approval request. All data reports are available without restriction after monograph approval, subject to the five year provision discussed below.

Because data is released prior to approval of the monograph, the participation of more individuals and entities in the process may, at least in some cases, slow down the approval of monographs. On the other hand, the disclosure of data allows more scientific knowledge to come to bear on the decision of approving a drug entity. Furthermore, the availability of all data after monograph approval is expected to reduce duplicative testing to support the safety and efficacy of a drug product, because the necessary studies for a drug entity are already available. Estimates of the degree of duplicative testing would obviously be useful in assessing the benefits of this provision. To date, no reliable estimates are publicly available.

Although the DRRA states that no one can use the safety and efficacy data submitted by an innovator to request the approval of a monograph, a study by the Economic Staff of the Food and Drug Administration concludes that, based on certain assumptions about the loss of market share by innovative ("research-intensive") firms, the degree of shift in sales to foreign firms, and the amount of sales gained by non-research-intensive firms, the disclosure of safety and efficacy data will still have a negative impact on pharmaceutical R&D expenditures (18).

The FDA study contains the following paragraph in the Executive Summary:

> "Full disclosure of S&E data is estimated to decrease U.S. pharmaceutical firms' R&D expenditures by $56 million or up to 4.7 percent of recent levels of R&D. The impact on R&D investment is a consequence of increased competition in the industry and the accompanying shifts in sales from innovators to other U.S. firms and to foreign firms. Innovative or research-intensive firms in the aggregate invest a higher proportion of sales into R&D than other U.S. firms. The estimated potential loss in sales of all U.S. firms is approximately $600 million, an event which would occur over a multi-year period." (18)

It is noted in the Executive Summary to the FDA study that the impacts given in the above paragraph do not take account of the possible "mitigating effects" of the May 17, 1978, version of the DRRA, such as the provision that the data cannot for a period of five years be used to obtain market approval for a drug product without the permission of the individual or entity that submitted the data originally. On the other side of the coin, however, is the fact that if one does not accept some or all of the assumptions of the FDA study, the sales loss, and in turn the loss in R&D funds, could be significantly greater.

The competition, through "intelligence" use (i.e., acquiring knowledge from) of safety and efficacy data, and through its use to obtain approval to introduce generics onto the market, could have another negative effect besides that on R&D expenditures. The incentive for innovators would be to shift the introduction of new drugs to foreign markets, thereby accentuating the "drug lag". Of course, the increased competition may increase innovation. It is difficult to estimate the consequences of provisions in the DRRA for post-marketing studies to, say, examine an adverse finding more carefully or monitor drugs after approval. These provisions are discretionary; hence, the number of drugs to which they would apply is impossible to estimate. Also, costing out such requirements is equally difficult because of limited U.S. experience. On the whole, however, it might be anticipated that marketing approval for some drugs would be granted earlier with the availability of these provisions. Hence, there would be a possible time savings, but at some cost. This cost for post-marketing studies could, however, be more than offset by increased revenues. This provision is in the time and cost expended category because the argument that it will cost appears stronger than the argument that it will save since the latter argument is more conjectural in nature.

The patient package insert (PPI) provision (this provides that patient information on dosage, adverse effects, etc., would be included with prescription as well as over-the-counter drugs) of the DRRA appears to have gathered more attention on the cost impact side than is warranted. The PPI should save expensive physician time at a small cost per prescription. However, as long as no hard figures exist, the cost of PPIs will undoubtedly continue to be an issue.

And, finally, there is unit-of-use packaging (i.e., certain drugs may be required to be packaged in quantities used in an "acceptable treatment regimen"). This is again a discretionary provision. How costly? Even if the number of drugs that would fall under this provision were known, it is necessary to estimate the cost of switching the pharmaceutical production and marketing system over to unit-of-use packaging methods. This would require some detailed cost work.

Summary and Conclusions

It can be seen from the above discussion that there are some potential time and cost savings associated with the DRRA that are expected to contribute to the R&D effort of pharmaceutical firms. However, there are also some potential time and cost losses associated with the DRRA. Furthermore, there is a paucity of quantitative estimates of those time and cost savings and losses.

Presently, no definitive conclusion can be reached on the economic consequences of the DRRA. Furthermore, it is never expected that all the monetary benefits and costs can be summed to arrive at such a conclusion, or to make an assessment of the impact on innovation resulting from these benefits and costs. However, there is an obvious need for more and better economic analysis.

A look at what has been done to date reveals that only one provision of the proposed Act, the safety and efficacy data release section, has been studied in any significant detail for economic impact. Admittedly, this provision is one of the most important, but the other provisions discussed in this paper could, either singly or in some combination, have an even greater economic impact and, consequently, impact on drug innovation. In addition, there are other provisions with seemingly less economic and innovative impact, not discussed above, which may be elevated to importance or added as the 1979 version of the DRRA is reviewed and revised by Congress.

I would like to make a plea. Although the DRRA is not the only force bearing on the success of the pharmaceutical industry and the issue, therefore, of drug innovation, it is potentially one of the most important pieces of legislation, and thus forces, to affect this industry. Therefore, I would like to see increased cooperation on the part of both industry and government with respect to data resources and studies of the DRRA. It all goes back to an emphasis on analysis that is designed to contribute to a policymaker's ability to make decisions, and not on analysis designed to win arguments.

Finally, not to overemphasize the role of economics in making decisions on issues such as those surrounding the DRRA, it may be that economics can and should play only a small part in these decisions. That is, perhaps such decisions should be based primarily on social grounds. Too much appears to be expected of economic analysis, particularly cost-benefit analysis. Normally only parts of a problem and alternatives to solving it are amenable to economic analysis. We should not expect more regardless of the recent surge in demands for economic impact analysis.

Literature Cited

1. Mitchell, Samuel A., and Link, Emery A. (editors), "Impact
    of Public Policy on Drug Innovation and Pricing; Proceedings
    of the Third Seminar on Pharmaceutical Public Policy Issues",
    pp. 47-82, The American University, Washington, D.C., 1976.

2. Mashaw, Jerry L., and Merrill, Richard A., "Introduction to
    the American Public Law System: Cases and Materials", West
    Publishing Co., St. Paul, Minn., 1975.

3. Schwartzman, David, "Innovation in the Pharmaceutical Indus-
    try", The Johns Hopkins University Press, Baltimore and
    London, 1976.

4. "Unhealthy Costs of Health Care", Business Week, September 4,
    1978, pp. 58-68.

5. Myrdal, Gunnar, "Objectivity in Social Research", Pantheon,
    New York, New York, 1969.

6. Hansen, Ronald W., "The Pharmaceutical Development Process:
    Estimates of Current Development Costs and Times and the
    Effects of Regulatory Changes", University of Rochester,
    Rochester, New York, 1977 (mimeograph).

7. Updegraff, Gail, "Some Thoughts on Professor Hansen's Paper;
    'The Pharmaceutical Development Process: Estimates of Current
    Costs and Times and the Effects of Regulatory Changes'", Food
    and Drug Administration, Rockville, Maryland, 1977 (mimeo-
    graph).

8. Reinsch, Susan, "Economic Impact Assessment of Proposed Rule-
    making—Non-Clinical Laboratory Studies; Good Laboratory
    Practices", Food and Drug Administration, Rockville, Maryland,
    1978 (mimeograph).

9. Pracon, Incorporated, "Study to Assess Impacts of Releasing
    Safety and Effectiveness Data on the Pharmaceutical Industry's
    Incentives to Invest In and Conduct Research and Development
    Programs", Food and Drug Administration Contract No. 228-77-
    8052, Vienna, Virginia, 1978.

10. Lasagna, Louis; Wardell, William; and Hansen, Ronald,
    "Technological Innovation and Government Regulation of
    Pharmaceuticals in the U.S. and Great Britain", National
    Science Foundation Grant No. RDA-75 19066-00, University of
    Rochester, Rochester, New York, 1977.

11. Peltzmen, Sam, "Regulation of Pharmaceutical Innovation; The 1962 Amendments", American Enterprise Institute for Public Policy Research, Washington, D.C., 1974.

12. McGuire, Thomas; Nelson, Richard; and Spavins, Thomas, "An Evaluation of Consumer Protection Legislation: The 1962 Drug Amendments: A Comment", Jour. Pol. Econ., (1975), Vol. 83, (No. 3), pp. 655-661.

13. Grabowski, Henry G., "Drug Regulation and Innovation; Empirical Evidence and Policy Options", American Enterprise Institute for Public Policy Research, Washington, D.C., 1976.

14. Department of Health, Education and Welfare, "Review Panel on New Drug Regulation", Government Printing Office, Washington, D.C., 1977.

15. Schwartzman, David, "The Expected Return from Pharmaceutical Research; Sources of New Drugs and the Profitability of R&D Investment", American Enterprise Institute for Public Policy Research, Washington, D.C., 1975.

16. H.R. 11611 and S. 2755, 95th Congress, 2nd Session, "Drug Regulation Reform Act of 1978", May 16, 1978.

17. Department of Health, Education and Welfare, "Drug Regulation Reform Act of 1978; Section-by-Section Analysis; H.R. 11611 and S. 2755", 95th Congress, 2nd Session.

18. Dworkin, Fay, "Impact of Disclosure of Safety and Efficacy Data on Expenditures for Pharmaceutical Research and Development", Food and Drug Administration, Rockville, Maryland, 1978 (mimeograph).

RECEIVED March 8, 1979.

Meeting the Challenge of the Toxic Substances Control Act with Technological Innovation

JOHN DeKANY and STEVEN MALKENSON

U.S. Environmental Protection Agency, 401 M St., SW, Washington, DC 20460

As most of you know, the Toxic Substances Control Act
(TSCA) was enacted in October, 1976. Several factors were critical in the drive for this law. First, there was an increasing
awareness of the threat chemicals can present to human health
and the environment. This threat was (and is) not adequately
understood because little data is available and the state-of-
the-art in assessing risk is rudimentary. This element of the
unknown added to the unacceptability of the situation.

Secondly, in many cases certain segments of society were being forced (sometimes unknowingly and involuntarily) to assume
substantial risks. Workers, consumers, and the general public
have been exposed to dangerous chemical substances at work, in
consumer products, and in the water they drink and the air they
breathe.

In general, the public was ill-equipped to respond to this
dilemma - it had neither information nor a vehicle to obtain it.
Interestingly, however, we can cite examples of isolated cases
where the public, when informed of a potential risk, was willing to go out of its way to control it. Consumers have been extremely reluctant, for example, to buy remaining inventories of
products utilizing fluorocarbon propellants. They have been
willing to accept the products in less desirable packaging as a
tradeoff for the increased measure of environmental safety associated with their use. Another indication of this phenomena
has been the premium prices consumers are willing to pay for
organically-grown food. Do not mistake this as a condemnation
of pesticides, but rather an indication of the genuine cost
people associate with uncertainty regarding unknown toxic effects of chemicals.

Understandably, responsible businesspeople are constantly
under competitive pressure to keep costs down and margins high.
It would have been extremely difficult for a company to carry
out an extensive testing program if their competitors did not.
This might lower return (at least in the short-run), and

correspondingly have negative impacts on the firms' competitive position in the marketplace.

In passing TSCA, Congress found this combination of circumstances to be unacceptable. The Environmental Protection Agency was given 4 major powers under the Act to work toward better understanding the problem and eliminating "unreasonable risks" from chemical substances. They are as follows:

1) Reporting - EPA can require chemical manufacturers to report certain types of data which will enable the Agency to more effectively assess the risks associated with particular substances. This includes information on chemical identity, use, production volume, exposure, and existing health and safety studies.

2) Testing - EPA can require manufacturers to perform health and safety studies on specific chemicals or categories of chemicals that the Agency feels may present an "unreasonable risk to human health or the environment."

3) Regulatory - TSCA gives EPA broad authority to regulate any chemical that the Agency finds presents an "unreasonable risk to human health or the environment." The Agency may take action at any stage of the chemical's lifecycle - manufacture, processing, distribution, use, or disposal, in order to eliminate this unreasonable risk.

4) Premanufacture Notification - The Toxics Act requires chemical manufacturers to give EPA 90 days notice before commencing commercial production on any new chemical substance. Through premanufacture notification, the Agency is charged with the responsibility of regulating unreasonable risks from these new chemicals before they occur.

As I have described, in passing TSCA, Congress charged EPA with the responsibility to prevent chemicals from presenting unreasonable risks to human health or the environment. At the same time, however, Congress directed the Agency to implement the Act so as not to "unduly impede technological innovation." Striking a balance between these two objectives is one of the incredible challenges we all must face in the coming years. In a sense, it is also one of our goals to address this issue here today.

The section of TSCA that will most directly effect innovation, research, and development in new chemicals is premanufacturing notification. Consequently, a more detailed description of this program would be appropriate.

Manufacturers proposing to produce a new chemical for commercial purposes for the first time must first submit certain types of information to EPA to enable the Agency to evaluate the potential risk attributable to that chemical substance. Examples of the information to be required include chemical identity, projected uses, production volume, and data on human exposure and environmental release. Additionally, manufacturers are expected to test new substances as necessary to assess their potential to cause specific adverse human health and environmental effects.

Based on this information (supplemented with data on substitute products and the projected economic significance of the chemical), the Agency will take one of the following courses of action:

1) Do nothing. This allows the manufacturer to commence production of the chemical upon the expiration of the 90-day notification period. It does not constitute an EPA endorsement of the safety or efficacy of the substance.

2) If the Agency feels insufficient test data has been submitted to allow a "reasoned evaluation" of the risk presented by the chemical, it can act to limit or prohibit manufacture of the substance until sufficient data has been submitted. In this event, EPA must specify the necessary tests. Action taken under this option would be subject to court review.

3) If the Agency feels the chemical presents an "unreasonable risk to health or the environment," it may regulate the chemical in such a way to eliminate the unreasonable risk.

EPA is conducting an extensive study in order to more fully understand the impact of the premanufacturing review program on innovation in new chemicals. Although the lack of data in this area is discouraging, we are doing the best we can to quantitatively evaluate the effect on both the input (in terms of R&D dollars) and the output (in terms of new chemical substances) of the innovative process.

There are two aspects of this program that will effect the research and development investment decision. First, the costs of premanufacture notification (including testing costs) will increase the investment in R&D necessary to develop and market new chemicals. The health and safety properties of a chemical must now be considered an intrinsic part of the new chemical development process, right alongside consideration of the substances commercial properties. Both are equal parts of the "total product". To the extent that this results in increased testing for health and environmental effects, the amount of investment required to achieve a given level of output from R&D will also rise.

Secondly, the additional uncertainty that a new chemical will be environmentally unacceptable will increase the risk associated with the investment decision. Given the increased data that will be available relating to a chemical's health and environmental effects, decision-makers will be more aware of any risks a new substance may present. In many cases, the manufacturer will be able to sufficiently control this risk through the use of safeguards - for example, controlling emissions or proper labeling. In some cases, however, risks may be unavoidable as a direct result of the chemical's use. I think we would all agree that it would be unreasonable for a chemical to be used as a detergent in commodity quantities if it were

found to be carcinogenic. To the extent that the increased
awareness of the chemical's toxicity resulting from premanufacture testing presents an additional uncertainty in the innovation process, the number of new chemicals being marketed in a
given year may decrease.

Both these factors - increased testing and additional uncertainty, will reduce the output of research and development
in the chemical industry (if measured by numbers of new chemicals
marketed) that would likely be achieved in their absence. It is
an undeniable fact that the market for some low volume, specialty
chemicals will not be sufficient to justify the expenditure necessary to perform adequate health and safety testing. It would be
foolish of me to stand before you and deny this.

But let me also be quick to point out that the impacts will
not be as significant as they at first appear. The number of
new chemicals is not a complete measure of the output of chemical innovation. It ignores qualitative factors about the chemicals, a very important one of which is the unintended environmental and health effects resulting from the use of the product.
In this respect, it is one of the goals of the premanufacture
review program to improve the quality of output of the innovative
process.

Furthermore, I think we will all agree that the implicit responsibility for assuring the safety of a chemical has always
rested with its manufacturer. All TSCA does is make this responsibility explicit. To the extent that a manufacturer has
responsibly dealt with this problem in the past (through testing and withholding undesirable chemicals from the market), the
incremental impact of TSCA will be minimal. It is the manufacturers who have habitually avoided this responsibility that will
be most impacted. In effect, Congress has said we can not wait
any longer for these firms to take this responsibility on
voluntarily.

The point I would like to emphasize is that EPA is sensitive
to the effect of its programs, particularly premanufacture notification, on the development of new chemicals. The Agency is
actively seeking ways to mitigate this impact, and several
possibilities are already under investigation. One alternative
involves some form of financial assistance to developers of new
chemicals. A fund could be established by the chemical industry
or Congress which could help finance health and environmental
testing of new chemicals. Manufacturers could pay back the
fund according to the commercial success ultimately achieved
by the chemicals for which testing was in part financed by the
fund. Another program under consideration by EPA is the offer-
ing of technical assistance by the Agency in the designing of
test programs and the filing of premanufacture notices. I am
not hesitant to say that you may contact me personally with any
additional ideas to help in this area.

I can safely say that the tradeoff between health and en-

vironmental protection and technological innovation is excruti-
atingly difficult to make, but it is one we must make. The
larger question then becomes, "what parts can we all play to
optimize the outcome?" Ironically, the answer rests in part in
seeking innovative and creative responses to the problem.

Let me first answer this question from the perspective of
the Environmental Protection Agency. The first positive step
we can take is to recognize the natural tension that exists
between the cost of information and the value of information in
addressing risks to be presented by chemical substances. From
a purely scientific viewpoint, more data is always better. However, data is not free and its potential usefulness must be
carefully weighed against its cost. We can be sensitive to this
by promulgating responsible test guidelines that ask only for
test data appropriate for assessing the reasonableness of the
risk presented by a particular substance given its unique identity, structure, uses, and exposures.

Secondly, EPA seeks a cooperative, informal relationship
with industry. Solutions to difficult problems are easier to
reach when people are working with each other, not in opposite
directions. We will work hard not to bog industry down with unnecessary administrative and technical requirements.

Thirdly, the Agency will act only when necessary under the
regulatory authorities granted under Section 5 of TSCA. Consistent with the principals of Regulatory Reform, we are constantly
looking for innovative alternatives to command and control regulations. A good example of this is one of the approaches the
Office of Toxic Substances is exploring with respect to non-
propellant uses of chlorofluorocarbons. A system of marketable
permits sold to the highest bidder could perhaps be used in this
case to ration fluorocarbon emissions among its most valuable
uses.

Let me now turn to industry's role in minimizing the adverse effect of TSCA on innovation. I would urge recognition
and acceptance of an important objective of Congress in passing
the Toxics Act to assess health and environmental risks associated with new chemicals prior to their initial manufacture. By
institutionalizing a testing program that parallels new chemical
research as early as feasible in the R&D cycle, chemists can
concentrate their efforts on chemical structures with few or no
toxic properties. In this way, firms can avoid investing large
efforts in chemicals environmentally unacceptable for anticipated uses.

Secondly, firms should cooperate with EPA in spirit and
action by moving voluntarily to mitigate risks (when present)
from toxic new chemicals. Appropriate actions might include
taking precautions and safeguards to limit exposure to humans
or the environment in manufacture, use, and disposal. I can
cite many examples where chemical companies have faced environmental problems in certain of their activities, and with the

help of a little innovative thinking (and sometimes some technical and technological research) have turned the problem
around into a profitable opportunity. In one case, Ontario
Paper Company was producing large amounts of unwanted chemical
byproducts from a particular manufacturing process. Chemists
there found a way to convert lignum to vanillan, thus eliminating the disposal problem and providing a source of revenue at
the same time. In another instance, Union Carbide developed
the "Brodie Purifier Process", which cut production costs of
certain high purity organic chemicals by 20% to 50% and reduced
waterborne wastes at the same time. Allied Chemical's new process for manufacturing aluminum sulfate cuts production costs,
reduces process wastes, and eliminates discharge all at the
same time. I could continue with examples, but the important
thing is that through innovative technical and technological
thinking, many problems can be controlled and disruptions to
the R&D process can be minimized.

A critical role in the successful tradeoff between controlling risk and protecting innovation will also be played by
toxicologists - whether in government, industry, universities,
or elsewhere. Although we all might agree that the field of
toxicology is advancing very quickly, the state-of-the-art is
still archaic. The development of cheaper, more reliable
screening tests for various toxic effects is critical to the
success of this program.

We must all work together and share the burden in supporting this effort to achieve the dual objectives of maintaining
innovation in the chemical industry and controlling unreasonable
risks to health and the environment from these same chemicals.
Some compromises must be made from each objective, but working
together we can achieve the optimal solution.

RECEIVED March 21, 1979.

The Effect of Government Regulation on Innovation in the Chemical Industry

ARTHUR GERSTENFELD
Department of Management, Worcester Polytechnic Institute, Worcester, MA 01607

HOWARD K. NASON
I.R.I. Research Corporation, 7800 Bonhomme Avenue, St. Louis, MO 63105

This paper addresses issues concerned with the effects of government performance regulations on innovation, (as differentiated from economic regulations) with particular focus on the chemical industry. There is perhaps no other topic more timely these days than that of government regulation and its effect on what generally is conceded to be a lagging innovation process in the U.S. There are scarcely any meetings of business persons, government officials, or academics where this topic does not emerge as a central concern for today's economy.

The concerns are not limited to the borders of the United States since regulatory differences are now being cited as an important factor affecting international balance of trade. It is clear that if some area of the U.S. economy has imposed on it more stringent requirements than a foreign counterpart the U.S. regulations must result in increased costs, hence an unfavorable trade pattern. However, for the purposes of this discussion we shall limit our attention to three aspects, namely growth of performance regulations; unintended consequences; and prescriptions for improvement.

I. Growth of Regulations

Prior to 1960 there were few performance regulations affecting chemicals in industry and the environment. Some of the legislation that has since come into effect includes: (1)
The Clean Air Act
The Energy Supply and Environmental
    Coordination Act
The Clean Water Act

0-8412-0511-6/79/47-109-173$05.00/0
© 1979 American Chemical Society

The Federal Environmental Pesticide Control Act
The Occupational Safety and Health Act
The Federal Insecticide; Fungicide, and
    Rodenticide Act
The Mine Safety and Health Act
The Fish and Wildlife Coordination Act
The Coastal Zone Management Act
The Hazardous Materials Transportation Act
The Marine Protection Research and
    Sanctuaries Act
The Resource Conservation and Recovery Act
The Solid Waste Disposal Act
The Toxic Substances Control Act, and
The Transportation Safety Act

There is little doubt in our minds that economic
historians will identify the time from 1960 to the
present as "The Regulatory Period". Regulation today
has not only increased in volume but has increased in
breadth (2). One used to equate regulations with
"Regulatory Controlled Industries" i.e., transportation, utilities, etc. However, there is scarcely an
industry today that is not affected by the spectre of
government regulations. The chemical industry has
been particularly affected.

II. Unintended Consequences

In order to examine the unintended consequences
from this large growth of government regulation we
shall first consider the major forces that have caused
this growth to appear. Rising incomes often result
in demands for social legislation. These demands have
been coupled with engineering and science sophistication and change is coming about rapidly. New products
and processes constantly appear with ever decreasing
product life cycles, with demands for requirements
often exceeding the original intention.

Focusing on unintended consequences, it has been
pointed out that although we desperately need better
medicines, the current state of drug regulation is
standing in the way of that objective (3). There is
essentially no area of medicine that does not suffer
from inadequate drugs. Cancer patients receive little
help from present therapies and schizophrenics would
welcome treatment that does not carry with it the risk
of irreversible neurological damage. One consequence
of current regulations is that it now takes a U.S.
firm about 8 years and $54 million to bring one of its
drugs to the U.S. market (4). Recent studies show
that many new drugs are available for the treatment of

the afflicted from 3 to 15 years sooner in other countries, such as Great Britain, Canada and Germany, than
in the U.S. Some attempts have been made to calculate
the effects in lives saved vs. damage from unantici-
pated side effects, but more definitive data of this
kind is needed. The effect is, however, significant.

A great threat to chemical innovation is inconsistent government regulations, often as dysfunctional
as the regulation themselves (5). Inconsistency and
indecision by Federal Agencies cause companies to
withdraw financial support from projects at critical
times. Regulatory inconsistencies leave company management unable to predict whether a new product or
process will be acceptable. Nason has stated that
regulation-driven changes can have positive effects on
innovation, though at great economic and social costs.
(6). Examples include the development of more sensitive and reliable automatic instrumentation for monitoring chemicals, radiation and biological materials
in the environment, of safety-or-environment-related
add-on equipment for vehicles, of pollution-control
technology and of safety-related equipment for use in
industry, mining and the home.
A major concern is the effect of regulation on
the innovation process itself. While Hill, (7) in a
1974 study of the chemical and allied products industries, concluded that "although much of the literature
emphasizes the possible deleterious effects of regulation on innovation, examples of regulations which
stimulate innovation may also be found", the concensus
today among industrial research administrators is that
the overall effect is pernicious (8). R and D aimed
at innovation increasingly is being squeezed out by a
growing proportion of non-discretionary work made
necessary by regulation in a total environment of a
fixed, or in some cases decreasing, resource pool.

III. Prescription

In a new book to be published in late 1978, Ger-
tenfeld (9) presents a seven point prescription for
lessening some of the deleterious effects from government regulations. In this paper some of those ideas
will be listed and some new ideas added with the objective of ameliorating the effects of government regulation on innovation.
1. Efforts to evaluate the entire economic impacts of regulations before enactment is essential and
could yield substantial positive results (10).

2. Improved consistency within government could provide industry with the guidelines so necessary to encourage the needed R and D efforts.

3. The concept of accepting some inevitable risk (inherent in all products and processes) must become a part of the decision-making process, since our current path toward a "no-risk" society creates a climate that is the very antithesis for innovation and is, in any event, unattainable at any cost in the real world.

4. Information transfer must take place between industry and government on a continual basis and must start at the very beginning of a regulatory movement.

5. Government regulators must become more familiar with industry problems and perhaps it is time to consider a one year sabbatical to be spent in industry for each government regulator assigned to a specific industry.

6. Similar to zero base budgeting, there should be zero base regulations so that a regulation cannot be allowed to build on a previous regulation but rather each should be considered from a zero baseline. Application of the "Sunset Principle" to regulation has been advocated widely and is under study by the Congress.

7. Careful, rigorous societal impact analyses of both primary and secondary effects should be evaluated prior to the enactment of each and every regulation.

8. Periodic assessment of regulations and their impact on innovations should be a standard and regular procedure. It has become far too easy to allow for an accumulation of regulations which has resulted from a reward system within government which encourages increasing legislation with no rewards for lesser controls. A process to correct for experience is badly needed.

9. Conflicting agencies often issue conflicting regulations resulting in lessened innovations. A clearinghouse system must be devised so that compatibility can be obtained.

10. Small business, which has been particularly hurt by performance regulation requirements, should have special systems available so that reporting requirements and other administrative costs connected with regulations can be decreased.

11. Research programs and experiments should be utilized so that more of the uncertainty in connection with the effects of regulation can be reduced.

In conclusion, an example of a form of economic deregulation will be used to chart a course for similar actions on performance regulations. While the

Senate has passed a major bill giving airlines more authority to cut fares and add new routes, the Civil Aeronautics Board has relaxed its rules so much that a form of airline deregulation now exists. This has resulted in an abundance of new low fares, and the entry into new markets of competing airlines. The overall result of this decreased regulation has been more air travelers and higher profits for the carriers. While we recognize that not all cases are to clear cut, we do believe that similar positive results could be obtained by seriously considering the points raised within this paper and by taking a careful reappraisal of the unintended as well as the intended consequences from government regulations.

Literature Cited

1.   Corn, Morton, Impact of Federal Regulations on Engineers", CEP, July, 1978, pp. 24-27
2.   Leone, Robert A., "The Real Costs of Regulation", Harvard Business Review, November - December, 1977, pp. 57-66
3.   Lasagna, Louis, "The Development and Regulation of New Medications", Science, Volume 200, May, 1978, pp. 871-873
4.   Ibid.
5.   Throdahl. Monte C., Chemical and Engineering News, September 19, 1977, pg. 14
6.   Nason, Howard K., "The Environment for Industrial Innovation in the U.S.,", Technological Innovations: Government - Industry Cooperation, Gerstenfeld, Edit., New York: Wiley Interscience, (in press)
7.   Hill, Christopher T., et al, "A State of the Art Review of the Effects of Regulation on Technolgoical Innovation in the Chemical and Allied Products Industries", National R & D Assessment Program, NSF RDA 74-20086 A01, February, 1975
8.   Manners, George E., Jr., and Nason, Howard K., "Trends in Industrial Research", National Science Board Planning Environment Review, 1978, Volume I., pp. 45-49, NSB-78-191, June, 1978
9.   Gerstenfeld, Arthur, "Government Regulations and Innovation", Technological Innovation: Government - Industry Cooperation, Gerstenfeld, Edit., New York: Wiley Interscience (in press)
10.   Kramm, Robert F., Nagy, Stephen F., and Nemec, Joseph, "Complying with Proposed Regulations: Estimating Industry's Costs", Business Horizons, August, 1977, pp. 86-91

The opinions expressed are those of the authors and do not necessarily represent the views of the institutions with which they are affiliated.
RECEIVED March 8, 1979.

Regulation and Innovation: Short-Term Adjustments and Long-Term Impacts

GLENN E. SCHWEITZER

Program on Science, Technology, and Society, Cornell University,
Ithaca, NY 14853

During the past few years the chemical industry has responded
to a wide range of environmental and health regulations without
significant changes -- at least from a national perspective -- in
the current availability and costs of products dependent on chemicals, in employment opportunities, or in the growth or configuration of the industry. Of course, there have been changing empha-
ses in product lines in response to environmental concerns, a few
products have been abandoned, and environmental control costs have
been a factor in some plant closings. Nevertheless, from the public's viewpoint, the industry continues to operate at the forefront of technological opportunities in providing a wide variety
of products for our ever advancing standard of living.

Indeed, the industry has exhibited a remarkable degree of
technological resiliency in adjusting to the dramatic upsurge in
regulatory requirements. Much of the success in significantly reducing effluents and emissions in response to air and water pollution limitations of the early 1970's is attributable, at least in
part, to the earlier industrial neglect of technological opportunities for curtailing environmental discharges, both in operating
old plants and in designing new ones. Similarly, when confronted
with requirements several years ago to reduce worker exposure to
carcinogens, the industry demonstrated technological ingenuity on
many fronts -- in the rapid introduction of substitute chemicals,
in new and modified engineering processes that bypass use of the
troublesome chemicals, and in vastly improved engineering and related approaches to containment of these chemicals.

In short, the immediate economic impacts of regulatory requirements have frequently been overestimated by spokesmen for both
industry and Government who have not fully anticipated the technical ingenuity of both management and engineering staffs when
near-term profitability is at stake. However, from the perspective
of both individual companies and of the industry, the immediate
impacts of regulations can be almost trivial in comparison with
the longer term impacts of these same regulations within an industry that operates on a global basis and on the forward edge of

a constantly changing technology. Unfortunately, almost every
regulatory impact assessment concentrates solely on the immediately apparent impacts on the "tip of the iceberg" while the impacts
on the submerged aspects -- and particularly research activities
-- can have a major effect on the rate and direction of industrial
production in the years ahead.

Technological Penalties Associated with Environmental and Work-place Controls

While responses to environmental and workplace standards frequently stimulate considerable innovative activity among the environmental and chemical engineers, such activities are not without their technological penalties. Compliance with regulatory
requirements frequently requires the diversion of financial resources and technical manpower from other activities, including
innovative activities directed to product or process improvements.

Examine, for example, the industrial response to the indict-
ment of vinyl chloride as a serious environmental and workplace
hazard in 1974. Almost every company operating vinyl chloride or
polyvinyl chloride production facilities diverted many engineers
to tighten the engineering controls required to reduce vinyl
chloride leakages. They succeeded in significantly reducing emissions in a very short time. At the same, time, however, many of
these several hundred engineers had been diverted to work on the
vinyl chloride problem from other product and process improvement
activities. Indeed, in some companies major development projects
were postponed since the key personnel had been diverted from
these projects. Also, the equipment and related costs resulted in
diversion of financial resources from other activities, including
the support of research and development programs. In short, im-
pending regulatory decisions on vinyl chloride resulted in the
rapid upgrading of chemical engineering approaches in a number of
plants, but at the same time technological progress in other
areas was delayed.

There are a few, but not many, examples of engineering innovations introduced in response to regulatory requirements resulting in overall cost savings as the result of recovery of materials
or other newly introduced efficiencies. More generally, a small
portion of the control costs will be recovered -- perhaps ten
to twenty percent -- as the result of improved plant performance.
In retrofitting old plants the percentage of costs that is recov-
erable is likely to be lower; in designing new plants, it may be
somewhat higher.

The costs of compliance with pollution abatement regulations
have been documented in many company, industry, and Government
studies. These costs obviously impact on company growth, investment decisions, and allocation of resources among competing
company priorities. Such increased costs of company activities
impact on technological innovation in several ways. Upgrading of
production processes may be postponed. Investments in facilities

or equipment needed for introducing new products or processes may
be deferred. Finally, research and development budgets may be
reduced or perhaps not increased as would otherwise have been the
case.
    A less obvious interaction between regulatory compliance and
innovation relates to the role of management in the innovation
process and the increasing amount of management time devoted to
workplace and environmental requirements with less time available
for considering new discoveries and concepts. The innovation process requires a number of risk-laden decisions. Thus, careful
management attention to the details of such decisions can often be
critical to the successful development and commercial introduction
of new approaches.

What Is Technological Innovation?

    Most industrialists consider innovation to be synonymous with
development of a new or improved product or process that yields a
profit. Under this definition, a chemical company would not consider the following activities as innovation: use by the company
for the first time of off-the-shelf technology; a company discovery which is successfully commercialized by a competitor; development and use of new engineering technologies to satisfy pollution
control requirements. These industrialists emphasize the many
steps involved in the innovation process in going from discovery
to profit, and they consider regulatory requirements as hurdles --
and perhaps necessary hurdles -- along the path to successful
innovation.
    At the other extreme, public interest groups could argue that
any discovery that benefits society in any way should be considered as innovation. Thus, a routine toxicological test that
develops new information about a compound would be innovation.
Identification of impurities associated with a compound would be
innovation. Epidemiological studies would be innovations.
    Section 2 of the Toxic Substances Control Act states that
regulatory authority "should be exercised in a manner as not to
impede unduly or create unnecessary economic barriers to technological innovation . . ." The legislative history suggests a
definition close to the definition of the industrialists. However,
innovation needs to be examined more broadly than from the perspective of a single company or the success or failure of a single
project. Thus, if environmental engineers introduce new techniques to reduce the cost or improve the effectiveness of pollution control, such techniques should probably be considered as
technological innovation. Similarly, if toxicologists develop
cheaper, faster, or better biological screening tests, such developments should be considered as innovation. On the other hand,
detailed characterization of the biological, physical, or chemical
properties of compounds using standard methods should probably not
be classified as innovation.

Research and Development Trends in Large Chemical Companies

The rapid growth in R&D that characterized the larger companies a few years ago has subsided. At the top of the list of the causes for a levelling off of R&D expenditures in recent years are two interrelated factors: (a) overinvestment in R&D during the 1960's and a subsequent retrenchment to a more realistic level, and (b) growing maturity of the chemical industry with fewer opportunities for diversification. In some companies, environmental control costs have also slowed R&D growth.

As the direct result of regulatory concerns, the objectives and orientation of R&D activities are changing significantly, and the mix of researchers is also changing.

One of the most discernible changes within R&D budgets is the growth of expenditures for environmental and health activities. These expenditures typically exceed ten percent of the R&D budget, largely for evaluations of the health effects of compounds. Significant additional funds, sometimes exceeding another ten percent, are also being directed to the search for substitutes for compounds that have become the targets of regulatory agencies. This realignment of R&D budget priorities has necessitated hiring of additional environmental and health specialists. Sometimes additional positions have been made available to the R&D units, but more often the new positions have been accommodated within an overall R&D personnel limitation.

With regard to the remainder of the R&D effort, several noticeable changes in orientation are occurring. Perhaps most significantly, greater emphasis is being placed on improving established products and in broadening their uses, with less emphasis on the development of new products. For example, in one company new ventures commanded 25 percent of the R&D budget in the mid-1960's but now command less than ten percent. In another area, most companies are reducing the number of newly synthesized chemicals in favor of more detailed characterization of the chemicals that are synthesized.

Many of these changes are a direct response to existing or anticipated regulations. A principal concern which is resulting in an increasing percentage of the R&D effort being devoted to defensive research on established products is the lengthening of the R&D cycle, and the attendant increase in risk. The longer the cycle, the greater the likelihood that market factors, achievements   of competitors, or new regulations will inhibit successful commercialization.

Some companies have decided to avoid certain classes of compounds in their investigations simply because of the possibility that they will be plagued by regulatory problems due to the general character of their molecular structures (e.g. chlorinated hydrocarbons). One company has abandoned about 100 commercially interesting compounds since they have appeared on lists of suspected chemicals. Another company is backing off on all uses of chemicals which bring the chemicals in close proximity to food supplies or drinking water. Still another company has decided to redirect its R&D efforts almost exclusively to new uses of chemicals that are already in commercial usage. In short, while exploratory research in the 1950's and 1960's was characterized by attempts to expand understanding of all aspects of chemistry, some areas are now largely off limits.

The number of new molecules that are being commercialized has declined in recent years. This decline is particularly noticeable when considering new chemicals intended for high volume, long term markets as contrasted to new chemicals which are produced in small batches in response to the needs of small markets, frequently limited to one customer. There is now clearly a trend within large companies to emphasize a very limited number of new chemicals with high volume markets rather than investing substantial R&D resources in larger numbers of small volume chemicals. Meanwhile, the small companies continue to be sources of many batch-lot chemicals used as starting materials by the large companies.

The sequence, timing, and costs involved in the many steps from synthesis to commercialization of new molecules are changing. Preliminary testing for biological activity (e.g. Ames test) is far more commonplace now and is usually undertaken much earlier in the R&D cycle than was the case several years ago. Meanwhile, detailed efficacy, feasibility, and market testing are often delayed pending more detailed evaluations of possible health effects. Inevitably, many molecules are abandoned earlier in their potential lifetimes as the result of suspected effects, and the overall length of the R&D cycle is being extended.

In the past, major new chemicals have often had R&D lead times of seven to ten years. In such cases, some aspects of newly instituted environmental assessments (e.g. a portion of the time required for long-term chronic toxicity tests) can be conducted in parallel with other R&D activities. In other cases such as batch-lot production activities, new test requirements simply extend the R&D cycle for the length of the test program.

Large companies have formalized the R&D process to an unprecedented degree. Environmental checkpoints are usually built into the entire cycle. In one case, the corporate environmental staff issues an R&D "permit" identifying potential problems that must be addressed in each R&D project.

Another concern relates to the necessity to obtain Federal or state pollution control permits for pilot plants. This requirement is further delaying the commercialization process as well as raising costs which are often charged to R&D budgets.

Most research directors are clearly becoming more conservative in their approaches to new chemicals. They are not eager to become embroiled in hassles with the regulatory agencies. Should questions develop as to the acceptability of new chemicals, these directors are usually inclined to devote their efforts to other products. Indeed, there are cases of large companies abandoning a

complete line of products (e.g. dyes), with regulatory concerns
being a major factor in the business decisions.

Perhaps of even greater concern is the dampening effect of
regulations on the enthusiasm and inquisitiveness of the R&D scientists. While synthesis of a new chemical is relatively easy,
translating a new molecule into a commercial success is not easy.
One critical element in success stories is an individual researcher who is willing to devote his energies and reputation for a number of years to helping overcome a variety of technical and business difficulties on the path to commercialization. As the regulatory difficulties increase, fewer researchers are willing to devote their efforts to this type of activity with increasing odds
of failure.

Changes in Corporate Approaches that Affect Technological Decisions

Environmental regulations now constitute a regular agenda
item at the meetings of most Boards of Directors of the large
chemical companies. The impacts of environmental requirements
permeate the entire corporate structure. Staffs of health and
ecology specialists have expanded rapidly, and medical departments
have been enlarged. The competition for toxicologists in particular is resulting in unprecedented salaries for these specialists.
Concurrent with these internal company adjustments, some companies
are giving greater attention to the public relations aspects of
environmental consciousness, including the encouragement of publication of internal company scientific findings, the release of
data on environmental control expenditures, and the publicizing
of internal company environmental policies.

There are many examples of how chemical companies are changing as the result of regulatory requirements. Two developments
that may become industry-wide trends are particularly interesting.

As the result of regulations calling for prompt reporting to
EPA of any discovery within a company that a chemical manufactured
or processed by that company may present a "substantial risk,"
many companies have established extensive internal reporting systems to bring such discoveries to the immediate attention of top
management. In the past, heavy reliance was placed on the local
doctors at the plant sites and on the toxicological staffs to
handle as appropriate new information on chemical hazards. Now
with the establishment of formal internal reporting systems, the
sensitivity of corporate staffs at all levels to environmental and
health concerns is at an all time high.

Many large companies are becoming increasingly selective in
purchasing chemicals from small suppliers who do not follow sound
environmental or worker protection control procedures. This attitude is directly related to the problems associated with the production of kepone by Life Sciences, Inc., for use by a single
customer, Allied Chemical Company. Similarly, on a number of recent occasions large chemical companies have withheld sales to

small customers who do not have the environmental wherewithal to handle the chemicals in a safe manner.

The Changing Regulatory Framework Surrounding Technology Choices

About once a month, a new legislative action, court decision, or regulatory proposal modifies the legal framework surrounding regulatory proceedings. With each new Congress, there is an increasing desire to "legislate" regulatory actions directed to specific products and problems and to increase the precision of the criteria to be used by the agencies in reaching controversial decisions. Many of the recent procedural requirements written into regulatory legislation have been designed to strengthen the hand of the public interest groups. Perhaps most importantly, more and more attention is now directed by the regulatory agencies to procedural matters, often at the expense of substantive issues. Technical personnel are increasingly insulated from the negotiation and decision-making processes, as lawyers become more important. Finally, the complexity of the regulatory process inevitably increases.

The courts are becoming more heavily involved in toxic substance cases, thus forcing greater attention in the administrative proceedings to building a record. However, few judges are content simply to review procedural adequacies and the completeness of the record and to insure that decision-making has not been arbitrary and capricious. Rather, they are no longer hesistant to substitute their societal judgements for those of regulatory administrators in controversial decisions.

Three recent actions involving the courts are particularly relevant to current concerns over chemical control, namely:
-- the discussion of the nature of scientific evidence accompanying the decision of the Court of Appeals concerning the removal of lead from gasoline.
-- the denial of the liability claims of Galaxy Chemical Company against a doctor who on the basis of very slender evidence publicly accused the company of contributing to an alleged increase of cancer rates.
-- the current legal suits of a number of former employees of American Can Company, who are alleging increased bronchial problems attributed to their employment with that company, against many of the chemical suppliers of that company after the workers had exhausted worker compensation claims against their direct employer.

With regard to the administration of regulatory programs, toxic substances legislation is resulting in a more introverted Government. The agencies now seem more concerned with internal coordination and internal negotiations and less sensitive to developments in the private sector and to the need for and impact of regulations. As the regulatory agencies continue to grow, as their programs overlap to a greater degree, as their legisla-

tively mandated tasks increase, and as decisions become more complex, the limited time available to top management is increasingly
devoted to intra-agency and inter-agency negotiations and coordination. Further, the continuously changing leadership of the
agencies is always low on a learning curve which is quite long in
view of the complex character of the chemical industry. Not sur-
prisingly, these officials are more comfortable in internal discussions than exposing their uncertainties to external scrutiny.
Finally, concerns over potential conflicts of interest are a significant deterrent to bringing the technical expertise of the
chemical industry into the decision-making stream, either through
personnel appointments to Governmental posts or through effective
Government-industry interactions.

As a result of the inward looking tendencies which are becoming more commonplace throughout the Government, principal
forums for meaningful interactions between Government and interested parties, and particularly the industrial sector, are increasingly limited to highly structured public meetings and administrative hearings. This development has several drawbacks.
The likelihood of adversarial confrontations over minor issues is
greatly increased. Suspicion over Government motivations runs
high. The receptivity of Government to external views is reduced
since many compromises have already been made within the agencies
prior to public scrutiny of regulations, and Government officials
are not anxious for these compromises to become "unstuck". Finally,
the range of alternative approaches that can be realistically considered is very narrow given the usual strictness of the ground
rules surrounding such public sessions.

Meanwhile, the role of the scientist is changing. On the one
hand, scientists are being asked to provide precise estimates of
chemical risks often based on very sketchy laboratory data. Then
they are frequently excluded from the deliberations leading to
determinations as to whether the risks are acceptable to society,
only to be called into legal proceedings later to help defend such
value judgements. As the result of pressures from the legal pro-
fession to be as clear as possible as to risks, and particularly
with regard to possible carcinogenic effects, many scientists are
now taking sides in very controversial debates (e.g. carcinogen
threshhold vs. no threshhold) even when they believe that clear
cut positions may be distorting scientific reality.

The inspections by Government to insure compliance with Good
Laboratory Practices are resulting in an upgrading of shoddy practices in many laboratories. However, this intrusion into the inner
sanctum of the scientific establishment is indeed a revolutionary
challenge to the long held concept of scientific integrity. At
the same time, the increasing scope of laboratory tests proscribed
by Government -- while setting a minimum standard which must be
achieved by all -- will inevitably discourage some innovative
efforts by companies to explore other approaches to toxicology
which in the long run might have proven more effective than the

accepted test requirements. In this regard, there probably is
still time to build into Governmental regulations flexibility
which recognizes that there may be better and cheaper ways to conduct tests and which rewards industry for devoting efforts in this
direction.

Thus, regulation is impacting on R&D in many ways. Increasing attention is being devoted to very visible changes in R&D
activities in response to regulatory trends. However, there are
also more indirect impacts that will be important in the years
ahead. These indirect impacts are already developing their roots
in the changing legal and administrative apparatus surrounding the
regulatory process and in the changing attitudes and approaches of
the many participants in chemical activities.

Modifying the Legislative Base

Fundamental to significant improvements in the regulatory
process is a reshaping of the legislative base which drives the
regulatory activities of the executive agencies. At the top of
the priority list should be (a) a recasting of the objectives of
concern, and (b) the establishment of mechanisms which will help
decision makers understand the impact -- both positive and negative -- of regulations on society.

Specifically, Section 30 of the Toxic Substances Control Act
should be recast. This provision requires an annual accounting to
Congress of regulatory actions taken by EPA but does not even
refer to the far more important issue, namely, the impact of the
law -- either directly as a result of these actions or in other
ways -- on health and the environment and, at the same time, on
other societal concerns. Until the Congress recognizes that the
number of regulations that are promulgated may have little relationship to the state of the environment, a preoccupation with the
weight of the Federal Register will continue to take precedence
over more meaningful health and environmental concerns.

Closely related to the need for a refocusing of legislative
objectives is the need for a legislatively mandated Commission to
evaluate the impact on society, including the chemical industry,
of recently enacted legislation and to present recommendations for
mid-course corrections in the legislation that will surely be in
order in several years. Quite understandably the complexities of
the chemical industry defy an easy and quick grasp by lawmakers of
the impact of legislation on the technological base that underlies
15 percent of U.S. industry and that affects every consumer. A
serious effort to improve such understanding, directly involving
at least a few of the key Senators and Congressmen, seems essential. Given the stakes involved, both environmental and economic,
such a study effort, even if only partially successful, should
serve societal interests in many ways.

Finally, prompt steps are needed to alter some of the provisions of the Toxic Substances Control Act which divert attention
from the main problems at hand and can only lead to long and

protacted legal confrontations with little environmental payoff.
Specifically, a lower chemical production limit (e.g. one or ten
pounds per chemical per year per manufacturer) should be adopted
for applicability of this new law in the absence of indications
that in specific cases the lower limit should be removed. At
present, even a few grams of a chemical produced for commercial
purposes is automatically subject to a variety of legal provisions. It is certainly true that a few grams of a poisonous chemical can be a problem. However, there are more than enough problem chemicals produced in much larger quantities that need attention rather than complicating the research and related issues that
inevitably arise in dealing with all chemicals produced in such
small quantities. Secondly, the extensive requirements for immediate publication by EPA in the Federal Register of the receipt of
premanufacturing notifications and of the reasons for not taking
regulatory actions under several legal provisions are simply in-
viting unnecessary adversarial confrontations when the resources
involved could be better expended in dealing with more significant
issues. Criteria could be easily established concerning the need
for and frequency of Federal Register notices.
       Clearly, the area of testing of existing chemicals will be
fraught with scientific uncertainties and controversies over priorities and cost sharing. This is precisely the area where industry has a story to tell, an opportunity to help shape future
approaches, and an opportunity to help reduce the adversarial tensions that characterize Government-industry relations at present.
Specifically, the large companies should pledge themselves to a
prompt doubling of the budget of the Chemical Industry Institute
of Toxicology, with the "expectation" that Government would recognize such testing as just as important as testing in response to
Federal Register notices. Perhaps the lawyers from industry
would want to provide a little protection by coupling this initiative with a citizens petition to EPA concerning the specific chemicals to be tested.
       Should such an initiative work -- i.e. not only result in
needed testing but also gain recognition that such voluntary
actions count in the Government report card -- then a second
initiative under Section 6 of the new law should be considered.
Specifically, industry might commit itself to preparation and distribution of safety data sheets, reflecting available health and
environmental data, on all chemicals that are sold. Again, the
Government would be expected to recognize such an initiative as an
important complement to the current limited regulatory approach
under Section 6 of placing limitations only on polychlorinated biphenyls and selected chlorofluorocarbons.

The Carcinogen Issue

       The uncertainty as to the Government's approach to carcino-
gens is currently having a major dampening effect on research
activities of a number of companies. While prompt articulation of

a Government-wide policy is therefore very important, the current
approach of OSHA needs some modification to reflect sound science
and improved public administration.

The OSHA concept of categorizing chemicals which exhibit carcinogenic tendencies on the basis of demonstrated potency has elicited broad support. However, the categorization schemes that are
adopted should be uniform throughout the Government. EPA, CPSC,
FDA, and DOT are in the midst of addressing the carcinogen issue.
Therefore, the final OSHA set of standards should be coupled to
equally formal actions by the other agencies directed to a consistent approach for categorizing carcinogens according to their
demonstrated potency. Each agency, of course, must then determine
the appropriate regulatory response to chemicals in each category
depending on the exposure levels and statutory requirements concerning economic impact.

Secondly, the concept that one or two animal experiments
should be the overriding determinant of potency regardless of
other available evidence is not sound. While certain types of
test results may strongly suggest certain levels of potency,
guidelines rather than rigid test result criteria should be established for each category, with the category assignment made on a
chemical-by-chemical basis after consideration of all relevant
evidence. While OSHA's motivations in attempting to automate the
categorization system are understandable, responsible policy decisions should be made on the basis of all available evidence, recognizing that in some cases results of a single test may be far
more significant than all the other evidence combined.

Finally, with guidelines in hand, the task would then be to
place individual chemicals into appropriate categories. This is
a scientific task that should be undertaken by the best available
scientific talent in the country. Further, this task should be
undertaken in a manner that will serve the interests of all concerned Government agencies and not just OSHA. Therefore, an expert scientific panel, drawing members from both the public and
private sectors and with the full support of OSHA and other regulatory agencies, should be established under the aegis of the
Council on Environmental Quality. This Panel would recommend for
Government-wide action the appropriate category for each chemical
associated with carcinogenic tendencies. With regard to OSHA,
these recommendations should then trigger the appropriate workplace standard for the category of chemical. Should the Secretary
of Labor disagree with the Panel's recommendations, he would of
course have the option of separate rulemaking processes in those
cases of disagreement.

As Government agencies grow larger, there is an increasing
reluctance to entrust any responsibility to groups not under the
direct control of the interested agency. In this case, where the
issues are scientific and where much of the nation's best talent
is in the private sector, the public interest rather than frag-

mented interests of individual Governmental offices should be recognized and an appropriate organizational response developed. The stakes involved in the OSHA regulatory proceeding are substantial, not only in terms of worker risks, but also in terms of our economic welfare and the processes of good Government. While the Department of Labor's desire to promulgate a standard without delay is commendable, it is essential that the complexities of science, the interrelationships of Governmental programs, and the appropriate role for individual Government offices be carefully weighed prior to reaching a final judgement as to the workplace standards that will best serve the public interest.

Literature Cited

Draft Economic Impact Assessment for the Proposed Toxic Substances Control Act S. 776, Environmental Protection Agency, June 1975.

Study of the Potential Economic Impacts of the Proposed Toxic Substances Control Act as Illustrated by Senate Bill S. 776, Manufacturing Chemists Associaton, June 26, 1975.

Legislative History of the Toxic Substances Control Act, Prepared by the Environment and Natural Resources Policy Division of the Library of Congress, U.S. Government Printing Office, December 1976.

Preliminary Assessment of the Environmental Problems Associated with Vinyl Chloride and Polyvinyl Chloride, Report on the Activities of the Vinyl Chloride Task Force, Environmental Protection Agency, September 1974.

Voluntary Environmental Activities of Large Chemical Companies to Assess and Control Industrial Chemicals, Environmental Protection Agency, EPA 560/4-76-009, September 1976.

Gee, Edwin A. and Tyler, Chaplin, Managing Innovation, John F. Wiley, 1976.

Nason, Howard K., Steger, Joseph A. and Manners, George E., Support of Basic Research by Industry, Prepared for the National Science Foundation (NSF-C76-21517), 1978.

"R&D Expenditures of Leading Chemical Companies," Management Bulletin, E. I. DuPont Public Affairs Department, September-October 1977.

Quinn, James B., "U.S. Monetary Policy: A Heavy Hand in Technology," Technology Review, October/November 1976.

Ashford, Nicholas A. and Heaton, George R., "Environmental and Safety Regulations: Reasons for their Adoption and Possible Effects on Technological Innovation," Testimony to Senate Commerce Committee, June 23, 1975.

"Views of Industry R&D Vice Presidents on Federal Policy and Industry R&D Innovation," As Expressed to Dr. Frank Press, Director, Office of Science and Technology Policy, October 25, 1977.

Wiedenbaum, Murray L., "Government Regulation and the Slowdown in Innovation," Presented to the Chemical Forum, Washington, DC, October 11, 1977.

Evaluation of the Possible Impact of Pesticide Legislation on Research and Development Activities of Pesticide Manufacturers, Arthur D. Little, Inc., Prepared for the Environmental Protection Agency, 1975.

"Identification, Classification, and Regulation of Certain Toxic Substances," Occupational Safety and Health Administration, 29 CFR Part 1990, October 4, 1977.

"Regulatory Analysis of a Proposed Policy for the Identification, Classification, and Regulation of Toxic Substances Posing a Potential Occupational Carcinogenic Risk," Department of Labor, October 17, 1978.

"OSHA Proposal for the Identification, Classification, and Regulation of Toxic Substances Posing a Potential Occupational Carcinogenic Risk," Report of the Regulatory Analysis Review Group, October 24, 1978.

"Letter from Edward Strohbehn to Eula Bingham on OSHA Generic Carcinogen Proposal," Council on Environmental Qualty, October 24, 1978.

"Technological Innovation and Health, Safety and Environmental Regulation," Office of Technology Assessment Proposal 78-11, September 1978.

"Domestic Policy Review of Industrial Innovation: Work Plan," The Domestic Council, The White House, September 18, 1978.

"Detailed Guidelines for Analyzing Economic Impacts," Environmental Protection Agency, July 11, 1978.

RECEIVED March 9, 1979.

INDEX

INDEX